Praise for *The Perfect Score Project*

"An insightful, clear-eyed guide to one of the most onerous experiences college-bound teens and their parents face." —*Parade*

"*The Perfect Score Project* is as much a personal and familial journey as it is an informational guide on how to navigate the dizzying test-prep options and succeed. . . . [Stier's] insights are both humorous and invaluable."
—*Journal News*

"The book is a fascinating read. Many insights and strategies can be learned here, from 'bubbling' techniques to guessing strategies. Woven into Stier's experiment is both a mother's story and a sharp appraisal of the industry of college testing." —*Library Journal*

"More than just a guide to succeeding at 'the test,' it's a primer for succeeding at life. Stier deftly connects success, mindset, and habit. *The Perfect Score Project* is the book every parent should read before diving into SAT prep."
—**Shawn Achor, *New York Times* bestselling author of *Before Happiness* and *The Happiness Advantage***

"Debbie Stier has accomplished the equivalent of moving mountains: she has made taking the SAT a fascinating, irresistible adventure. It will have teens, their parents, high school guidance counselors, SAT-prep centers, and colleges reconsidering everything they think they know about the SAT and the world of test-prep. Debbie's entertaining, pioneering, and eye-opening book is a page turner that will grab you from the beginning. And it may just inspire you to follow her lead and strive for a perfect score too." —**Emily McKhann, cofounder of The Motherhood and author of *Living with the End in Mind***

"This book is about motivation and hard work and parenting, but above all it's about forming the deepest bonds of family connection. Here, the test Debbie took over and over and over again becomes a metaphor: she chooses to do the hardest work of her life and it pays off in a thousand different ways."
—**Laura Zigman, author of the national bestseller *Animal Husbandry***

"Debbie Stier's tips, lessons, and no-nonsense insights are insatiably useful. Her story is genuinely moving—not just a woman's obsession with a test, but a mother's love for her son. A perfect 800 in my book!" —**William C. Taylor, cofounder of *Fast Company* and author of *Practically Radical***

"*The Perfect Score Project* is a break-the-mold book. Whereas the college application process, and in particular SAT preparation, fills parents and students with anxiety and a sense of being overwhelmed, Debbie's experiences and hard-won insights offer much-needed clarity." —**Ellen Galinsky, president of the Families and Work Institute, and author of *Mind in the Making***

"Jam-packed with truly sound advice for conquering test fatigue, understanding superscoring, overcoming performance anxiety, and perfecting the 'fine art of bubbling.' Enjoy Debbie's cautionary tale of obsession and taking seven SATs—but don't try this at home!" —**Christine VanDeVelde, coauthor of *College Admission: From Application to Acceptance, Step by Step***

WHAT READERS ARE SAYING

"I'm an SAT tutor and have been full-time since 2008. . . . My job would be a lot easier if all parents had to read this book." —**Vince Kotchian**

"Debbie Stier has a humorous writing style that makes this book an easy read. . . . I thoroughly enjoyed it, and if the author lived nearby, I would invite her to lunch!" —**Patricia D. Brown**

"Some of the best advice for anything comes from those with experience in their area, who have 'been there, done that,' and *The Perfect Score Project* is the story of someone who's been through it all." —**D. Dent "Aragorn"**

"It is hard to put into words how floored I was by *The Perfect Score Project*. . . . This book is not just about the exam system." —**Terri Shanahan, MFA, MEd**

THE
Perfect Score
PROJECT

*One Mother's Journey to Uncover
the Secrets of the SAT*

DEBBIE STIER

HARMONY

BOOKS • NEW YORK

Originally published in hardcover in the United States by Harmony Books
an imprint of the Crown Publishing Group, a division of Random House
LLC, New York.

Library of Congress Cataloging-in-Publication Data is available upon
request.

ISBN 978-0-307-95668-2
eBook ISBN 978-0-307-95669-9

Printed in the United States of America

Cover design by Michael Nagin
Cover photography: Fuse/Getty Images

10 9 8 7 6 5 4 3 2 1

First Paperback Edition

For Ethan,

who taught me more about being a good mom

than I ever taught him about the SAT.

Thank you for sharing this journey.

CONTENTS

PROLOGUE

Freaky Friday

*Nothing will distract me. If there's a fire, keep working. If some-
one throws up, don't move. And no freaking out. Skip and come
back; shorter is better. Backsolve, plug in, VPP; make sure to
answer the question they're asking . . .*

It's December 3, 2011, and the line at this middle-class suburban
high school in Dobbs Ferry, New York, is short today, not like the last
time I was here, nine months ago, for SAT No. 2. Everyone seems more
relaxed. Or maybe I'm just more relaxed, since this will be my seventh
SAT of the year. I am a veteran.

Back in March there was more nervous energy in the halls, kids on
edge, some of them anxiously rehearsing the names of literary characters
to use in their essays:

"What's the boss's name in *Glengarry Glen Ross*?"

"Write about Blake."

"You pre-thought-out your essay?"

I overheard one kid telling a friend, "I'd get a 2400 if my driver's ed
teacher was the proctor."

On the other hand, I don't see the girls in flannel pajama bottoms today; at the March test, that's what they all were wearing. This December crowd seems less nervous but more serious, too.

Okay, the essay. What do I need to remember . . . What is the thesis? Don't forget to circle back to your thesis in every paragraph. Write it at the top of your answer book, like Erica said. Don't forget to do that. And use good vocab—"anomaly," "redolent," "circumspect," "jingoistic"—try to weave in a few of those. Leave a few minutes at the end to double back and check grammar. No pronoun errors, for godsake. Answer the question—yes or no. Agree or disagree. Declare, don't waffle. Think: "debate team." Convince the essay grader—build a case.

I want a 12 so badly I can taste it.

A Doogie Howser look-alike is in line in front of me. "It's my third time," he says to his friend.

"You're kidding, right?" the friend asks. "You've taken the SAT *two* times, already? You're only a sophomore."

The friend seems impressed. Or maybe that's stress I hear in his voice, I'm not sure. I'm only half paying attention. I'm in the zone, focused, running down my mental checklist of what I need to remember for the essay:

Don't forget to work in a counterexample at the end. And use a metaphor, if possible, and a literary example—enough with the Tiger Mom. She hasn't delivered that 12. Use The Things They Carried *by Tim O'Brien— that's what John, the super-methodical tutor, told me. Actually, he said to use an obscure poet, but that if I couldn't think of one, Tim O'Brien was a better choice than the Tiger Mom. Please, God, no technology prompts.*

The Future Is Always a Surprise

Four years earlier:

"Tell your mother," she said, guiding my twelve-year-old son, Ethan, into the conference room. Her hand rested gently on his shoulder, as if to say, "Don't worry, I've got your back." This was the school psychologist, and she'd just finished a round of psychological testing on my son, a legal requirement if Ethan's status as a student with a disability was to be maintained in the coming school year.

Ethan's disability is what I'd describe as a mild case of garden-variety ADHD, the kind without the behavior problems. Ethan's an easygoing kid: he's happy-go-lucky but disorganized, and needed a lot of "refocusing" during those early years in school. To my mind, ADHD is what we used to call "boys." Now we have treatment for the condition and legally required "accommodations" at school.

There were a handful of school administrators sitting around the table, gathered there on a spring morning for the annual review of Ethan's 504 plan. Ethan scanned the adult-filled room sheepishly, then looked down at his shoes. Finally he looked at me and spoke.

"Mom," he said, "I'm fine with B's."

The room was silent—for a moment—and then the door opened and Ethan's math teacher bounced in with a spring in his step, like Tigger in *Winnie-the-Pooh*.

"Ethan's the classic underachiever," he announced, as if to say, "No big deal, just reporting an observation for the record."

"I'm fine with B's" and "Ethan's a classic underachiever": I was the only person in the room experiencing a disconnect. Everyone else seemed to think underachievement was fine if you were getting B's. Or maybe not even B's; later on I talked to a family who got the same line about their son, another ADHD underachiever, who was getting C's. And these were high school C's, which count.

After the math teacher's report, the conversation turned to me and how I might learn to accept my twelve-year-old son's expectations for himself.

When I got to my car, I cried.

I was worn ragged from years of doing battle with the schools over every scrap of common sense. There had to be an easier way. It was simply not possible that I was the only mother upset that her son was not living up to his potential, no matter what the school said. Surely there was an alternate universe where mothers were surprised to see a C on the report card after they'd been assured by their sons that they had all A's.

"I don't know how that happened," Ethan would say, and he meant it. He *didn't* know, not until his mom called the school to get the story, which was usually some variation of: "He didn't turn in his homework," or "He had all A's, except for one test where he got an F. That brought his grade down to a C for the semester."

Ethan always managed to look on the bright side, no matter how many times this happened, and it happened constantly because he could never anticipate the problems before they arrived. His school life was like *Groundhog Day*, which is how I knew the seventh-grade special ed teacher was dead wrong when he called me in to give me a lesson in parenting. He said (I am quoting) I should "take away Ethan's safety net" and "let him fail a little" as he handed me a xeroxed sheet of instructions from Outward Bound to clarify the theory. Intentionally letting a child fail might work with a kid who can see beyond the next five minutes, but that kid was not my son in seventh grade. To Ethan, the future always came as a surprise.

I had had enough. For me—and this was where I parted ways with the school—the issue wasn't grades. I would have been proud of Ethan's B's if the math teacher had bounced in and said, "Ethan's a hard worker." But that's not what he said, and it wasn't what I was seeing. Ethan was taking the easy path, and the school was in his camp. The administrators thought Ethan, a happy-go-lucky, disorganized middle school boy with ADHD, should determine his own academic goals.

I had about one gasp's worth of fight left in me, so I called my friend Catherine. Catherine was another mom in the district. We'd met (and bonded) in the comments of a disgruntled mother's blog post (that disgruntled mother may have been me—I can't quite remember).

Catherine was no fan of the middle school. Whenever the subject came up she said the school motto should be *Your child: not the little genius you thought he was.* Catherine's husband, a professor at NYU, was equally disaffected, and after wrangling with the administration for three years, they had called it quits and taken their son Chris out of the district.

Chris was one year ahead of Ethan, and Catherine had been urging me for months to "Call Mr. Lauber."

Mr. Lauber is the director of admissions at Fordham Prep, a Jesuit high school in the Bronx where Chris was finishing his freshman year. I hadn't called, because I didn't think my father would approve. "We're not Catholic," I'd tell Catherine. Her family wasn't Catholic either, but she was way past the issue of sending her son to a Catholic school, and she didn't seem the least bit concerned about the two-train commute down the Hudson River with a layover in Harlem every day, either. That's not the kind of thing most parents who live in the suburbs would even consider.

Catherine's advice that day was the same: Call Mr. Lauber.

I decided I would.

By nightfall I'd collected myself and was ready to have the conversation with my father.

"Oh, the *Jesuits*," he said, when I told him. "They're wonderful educators." Which surprised me. I had been expecting resistance. Apparently my father was tired of the struggle, too.

The next day, which happened to be the day after the last day of Fordham Prep's school year, I made an appointment with Mr. Lauber for Ethan and me to come in. Mr. Lauber asked me to bring a copy of Ethan's report card.

The next morning, Ethan put on a jacket and tie and we drove to the school, where we found Mr. Lauber sorting textbooks. He teaches Greek and Latin in addition to his duties as the director of admissions. Everyone at the school has more than just one job, as far as I can tell.

We sat in Mr. Lauber's office and he asked Ethan a few questions about school and things he liked—icebreaker questions. Ethan seemed nervous.

Then he asked to see Ethan's report card. I handed it to him and he looked it over while Ethan and I sat quietly, waiting for the verdict.

"It's okay," he said. "Not great."

I explained to him that the C in science was an error and that I was in the process of having it corrected, as if that one grade were the deal breaker.

"I'll tell you what," he said, looking at Ethan. "Take the SSAT, and if you do well, you're in." Then he added, "Do you *want* to come to Fordham Prep?"

"Yes," Ethan said, though I'm pretty sure what he really meant was "I know it'll be good for me, but I don't really want to work any harder."

The SSAT (not related to the SAT) is one of the entrance exams required for admission to private secondary schools. By that morning in Mr. Lauber's office, there was one test date left—in June—before the next school year. Ethan would have exactly one shot.

We picked up a copy of the SSAT study guide on our way home so he could prepare. I wouldn't swear on my mother's life that Ethan "studied" for the SSAT, though he did crack the book every day, which was exciting to see. He seemed to know, somewhere inside, that he needed to be functioning better. Otherwise he would have balked, and he didn't. He was trying.

Three weeks later, of course, in true Ethan fashion, we had a worst-case-scenario experience on test day. Ethan had gone out with his friends for pizza the night before the test and woke up a few hours later with a terrible case of food poisoning.

The next morning at the crack of dawn, I drove him across the county to a testing center, where he took a mini-me SAT. He'd stopped retching by the time we got there, but he took the test on fumes, praying the whole time he'd make it through without throwing up. When I picked him up afterward, he was positively green, but he had survived.

And he had scored just above the line Mr. Lauber had drawn. He was in.

When I told my parents I'd be sending my non-Catholic suburban son on two trains into the heart of the Bronx each morning come fall, I was ecstatic. (I had decided on the two-train commute because Ethan would be riding with Chris, who had been making the trip for a year, and Ethan couldn't take the afternoon bus in any event because he would be staying late for sports.)

Leaving the safety of the suburbs every day was quite an adventure for my little boy, and the commute produced a whole new realm of mishap to manage from my corporate office in Manhattan. A few months into the school year, Ethan mentioned that he and Chris were leaving the Harlem station, where they had to change trains, to get breakfast at a local bodega, so there was that to worry about. The ride home was even more suspense filled because, as it turned out, Ethan and Chris often took different trains after school, so Ethan had to manage that leg of the trip on his own. There were days when Ethan fell asleep on the ride home, waking up discombobulated and an hour past our station, with no idea what to do. I had to teach him to set his watch alarm before nodding off. And there were a few frantic calls that he'd gotten on the wrong train altogether and needed to know how to get back on the right one. I'd sneak out of meetings and Google the answer, then we'd text each other until he was safe and sound on the correct Metro North train to our town.

One night he got off the train after track practice holding his pants up with his hand, even though he'd worn a belt to school. Belts are part of the Fordham Prep uniform.

"Ethan," I said. "Those aren't your pants!"

"Yes they are," he insisted for the whole ride home. We bickered about it until we were inside the house, where I made him show me the tag, which of course revealed that the pants were a few sizes larger than the ones he'd worn to school. He'd mistaken his khakis for a bigger kid's pants in the locker room after track practice. I still feel bad for that other boy, who's probably scarred for life after having to squeeze into pants three sizes smaller. (We never did figure out whose pants they were.) A few months later, the same thing happened with someone else's sneakers.

Despite the mishaps, Fordham Prep was the perfect school for Ethan. Perfect in every way except for the fact that, although I could see that Ethan was working harder, his grades did not improve. He continued to get mostly B's with the occasional A and C thrown in for good measure.

At times it seemed as if Ethan couldn't catch a break. Freshman year there were the concussions—three minor ones in one month—which rendered my unfailingly optimistic son mildly depressed and out of focus for several months before he was himself again.

Sophomore year things were looking up until November, when Ethan came down with a case of mononucleosis so severe he was like Rip Van Winkle. I have never seen anyone sleep that much in my life: sixteen hours a night, every night, for an entire year, which, believe me, is *terrible* for the GPA.

Which brings me to the story of how I came to take the SAT seven times in one year. By the end of Ethan's sophomore year, heading into the all-important junior year, I had a son with a B average, taking non-honors courses and not excelling in extracurriculars (though he is a very good piano player).

I had seen more studying going on during those first two years of high school, but there was a lot of convalescing, too, not to mention the socializing and the video games. Ethan was a "normal" kid who got B's and C's, not one of the stressed-out strivers you read about.

In fact, he was just like me when I was in high school. And while it was true that I'd had a successful career despite my average grades and scores, the world was different now. When I graduated from college, in 1989, unemployment had been falling sharply for six years straight, and the world was brimming with opportunity. Twenty years later, the land I would be sending my little tadpole into was a different place. At summer's end, the middle of the Great Recession, millions were out of work and the news was filled with worry that we were heading into a double-dip recession or, worse, that we were already in one. That August, the economy created no new jobs at all.* The days when you could la-di-dah

---

* The August 0 was eventually revised upward to 104,000, still well below the number needed to absorb all the new high school and college graduates looking for their first jobs. But as Ethan returned to school, the official number of net new jobs was 0.

your way out of Bennington, into the Radcliffe publishing course, as I did, and from there to a guaranteed starter job in the industry—a job, not an internship—were gone.

In truth, I was only subliminally aware of how bad things were. I was keeping my head down, avoiding the news. Not intentionally—my conscious thought was that I was too overwhelmed by work and family to read the paper, and I was. But looking back I see myself hunkered down. Which was probably just as well.

So I didn't know the numbers, not then, *but I could feel them*. I could feel that I would be sending two children into a hard world. The older of those children, Ethan, was a boy who was "happy getting B's" and had gotten an awful lot of them.

And I didn't have two nickels saved for college. Budgeting is not my forte—though I am a master worrier, and a warrior—and I needed a plan for Ethan to go to college: how to get in *and* how to pay for it. But judging from everything I read, B students didn't seem to attract a lot of merit aid. There was nothing we could do about that now; by the end of sophomore year, a student's GPA is pretty much locked in. Was I supposed to call the colleges and let them know about my son's concussions and mono? Of course not, but doors had been closed.

I was beginning to feel frantic, which is why I started poking around the SAT. The test seemed to offer a last-ditch chance to turn things around.

Somewhere in that search, I read an article about SAT scores and merit aid. "High scores = money." That was the gist.

A possibility presented itself. Ethan could study for the SAT, earn high scores, and get a scholarship at a decent school somewhere.

Of course, most of the people I knew in my small town hated the idea that I planned to train my son to get top SAT scores, but what choice did I have, really? I feared for my son's future. The fact that I had managed to succeed despite mediocre grades was irrelevant. Those were kinder, gentler times.

So I cooked up a plan that took on a life of its own.

I

THE PERFECT DO-OVER

How It All Began

I'm a forty-eight-year-old mother of two teenagers, and this whole crazy "perfect score project" started out as a scheme to rescue my kid from . . . *sliding by.* I thought maybe I could motivate Ethan to care about the SAT, just a little, if I climbed into the trenches myself.

Initially, though, the number of test-prep options left me agog (over a million on Google). My *original* idea was to try out twelve different methods of test prep the year before Ethan would be taking *his* first SAT. But as I saw how vast and complicated the realm of SAT prep appeared to be, I kept adding layers to the idea. What was at first simply the notion of taking an official SAT at school with the kids mushroomed into a vow to take the test every time it was offered in 2011 (seven times in all). And I'd try out different locations for each test, which turned out to be a total of five. (I didn't anticipate the issue of test centers booking up early and ended up having to repeat a few). I wanted to see if the location played any role in the test experience, so I chose schools ranging from an elite private school in the suburbs to an urban public school in the Bronx.

My journey would start with the first SAT of 2011, on January 22, and Ethan would take *his* first SAT exactly one year after me—in January of 2012. We'd overlap in our preparation about halfway through the year because (a) juniors take the PSAT in the fall (October of 2011 for Ethan; SAT No. 5 for me), so he'd need to study; and (b) I know my son well enough to realize he does better with some spare runway to build momentum.

In spite of the escalating nature of the project, I was excited about the "study together" part and assumed that by halfway through the year, with four SAT experiences under my belt, I'd have my bearings and be able to adroitly show my son "the SAT ropes."

Let's clarify something from the start, though: I did *not* expect Ethan to pull off a perfect SAT score (though I wouldn't have discouraged him from trying had he wanted to do so of his own accord). I found that by putting the pressure on myself, not on him, I was able to hold the bar reasonably high without having to nag or push (too much). I was "modeling" the behavior that I was hoping to cultivate in my son. In the end Ethan came up with his own number, which we both agreed was the right one.

The Question of the Day

Daunted by the million hits on Google, I started with the College Board Question of the Day. My friend Catherine told me to sign up. She was a year ahead of me with her son Chris and was studying for the SAT alongside him, and I thought it looked like fun. You could say Catherine was my first SAT mentor.

The first week I tried answering the Question of the Day I got most of the questions wrong, which was unnerving. Now, granted, I was trying to answer on the fly from a BlackBerry while cooking breakfast and getting kids out the door—but still, it was upsetting. The second week I decided to focus and see if I could answer the questions if I paid attention. I did better, though I still missed the few math questions. I *was* encouraged, though.

By week three, I was so into it that I gave myself permission to take the later train to work if I needed a few extra minutes to get the question right. I'd become hooked on these questions. What began as a little fun with the Question of the Day had developed into a full-blown habit. My fourth week, I hit the jackpot: all seven questions right. I was over the moon. I told my children, friends, and family, made an announcement on Facebook and Twitter—even went so far as to write a blog post, declaring to the world: *I'm going to get a perfect SAT score!*

There was no turning back.

The Wrath of Perfectionism

From the beginning, that word "perfect" had people riled up—so much so that I started to feel self-conscious. I'd backpedal if I sensed someone was going to take issue with the word, and I'd lean on the "project" part, to ease people's anxiety about "perfect."

"What? Do you think the person who wrote *The Happiness Project* is *happy*?" I'd ask. "It's a *project*," I'd say. "It's about the journey."

I *almost* caved and called it "The Higher Score Project." One night, during dinner, I received a call from the marketing expert for the group that was designing my website. She told me that "the team" wanted me to know they all hated the word "perfect" and were in agreement that I should switch "perfect" to "higher": The Higher Score Project. I said okay, though it didn't feel right, and immediately logged on to GoDaddy, where I purchased every conceivable variation of HigherScore.com. Then I returned to the dinner table, where I told my kids the new name.

"You just lowered the bar—*a lot*," said my daughter, Daisy. Ethan nodded in agreement.

After word of the project got out in my very small town, I began to feel as though people were seeing me as "the mom who pushes her kids too hard." I was sure I could feel people staring when I'd walk into local shops and could practically hear what they were thinking. "There's that lady who's pressuring her son about the SAT." I'd try to convince myself it had to be my imagination, but then something would happen that would substantiate my fears. One time, I walked into a restaurant and a "friend" I hardly knew sidled up to me, a few glasses of wine into her evening, and whispered, "Don't worry, I don't believe what they say."

A few months after I'd finished my seventh and final SAT, I was waiting in line with some other moms to meet with the guidance counselor assigned to the juniors. It was parent-teacher conference night at Ethan's school, and the guidance line seemed longer than it had in prior years. I knew the woman sitting next to me a little better than the others because our sons were friends.

"So what's this SAT thing I hear you're doing?" she asked.

I didn't want the other parents within earshot to hear. They'd think I was insane.

"I took the test seven times last year," I whispered, "to see if I could motivate Ethan."

The woman looked perplexed, so I continued. "I was overwhelmed," I said. "I didn't know which prep class to sign him up for"—as if that explained why a middle-aged woman would subject herself, willingly, to seven SATs.

She still looked confused, so I went on digging my hole.

"It started with that Question of the Day from the College Board," I said, "and I don't know exactly how it happened, but before I knew what hit me, I was into it—like, *really* into it."

Out of the corner of my eye I noticed one mom lean in a little and another tuck her hair behind her ear, subtly. I could feel what they were all thinking: "Does this woman know something about the SAT?"

Right then, the guidance counselor opened his office door and a mother walked out confidently, her "what's next" checklist restocked. She was infused with a little more clarity than the rest of us, who were all waiting patiently for a turn with the college gatekeeper. The mother with whom I'd been whispering was called in next. She walked into the office, but before closing the door she turned around and asked—from clear across the room—"What's the *one* thing I need to know?"

I felt like Katie Couric had just asked me one last question before the commercial break.

God, I hope I don't embarrass my son.

THE ONE THING YOU SHOULD KNOW

- Taking full, timed practice SATs using College Board material (only) is an *essential* ingredient for success on the SAT.
- Mimic the actual test conditions as closely as possible, including the five-minute breaks and bubble sheets.
- It's critical to review all mistakes until you understand them so well that you are able to explain them to someone else.
- Keep track of how many questions you got wrong or guessed at and categorize them (e.g., three triangle problems wrong, four verb agreement mistakes).
- The SAT is every bit as much about performance on test day as it is about the knowledge being tested. Experienced tutors advise taking ten full practice tests prior to sitting for the real SAT, and the most exclusive test-prep companies have their students take fifteen or more full tests—*before* ever taking an official test. The College Board offers twenty-one practice SATs and plenty of extra practice problems, between the Blue Book and the online course.

A few weeks after declaring my goal, I had breakfast with an SAT tutor. I told her all about my plan: the perfect score, the different methods I would try, the various test locations, and so forth.

She looked at me with eyes of pity and didn't say a word.

"But I answered the Question of the Day right seven days in a row," I said. "Isn't that what I'll be doing on the SAT?"

She smiled, but remained silent, so I went on: "One year, twelve methods, seven SATs . . ." I couldn't get a word of feedback out of her. "But it's my lucky year," I said in a last-ditch attempt to shake loose some sort of reaction. My birthday was scheduled to fall on 11/11/11 that year, and I *was* feeling lucky.

Not a peep.

My lucky year didn't unfold at all the way it was supposed to.

Trying to Light the Fire

The project started as a way to help Ethan—to ignite a fire and motivate him—but not too far into it I got a teensy bit crazed. (Okay, maybe it was more like possessed.)

Call me crazy, but I enjoyed studying for the SAT as an adult and, yes, I do realize this is unusual, especially when you consider that my high school scores were abysmal. Actually, maybe an SAT obsession makes complete sense if you look at it through that lens. I'd always assumed I hadn't done well in high school because I hadn't tried hard, or cared. That was 1982, and things were different back then. Now I wanted to see what I could do if I did try and did care.

Looking back, maybe I should have called it "The Perfect Do-Over." But that insight didn't come until much later. At the time, this was about how I could salvage Ethan's thirteen years of education, at the very last minute, with the SAT.

I ended up salvaging a lot more than that.

2

BACK TO THE FUTURE

*There are many shitty things about being a grown-up. You have
to make money. You have to do taxes. You have to show up for
your bail hearings.... But one of the few upsides of being an
adult is that you NEVER have to take the SAT again.*

—DREW MAGARY, DEADSPIN

The SAT, circa 1982

I remember two things about my SAT experience in high school in
1982:

1. It felt like everyone had the playbook except me.
2. I was relieved to find the word "iota" in the analogies section
   (which no longer exists) because it was the *only* question I was
   sure of on the entire test.

My scores were *very* bad, and they had the effect of whittling down my
college choices to the "SAT-optional" schools of the day. I knew of only five
such colleges: Bennington, Bard, Sarah Lawrence, Hampshire, and Bowdoin. I didn't have the grades for Bowdoin, so I applied to the other four.

Out of this experience, I built a story that made sense: I didn't do
well because I didn't try, and I didn't try because I didn't care. *Of course*
I would have done better if I had studied.

As a mother thirty years later, I produced another story that made perfect sense—a story about helping my son perform well on the SAT. In this story, I was trying to rescue my kid from doing the minimum. I wanted to motivate him to study for the SAT without nagging. I didn't need my son to be a star, that wasn't the issue. I wanted him to go to a decent college, and I needed a way to pay for it.

Thinking about my son, I didn't remember any "trauma" or "unresolved issues" or "test anxiety" from my own SAT experience. Why would I? Low scores or not, I had gotten into college, where I had done well, and I had had a successful career in book publishing. I had no idea I was carting around any baggage. One day, though, I was enlightened by sheer serendipity.

A Treasure Trove of Truth

Years ago my parents delivered a box with my name on it, which they'd found in their basement. They told me to throw it out if I didn't want it, but instead I put it in my basement.

This was out of character for me. I hate clutter. I'm sparse. I feel a sense of accomplishment when I rid myself of things, and it doesn't even matter what those things are. I love the sensation of seeing Hefty bags filled with "stuff" waiting at the curbside for garbage men to pick up.

But for several years the box sat unopened in my basement.

When I moved houses, I brought it with me to my *new* basement, where it waited another year or two until I repositioned it in front of my office door, thinking that if I had to trip over it to get into my office I might open it, finally.

Cut to December 2010.

I had to register for the January 2011 SAT. I logged on to the College Board's website but, feeling nervous, found myself procrastinating. Casting around for something to do that did not involve registering for the SAT, I decided it was as good a time as any to open up that box.

Inside I discovered my very own treasure trove of truth, waiting for me after almost thirty years. The box was filled with water-stained letters, all stuck together in a unity of neglect. The letters seemed so grateful for the fresh air that they fluffed up in anticipation of enlightening their suddenly attentive reader.

The letters had all been written to me in the years 1982 and 1983, my junior and senior years of high school, the exact same period I was about to live through as a mother with my son.

Apparently, we used to hand-write long letters back then. I'd forgotten this. Some of the letters were over ten pages long. They were written on rice paper and yellow legal pads, in ballpoint pen that was smudged from having survived years of basement floods. There were love letters and notes from my parents, letters from best friends, and cards from my long-dead grandmother, who always signed off by saying she'd included a stamp so I'd write back.

There were pages and pages that reflected back to me things I must have said to my loved ones, and if I can distill the realization I was having into one line, it would be this: forget what you *think* you know—those memories are nothing more than wishes, lies, and dreams.

The letters made it clear that in fact I had had a great deal of anxiety around the "getting into college" process, including the SAT. And, judging by the expressions of concern in the letters, I had been making some bad choices. As an adult, I had believed for years that all I had been showing back then was normal teenage rebellion—not the extreme angst I was reading about now. Clearly, my teen years had been more difficult than I remembered, for me and for people who cared about me.

"Listen to me," my friend Martha wrote in 1982. "Look inside yourself and ask if what you're doing is fun. I tell you honey, it isn't. God, I wish you'd get your act together."

My father's letters read like time capsules, with references to Three Mile Island and *Terms of Endearment*. "It's not easy to step back and let you make your own decisions," he wrote.

The letters from my mother were the most surprising. I'd been telling people for decades how difficult she was, but her letters were downright loving, even—dare I say it—*warm*. "I want you to get a good education, Debbie," she wrote, her handwriting looking like she'd penned the words yesterday.

There were amends to be made.

And perhaps my obsession with the SAT had deeper roots than I'd thought.

Registering for the SAT

On December 16, 2010, I registered for the first of seven SATs in my lucky year.

Name:	Debbie Stier
Sex:	Female
Birth Date:	Huh, it never occurred to me until that moment that they might not allow adults to take the SAT. I wasn't sure if I should lie about my age (I'm not a good liar). I typed in the truth: 11/11/1965.
Test Center:	Masters School, Dobbs Ferry, New York. This was the Four Seasons of private schools. As long as they were offering it as a location, why not? Naturally, I assumed that "elite private school" equated to "best test conditions."
Test Date:	January 22, 2011. *Good,* I thought, noting that twenty-two was twice my lucky number of eleven.
Address:	Irvington, New York.

I'd moved to Irvington from New York City a decade before "for the children," just like almost everyone else in town. It's a bedroom community just north of the city, and the birthplace of "The Legend of Sleepy Hollow." I visited one Halloween and that was that. I was intoxicated by the festivities and all the candy; I felt like I'd discovered the Promised Land, where children scamper through grassy parks that are as beguiling as any painting you'd find in the Metropolitan Museum. It was the Garden of Eden—for rugrats.

CHOOSING A TEST LOCATION

Don't assume that "fancy school" means "best test location." Confirm the following with friends or contact the test center supervisor. (Each test center has a test center supervisor who is responsible for the test and can be found by calling the school and requesting contact information.)

The characteristics of a great test location:

- Classrooms, rather than gymnasiums or cafeterias, are used for testing.
- Full-size desks and chairs are used (versus chairs with attached tablet desks).
- There is a visible clock in the testing room, and a board that displays the "end time."
- Proctors abide by the official test rules.

These details may sound small, but they can make a big difference in your score. The College Board will allow date and location changes for an additional fee as long as the changes are made before the change deadline, which is noted on the admission ticket (usually about fourteen days prior to the test).

Bells and Whistles

During the registration process I clicked Yes to everything the College Board had to offer, putting over $150 on my credit card:

- SAT registration
- The *Official SAT Study Guide* (aka the Blue Book)
- The Official SAT Online Course
- Question-and-Answer Service (aka QAS). I wasn't sure exactly what this was, but yes, I wanted it. I wanted *all* the trimmings this time around.

It would take months before I found my sea legs and figured out how to make use of the tools, and even longer before I understood them well enough to explain them to someone else. The final step was to print my "SAT Admission Ticket," which I did, noticing that at the bottom it said:

Important Message:
Report to the gym. Please wear soft-soled shoes.

Very back to the future.

QUESTION-AND-ANSWER SERVICE VS. STUDENT ANSWER SERVICE

The Question-and-Answer Service (QAS) and Student Answer Service (SAS) are available for purchase at the time of registration and for up to five months after the test date. One or the other (not both) is available for purchase for each SAT. The QAS is more expensive and includes the SAT test booklet. The SAS is available the months when the QAS is not offered and is essentially an answer sheet without the questions.

Question-and-Answer Service (QAS):

- Detailed score report, including question type, level of difficulty, correct answer, and your answer

- **Includes test booklet**
- Available for tests: January, May, October
- Arrives in mail six to eight weeks after test date

Student Answer Service (SAS):

- Detailed score report, including question type, level of difficulty, correct answer, and your answer
- **Does *not* include test booklet**
- Available for tests: March, June, September, December

Both reports are worthwhile if you plan to take the SAT again. Knowing the question type and level of difficulty is useful information for preparation.

3

HIGH ANXIETY

Most people's feelings about the SAT and other standardized tests are not entirely rational. The tests have a power out of proportion to their actual content, and they awaken smoldering insecurities in the people who take them.

—DAVID OWEN, NONE OF THE ABOVE

Procrastination

There were five and a half weeks before my first SAT, and I was almost giddy with anticipation. I felt intensely motivated and couldn't wait to get ready for the test . . . which turned out to mean a frenzied "clearing of the decks" rather than the more traditional "test prep" involving actual study. There was laundry to do, mail to read, errands to do—and all of these things had to be done *first*, before I could sit down and open a book.

I was procrastinating. It was *productive* procrastination; it wasn't as if I was watching TV or relaxing. I wasn't! I was busy getting ready—*to get ready.*

CULTIVATE AWARENESS OF DISTRACTIONS

Psychologist Ben Bernstein compiled a nearly definitive list of "distracting activities" in his book *Test Success!*, many of which were all too familiar to me. Dr. Bernstein advises cultivating awareness of these distractions so you can nip them in the bud.

- Doing laundry
- Shopping online
- Complaining
- Answering e-mail
- Cleaning the house
- Paying bills
- Going to the gym
- Making lists

People procrastinate to avoid the pain of unpleasant tasks, but procrastination causes even more stress and poor performance to boot.

SAT No. 1 was supposed to be a baseline (i.e., no preparation), but of course, I planned to do a little bit of *secret* studying. No one needed to know my *real* baseline. I still hadn't decided which prep method to use; I just knew that I wanted to get my feet wet before test day.

By New Year's Day, I'd checked off every single item from my to-do list—the first and last time I've ever achieved a perfectly clean slate—and there was nothing left to do *except* prepare for the test. I had twenty-one days left.

Here's the weird part: at that precise moment of reckoning, when the skies cleared and the fields of obligation were laid bare of tasks, the rocket fuel that had provided me with enough strength to pick up cars as if they were Tinkertoys evaporated, and I was suddenly overcome by the most extreme fatigue I'd ever felt. I melted into a puddle on the couch.

Looking back, I'm sure that was the first of many signs I missed that I was suffering from test anxiety. I had no idea that "inert" could be a symptom.

PHYSICAL SIGNS OF TEST ANXIETY

To perform well, it's essential to remain calm, and recognizing anxiety's signals is the first step. Dr. Bernstein lists several symptoms in his book, including:

- You're overly tired or you can't sleep.
- You have a headache, a shoulder ache, or some other body ache.
- Your breathing is irregular: you hold your breath or you gasp for air.
- Your mind races.
- You want to run away.
- You speak too fast or too loud.

A few days later, when I realized winter break was over and my kids were headed back to school, I felt hysterical. Only seventeen days left until my first SAT. My friends and family kept calling to see if I was "preparing" yet (I wasn't), and they did me no favors with their queries even if they were calling out of concern. My father sounded seriously worried.

"*Dad*," I'd say, "I'm not studying on purpose. I need to get a baseline. *After* the test—that's when I'll study."

This calmed him down—a little.

It was as if all of us had been overcome by an acute case of group test anxiety. There isn't a person in my circle who does not know what a baseline is, or that if the point of the project was for my scores to *improve*, I should start with the lowest scores possible, not the highest. Rationally speaking, my job on this first test was to establish that low-score baseline. But none of us was being rational. It was as if I were sixteen again, facing the test, and my friends and family were facing the test through me.

That was the problem with blabbing my intention to conquer the SAT. I made people uncomfortable. There was "sympathy anxiety" from the low scorers, and apprehension from the high-scoring crowd, as though a perfect score from me could jeopardize their own status.

No one forgets an SAT score—ever.

My predicament was that I wanted to *appear* smarter from the get-go than I thought I might turn out to be. For decades I'd been making excuses about my high school SAT scores ("I'm creative . . ."), but I feared that maybe those high school scores were a legitimate measure of my intelligence—and what if I hadn't gotten any smarter over the years? No one needed to know that, especially my kids.

An honest-to-God naked baseline was too much, even for me. I *had* to brush up—for the children.

My bookshelves were already bloated with test-prep guides: the Blue Book, Stanley Kaplan, The Princeton Review, Gruber's guides, *Dr. John Chung's SAT Math*, Tutor Ted, *Outsmarting the SAT, Hack the SAT, Perfect 800, Up Your Score, Zen in the Art of the SAT*, and so on. Of course, part of that I chalk up to the fact that I'm a book nut; I shop for books the way some women shop for shoes. No matter what the problem, I'm always sure there's a book (or, more accurately, many books) that will tell me how to solve it, even if I don't have time to read them all. I'm comforted by their presence, and I like knowing that they're there . . . *just in case.* So I had built myself a cozy nest on the couch with all of my SAT books and office supplies (I *love* office supplies)—colored pens and stickies, highlighters and freshly sharpened No. 2 pencils—and when my nest looked like it was strong enough to support me in this secret cram session, I nestled in, ready to incubate for a few weeks before the test.

I was pretty sure I could consume massive amounts of information before test day. After twenty years in book publishing, I can read *very* fast.

DOES CRAMMING WORK?

According to cognitive scientist Daniel Willingham, cramming may help in the short run, but it does *not* have lasting effects.

- Research shows that spacing study time over several sessions leads to better retention of material than studying the same amount of time in one session. This is known as "the spacing effect."
- *Less* practice time is required if the practice is spaced.
- Cramming, also known as "massed practice," might allow you to remember material for one day, but research shows that there is a considerable drop-off of recall by the following week.

I started ricocheting from book to book, which wasn't unusual for me, though maybe I *was* a bit more frantic that day. I opened one book . . . too hard, so I put it down. Then I opened another . . . too easy, so I put that one down too. Then I tried another, spent a few minutes answering problems, and then switched books, again.

This is called "willy-nilly test prep," and it's very, very bad. It goes beyond not helpful and should be considered "harmful." I was growing more frenzied by the second—a whirling dervish, trying to be a "jack-of-all-trades" but mastering none. It was not a pretty sight, and my increasingly agitated state began to resemble the sort of test anxiety that I *was* familiar with (e.g., hysteria, panic, confusion).

I'd unleashed a beast—there was anxiety everywhere, and it felt boundless as I lay there alone on the couch amid my test-prep books and office supplies. In an effort to get control, I decided I should choose one thing and focus on that. I picked the essay. I flipped through the College Board's Blue Book, looking for an official essay prompt to practice with.

Can the daily actions of average people have a significant impact on the course of history?

I couldn't think of a single thing to say. Twenty years in book publishing and I was suddenly illiterate. It was as though, in my panic, I had induced my own amnesia. Just then my daughter, Daisy, came home, and as she walked through the door, I wailed, "I'm *freaking out!*"

Daisy looked at me without an iota of sympathy and said, "That's how I feel every day in school." Then she walked up the stairs to her room, yelling back down for emphasis: "Now you know how I feel."

My little study nest now felt more like a cage. I needed to escape.

I got into my car and started driving without any destination in mind. I wanted to drive out of my skin.

I parked about a quarter mile from my house, outside a yoga studio I'd always been curious about but had never had time to investigate.

I'd always been jealous of the "yoga people," envious of that look they all had, like there wasn't a thing in the world that was pressing. I wanted to feel that way. So, on impulse, I walked into the studio and, without even so much as trying a class, told the manager, "Sign me up for a year." I must have looked positively feral.

But through oms and chants, downward-facing dogs and happy-baby poses, I managed to climb off the ledge that day, and even had an epiphany during shavasana. My eleventh-hour revelation was that the best thing I could do to prepare for this first SAT was to learn how to relax—and to breathe.

I went to yoga every day until the first SAT, and ultimately yoga, not the Blue Book, became the first test prep I tried. In hindsight, I don't think it was such a bad plan.

4

SAT No. 1: THE MENTAL MARATHON

I've Arrived

Date: *January 22, 2011*

Scene: *Masters School, Dobbs Ferry*

I arrived at 7:15 in the morning. The SAT admission ticket said to arrive by 7:45, but I wasn't taking any chances. Already the foyer outside the gym at the Masters School was nearly three-quarters full—perhaps seventy-five students, all clustered together in two- and three-person pods. A few parents lingered near their children; everyone knew someone but me. Periodically, the head proctor announced that they'd be checking us in at 8:00 a.m. sharp.

I had no one to talk to for forty minutes. *An eternity.* I felt as though I were sixteen years old again—*awkward*. I fiddled with my phone, trying to kill time and fit in. Then I remembered the ticket said to leave cell phones at home, so I tucked the device away in my purse before anyone noticed. Speaking of purses, apparently it's not in fashion to carry a bag to the SAT—at least, not at the Masters School. The kids around me were all carrying stray pencils and a calculator in their bare hands. This felt positively reckless to me.

Where are their extra batteries?

The ticket instructions advised test takers to bring a calculator. I had brought *two,* plus a box of triple-A batteries because you never know. The ticket also specified two No. 2 pencils. I had two *boxes* and a sharpener, too, just in case. It must have been the mother in me.

Maternal instincts probably spurred me to overpack snacks as well. I thought long and hard about that snack bag, certain that proper sustenance was an essential prerequisite for success on the SAT.

Focusing on the wrong things is another sign of test anxiety, according to Dr. Bernstein.

THE THREE LITTLE BREAKS

Snacking is allowed during the three five-minute breaks. I attempted to sample everything I could think of that would enhance performance, from Red Bull to peanut butter, to everything in between. In the end, the list below is what I found to be most effective in warding off hunger and boosting energy, though it's possible that simply *believing* they are effective is the secret sauce.

- **DARK CHOCOLATE:** Try for 70 percent or higher cocoa content—for example, one Willy Wonka–sized bar.
- **WATER:** I'm *certain* water makes me think more clearly.
- **SLICED RED APPLE:** A story on calorie restriction in the *New York Times* reported that apples are superb at warding off hunger in people eating 25 percent fewer calories than they normally consume. Even people who, at the study's beginning, disliked apples ate them because they were effective. My "research" concurred: apples fill the belly.
- **LISTERINE STRIPS:** An energizing pick-me-up, like taking a shower. You get to start over, feeling refreshed.

Oh, the irony . . . Here I was, worried that my fellow testers didn't have enough pencils and snacks, and meanwhile they had all likely been receiving professional tutoring for months, testing each other on the one hundred most frequently used vocab words, going over literary examples for the essay, and swapping tips for working out algebra problems on their highfalutin calculators.

At 8:00 sharp, the proctor appeared in the foyer, announced that it was time for the test to begin, and like a border collie herded us through double doors that led to a card table where we presented our identification and test tickets. We were checked off a list, handed a test booklet, and told to find a seat.

Next to the check-in table was a stack of answer booklets. "Do I take one?" I asked. I was confused.

"We give them out when everyone's seated," the proctor said, noticing for the first time that I wasn't what he was expecting to see when he looked up. This was the first of many "What's *she* doing here?" looks I was to get that year. On test day, I always forgot I was different. I felt like a teenager.

The gym was lined with rows of tablet-arm desks, those desk/chair combinations with the little pork chop–shaped writing surface. According to the official SAT requirements, they pass muster (i.e., twelve inches by fifteen inches). According to me, they are too small to hold both SAT booklets—your test booklet *and* your answer book—comfortably, let alone two test booklets, a calculator, and two No. 2 pencils. I would go so far as to say it's worth driving farther to avoid a pork chop–desk experience.

But I didn't realize that then. I had simply made the assumption: fancy school = best option. I followed the crowd into the gym and sat in the first available seat, which happened to be in the middle of the large basketball court. Seating was self-serve, and, like high school kids everywhere, the test takers that morning were filling the seats starting from the back and moving row by row to the front. No one wants to sit in the front row in high school.

This time-honored seating procedure was the first irregularity of several I would experience taking the SAT. According to the official testing rules, seating is supposed to be assigned before students arrive. But of the seven SATs I took in 2011, I came across assigned seating exactly once. For every other test, students chose their seats. If you find yourself in that position, I'd advise sitting front and center. You want to eliminate as many distractions as possible, and having a kid in front of you stretching his arms back in your direction makes sustaining focus that much more challenging.

By 8:30 everyone was seated, and the proctor began reading from the official script: "Good morning," he said. "Today you're going to take the SAT . . ."

He read the same way all the other proctors around the world—175 countries, three million students, seven Saturdays per year—are instructed to read the text: *verbatim*. It took a few tests for me to realize that even the pauses are standardized: "Remove everything from your desk . . ." Pause. "Store devices away now . . ." Pause. Eventually, the proctor would get to "If you brought a backup calculator or extra batteries, get those out and put them under your seat in plain sight . . ."

CALCULATORS AND THE SAT

In 1994 the SAT math section was changed, and students were allowed to use calculators for the first time. Every question *can* be solved without a calculator, but the College Board recommends that you bring one you're comfortable using, along with spare batteries.

- **PERMISSIBLE CALCULATORS:** Scientific, graphing, four-function.
- **NOT PERMISSIBLE:** Typewriter-like keypads; anything that makes noise, uses tape, or needs an electrical outlet; cell phones; organizers; and anything that can access the Internet.
- **CALCULATOR MALFUNCTIONS:** Students are allowed to replace batteries or use an approved backup calculator.

- **MOST ADVANCED CALCULATOR ALLOWED:** The TI-89 *does algebra*. It's also intimidating, and you need a lot of practice to become comfortable enough to operate it on test day. You need to know where the functions are, the same way a touch typist knows QWERTY.
- **MULTIPLE CALCULATORS:** Students may use more than one calculator—for example, the TI-89 for algebra questions and another calculator for the rest.

Most kids that day were using a Texas Instruments TI-83 or 84. As for me, I'd brought a fifteen-year-old, no-frills freebie from the bank, a corporate thank-you for opening an account. Absurdly, I found myself feeling mortified by this fresh evidence of my outsider status. If you've forgotten what it was like to be a teenager, take the SAT. It comes back fast.

After the directions had been read, we began the test. Elsewhere, in hundreds of schools up and down the Eastern Standard Time zone, thousands of students began theirs, too. An hour later, and then every hour after that, the SAT rolled out to the next time zone and the next, moving around the world like a wave at a baseball game.

Showtime

The first section is always the essay. You have twenty-five minutes to respond to a prompt, cramming your most profound, original, and grammatically correct ideas onto two pages.

If you finish early, you can't turn to another section, a rule that holds for the entire test. A section is a section: no "flipping," as they say.

I scored a 9 out of 12. I'd had no idea what I was doing, so I was okay with a 9 and assumed that with practice I'd score a 12. So the many 10's that came later hurt much more than the initial 9. Incidentally, you *can* score an 800 on the writing section with a 10 on your essay (or even a 9, on occasion, depending on the curve of the test that month). But to hit

800 with a 9 or 10 on the essay, your multiple-choice score on grammar has to be perfect. You can't make a single mistake.

The prompt that morning asked if an idealistic approach was less valuable than a practical one. I wrote what I thought they wanted: an essay about Martin Luther King Jr. and Rosa Parks. I'd never written a timed essay on a standardized test before, but Catherine's son Chris had been espousing some ridiculous rule about using Martin Luther King Jr. in every essay, no matter what the topic was. The one time he actually did this (on his third outing), he scored an 11. The theory took on new meaning after his mother, Catherine, scored a 10 (prompt: Rules versus Freedom) when *she* took the SAT. Catherine has a PhD and teaches college freshman composition; she *grades* five-paragraph essays for a living. Plus the College Board has used passages from her books in the critical reading section. She told me she'd written her essay on law and economics (in South America, no less), citing Hernando de Soto's book *The Mystery of Capital*. And she scored a *10*.

The funny part was that when she told a friend about her 10, he said, "You must have had a bad day." That's how much authority the SAT has. People just assume the test is right. Catherine told him, "The scorers had a bad day, not me."

My feeling is that if a composition instructor and author with a PhD can't score an 11, then listen to the experts who tell you to shoot for a 10 and spend the bulk of your time studying for the multiple-choice section, where the scoring isn't arbitrary.

I was midsentence when the proctor said to stop work and put our pencils down. Twenty-five minutes never felt so short.

After the essay comes Section 2, which can be math, reading, or writing, and then the first of three five-minute breaks, at which point you're allowed to walk around, use the restroom, or eat a snack "in the designated area with your ID," though I never located a "designated area" for snacking at any of the test sites. Everyone ate everywhere, as far as I could tell.

Once everyone is seated after the break, the proctor reads out more instructions: "Turn to the back page and find the Certification Box.

Copy the requested statement in *cursive writing* (not print)." Always, at this point, in test locations across the country, scattered snickers break out across the room because everyone thinks they're the only one who can't write cursive. The truth is that many people can't write in cursive these days, especially those young enough to be taking the SAT. Of the 1.5 million students who took the SAT in 2006—the first year that the SAT included the essay—only 15 percent wrote the essay in cursive. Everyone else printed, many in block letters.

"Sign your full name as you would on an official document."

WHAT'S A CERTIFICATION STATEMENT?

The official statement, written in cursive, is intended to prevent test fraud. By signing your full name as you would on an official document, you're agreeing to the College Board's conditions, which include not taking the questions out of the room or discussing them with anyone by any means, including the Internet. These conditions cover the essay question too. You're not allowed to discuss it until after your essay has been scored and is available online.

All the rules and regulations are spelled out in *The Paper Registration Guide* and on the College Board's website.

During my year of testing, there was often one kid in the room—usually a boy—who had more trouble writing in cursive than everyone else. The rest of the test takers would finish copying the sentence, put down their pencils, and, inevitably, having nothing else to do, turn to watch the boy who was still working. The first time I took the SAT, the boy with the cursive problem was directly behind me, and it felt as if the whole room was staring, like that scene in *The Jerk* where Steve Martin walks into the restaurant alone and a spotlight follows him to the table while everyone watches. I could almost hear his heart pounding as he wrestled with that one certified sentence while the rest of us waited for him to finish.

The proctor stood over the boy and time froze until finally the proctor said, "Just do your best. Print, and connect the letters." *That poor kid.*

Luckily, there's no need for cursive once you get past the mandatory certification statement. From that point forward, the emphasis is on the fine art of bubbling: filling in the correct circles in those multiple-choice arrays, and knowing how to "grid-in" properly.

Bubbling Errors!

Over the course of the year I developed a bubbling obsession. That might sound crazy, but proper bubbling is a legitimate concern on the SAT, as I learned early on. Some high schools actually hold mandatory bubbling sessions (I'm not kidding).

As far as I was concerned, there was no error more demoralizing than a misbubble, and the potential for a bubbling blunder was not to be underestimated. I wasn't so much concerned with "extraneous marks" (bad) or "filling in the circles completely" (good). Nor was I worried about "improper erasure marks," despite the College Board's frequent reminders on this score.

My own hang-up had to do with bubbling my answers *in the wrong section.* To be fair, the proctor does read a one-line warning alerting test takers to this possibility—but it's brief and buried amidst a lot of other directions:

"There will be more spaces on the answer sheet than there are questions. Be sure to mark your answers *in the correct rows.*"

Personally, I think they should read that line a few decibels louder than the others, so it gets people's attention. After making that very mistake *twice,* I became a compulsive bubble checker.

Here's the danger: The SAT *test booklet* is a separate entity from the SAT *answer book.* Both contain ten sections, but the answer book has forty bubbles per section and there are fewer questions per section in the test booklet. Sections have between fourteen and thirty-five questions. So even if you answer every question on the test, you will leave many bubbles blank. Of course, leaving bubbles blank goes against years of ingrained test-taking experience in school, where leaving an answer space (or a bubble) blank meant you hadn't finished the test. I used to tell the other moms I knew that the extra bubbles were an accident waiting to happen, and in my case that turned out to be true.

Taking my first two SATs, I was halfway through Section 10, nearly four hours into the exam, worn, weary, bleary-eyed, barely able to focus, when I realized mid-section that I had reverted to bubbling Section 9. It was as though my arm had a mind of its own and was determined to leave no bubble blank. But really, my exhausted brain had gone on autopilot, defaulting to a long-ingrained habit of filling in all the answers.

By my third SAT, I knew to be on the lookout for bubbling mishaps when I got to Section 10. But that frantic feeling of realizing I'd been bubbling in the wrong section left me with a yearlong case of "bubble anxiety." I'm sure I lost many valuable minutes checking and rechecking *all* of my bubbles . . . but then again, if you're shooting for a top score you probably can't be too cautious. One bubbling error and it's all over. Fortunately, a single error isn't as big a deal if you're shooting for the 600s.

There is another classic bubbling mistake to be aware of: forgetting to fill in the bubbles altogether. Many students circle or write their answers in the test booklet first, then, as they finish each page, transfer all the answers on the page to the answer booklet en bloc. This tactic saves time, but it, too, goes against ingrained experience telling you that once you've circled the answer, you're done. Catherine's writing score dropped from 800 to 720 when she forgot to transfer the answers from the last page of her test booklet. Even the experts can fall prey to this error. Elizabeth King, an exclusive SAT coach and author of *Outsmarting the SAT*, writes that she scored a 790 one year on the critical reading section because she "forgot to turn the page and accidentally omitted the last two questions in the final section!"

As someone who made careless bubble errors, I know that the brain can go on autopilot when fatigue sets in.

Beware of bubbling errors!

THE FINE ART OF BUBBLING
(AKA THE MOST IMPORTANT BOX IN THE BOOK)

There is nothing more frustrating than making a dumb mistake on the SAT. Careless errors such as misreading the questions or mis-bubbling the answers can be avoided with a good strategy and lots of practice. Below is one bubbling method that Stacey Howe-Lott, an SAT tutor in Seattle, teaches her students.

- Mark your answers in the test booklet.
- Draw a big circle around the answer you choose (circle the letter *and* the answer).
- Write the letter of your answer choice (in large print) to the left of the question. This allows for fast bubbling.
- Draw a large circle to the left of any question you skipped.
- Fill in the bubbles on the answer sheet each time you turn a page in the test book.

After the certification statement came Sections 3 and 4, then a second five-minute break, followed by Sections 5 and 6, then the final five-minute break, and finally a breakless homestretch—Sections 7, 8, 9, and 10—and the test was over.

"We will now collect your answer sheet and test book," the proctor announced. "Please sit quietly until you are dismissed." He walked through the aisles of seats collecting all the answer sheets, then did another lap to collect the test booklets, and we were sent on our way.

SAT TEST FORMAT

The SAT sections are ordered in various sequences, though every SAT consists of ten timed sections (nine sections for students with the extended-time accommodation):

- Section 1, 25 minutes: Essay (everyone)
- Section 2, 25 minutes: Critical Reading, Math, or Writing

- *5-Minute Break*

- Section 3, 25 minutes: Critical Reading, Math, or Writing
- Section 4, 25 minutes: Critical Reading, Math, or Writing

- *5-Minute Break*

- Section 5, 25 minutes: Critical Reading, Math, or Writing
- Section 6, 25 minutes: Critical Reading, Math, or Writing

- *5-Minute Break*

- Section 7, 25 minutes: Critical Reading, Math, or Writing
- Section 8, 20 minutes: Critical Reading or Math
- Section 9, 20 minutes: Critical Reading or Math
- Section 10, 10 minutes: Writing (everyone)

I'd survived the "baseline," barely. It felt like running a marathon without training first.

AN ALTERED STATE

Stamina

It was 1:15 in the afternoon when the proctor finally told us to put down our pencils. My brain hurt. The experience of having to focus so intently for so many hours was fatiguing beyond anything I remember experiencing in college—or, for that matter, during my entire decades-long career in book publishing.

Why does everyone tell you the SAT is a three-hour-and-forty-five-minute test? That's misleading! I arrived at 7:15 in the morning and walked out six hours later at 1:20. My brain was under duress the entire time, breaks or no.

Stamina and mental focus are a huge part of the SAT, so much so that I wonder whether the ability to stay focused for extended periods of time is as much a predictor of college readiness as is the content knowledge on the exam. A seventeen-year-old who can manage a four-hour multiple-choice exam with questions of the *"A. I and II are true, B. II and III are true, C. I, II, and III are true"* variety will have no problem surviving finals week.

I hadn't anticipated the level of mental fatigue I felt. True, the test had grown an hour longer since I had taken it in 1982, due to the addition of the writing section in 2005, but I think my exhaustion came from more than just the length and content of the test. A fair portion of my fatigue came from dealing with the graphic design of the test itself. The SAT is the opposite of user-friendly. The font is way too small (especially by the third hour), and there's too much print on each page and too little white space. Add to that the stress of having to flip back and forth constantly between the test book and the answer booklet (also printed in tiny type), and you suffer a level of wear and tear on the working memory that left me, by the time it was over, in an altered state.

Catherine felt dazed and overwhelmed coming out of the test, too, and she's not usually the type to get overwhelmed. She told me she was actively afraid, backing out of her space in the school parking lot, that she would hit someone, and she drove home in a state of hypervigilance because she was in no shape to be driving at all. She said it was like being drunk—only in reverse.

THE UNEXPECTED TRUTH ABOUT TEST FATIGUE

In March of 2005 the SAT changed in content and length and increased in time by forty-five minutes. Research was conducted to address concerns about whether the increased length affected test performance. The results:

- Increased test length *does not* affect test performance.
- Fatigue affects "low-stakes" tasks that are basic and repetitive.
- Fatigue *does not* affect "high-stakes" tasks that are varied and complex.
- Testers reported *feeling* more fatigued, but performance stayed the same.
- Findings were unclear for students with extended-time accommodations for disabilities such as ADHD.

On a brighter note, those six hours felt more like back-to-back sprints than they did one long marathon. It hadn't occurred to me that I would *like* having my time chunked up and monitored by a proctor, but I did. There was something comforting about the boundaries, as if someone had put up the kiddie bumpers at the bowling alley.

It wasn't until I stood up *after* the test that I realized just how beat-up I was. As I hobbled past the proctor on my way out the door, he stopped me. "Are you going back to college?" he asked with a smile and a nod of encouragement.

"Kind of," I answered. I hadn't thought of what to say if someone asked me that question, so I just said the first thing that popped into my head. "It's an experiment," I answered.

One section of the SAT actually *is* an experiment, as a matter of fact.

THE EXPERIMENTAL SECTION

One of the ten SAT sections is "experimental" and doesn't count toward the final score. The experimental section, part of the SAT since the first exam in 1926, is used by the College Board to field-test question types and entire sections on real students sitting the exam under real testing conditions.

The section—always one of the twenty-five-minute sections—is not identified to test takers until the score report is released (QAS or SAS). Test takers have no choice but to apply themselves fully to the entire test.

Test takers sometimes think they can spot the experimental section because it seems off-key somehow. When the test is over, students compare notes on the College Confidential forums, where they often identify the experimental section through a process of elimination.

Students with extended-time accommodations complete only nine sections, none of which is experimental.

In the parking lot, I fumbled for my keys. I needed food and hydration, and the sunlight was too bright. I couldn't remember where I'd parked my car.

All those years of real-life experience hadn't held up under testing conditions. Okay, maybe my years in publishing helped a little bit with the vocab—but they netted *nothing* in the mental endurance department.

Two high school boys walked behind me, bantering about how easy the test was. They were buoyant; I was limp. They sparkled; I was dazed and confused. That should have been a clue that I'd done something very wrong with my test preparation, minimal as it was. You don't get to bounce out of the SAT if you've been prepping on yoga and obsessing about what snacks to bring.

It took a few months before I realized how those boys had pulled it off. I'd recognize that gait anywhere now. They'd been *endurance training*—I'm sure of it. Everyone had been telling me, "Take *full* timed practice tests," but I thought I was different. I had grown-up commitments. Who has time to take a four-hour practice SAT?

Incidentally, *everyone* thinks they're different.

After my first SAT, I did start practicing by taking individual sections timed with a stopwatch. That's essential, but taking timed sections alone isn't enough to build the kind of endurance you need to bounce out of there like the boys bopping along behind me. For that, you really do need to practice taking full, timed practice tests. You need to build stamina, exactly as you do to run a marathon.

If I haven't said this before, now is as good a time as any: do as I say, not as I did.

What Is Hard Work?

After that first SAT, I was seriously concerned about Ethan's ability to concentrate for so long, especially given what I saw at home: a high school sophomore who was easily distracted, especially when tired. I was sure he needed to start preparing much sooner than he thought he did.

Of course, the larger issue was how to convince Ethan he needed to endurance train for a standardized test that, to his adolescent, ADHD brain, seemed light-years away. Early on, my attempts to lure him into studying were invariably met with resistance. It was the same dance we did for school: I'd push and prod, he'd get annoyed. And of course, Daisy was delighted to jump into the fray.

"No one studies as hard as Ethan," Daisy would say. Ethan would nod.

Trust me, he was not working that hard.

I guess it's a question of perspective: what *is* hard work? It seemed to me at the time that Ethan spent more time *telling* people how hard he was working than actually working. I overheard him a few times on the phone explaining that "my mom is making me stay home to study for the SAT" when I was doing nothing of the sort. It made for a good excuse if he didn't feel like doing something. People felt sorry for him.

I'm sure he didn't realize the implications of using phantom test-prep sessions as a polite way of saying no. Given all the studying he was supposedly doing, people were going to *expect* him to do well, which was by no means guaranteed. Middling scores you've spent years working to achieve are no one's idea of a success story. Meanwhile he was burnishing my local reputation as a demanding mother who pushes her kids too hard. I had always been cast in the role of family enforcer, and I felt my notoriety growing.

I kept telling him to tone it down with the "hard work" spiel or everyone would expect him to get great scores—and how embarrassing would *that* be if he didn't? "Do the opposite," I told him. "Tell everyone you're hardly working. Then they'll think you're really smart if you do well. That's what everyone else does."

My kids never believed me when I told them some kids start studying for the SAT in middle school. I told them about Tony Hsieh, the founder of Zappos and the author of a book I'd just read, *Delivering Happiness*. *His* parents had him start studying for the SAT in the sixth grade and take practice SATs throughout middle school and high school—and now he's a millionaire!

"I'd rather be happy," Ethan would say. "And studying for the SAT doesn't make me happy."

Cinderella's Slipper

I didn't set out to write a book about motivating a teenager. Lord knows, I'm no authority on matters of teenage parenting. However, one of the happy side effects of sharing this SAT experience with Ethan was that I did learn a few things about motivating a teen, and I don't think my n-of-1 experiences are unique. What worked with Ethan is the same approach I realize now I've seen work in other families. I just didn't understand what I was seeing.

My brother's best friend when we were growing up came from the happiest family I ever knew. They were the only kids I could think of who never rebelled, which my brother and I both found to be very odd. We rebelled for years, so I was always sure their rebellion must be imminent, but it never happened. For years, when we spoke of the family, one of us would say, sooner rather than later, "It's so weird they never rebelled, right?" My brother and I had been all too familiar with teenage rebellion and considered it to be normal.

When their name came up after my project was over, it occurred to me that they were a family who did projects together—*lots* of projects. One year, the father and son built a sports car together, from scratch. It took forever. And they were always doing family activities and taking family vacations together.

Then there was my friend Catherine. She had that same sort of magic with her son Chris. She talked about school and family on her blog, *Kitchen Table Math*, and all of the regulars seemed to be like-minded parents and educators who didn't think my idea of studying for the SAT with my son was so far out on a limb. They didn't necessarily think it was going to work in terms of motivating a teenager, but they didn't think I was crazy, either. Catherine studied for the SAT with Chris the year before he took the exam and raised his math score (and her own) by 100 points, though they never referred to what they were doing as "a project." They studied together at the kitchen table, just like they always had since he was age ten.

It was only after the project was over that I learned what the pixie dust was. I read a book by Gordon Neufeld and Gabor Maté called *Hold On to Your Kids: Why Parents Need to Matter More Than Peers*, and suddenly, it was as though Cinderella had found her slipper. The book explains teenage motivation in terms of attachment to *parents,* not *peers.* Teens who are more strongly attached to their parents than their friends are naturally motivated to value what their parents value, including a serious effort to prepare for the SAT. Unfortunately, most teens today are oriented to peers, not parents, and persuading a peer-oriented teen to start studying for the test a year before his friends are studying is a long shot at best. The authors explain that you've got to "hook" peer-oriented adolescents before they'll listen—not an easy task when you've raised a couple of latchkey teenagers.

In hindsight, Neufeld's theories seem so obvious. Everyone understands that peers and peer pressure pose nearly insurmountable obstacles to just about any productive behavior you're trying to instill in your teen. From the time our children enter middle school—if not sooner—we're locked in a struggle with other ten-year-olds for influence over our own kids.

Neufeld points out that parents competing with ten-year-olds for authority is a new historical development, and not a good one. Peer orientation, he says, is a fundamental source of problems ranging from bullying to drug use to academic failure. When you think about it, it makes sense: teenagers who care more about what their friends think than what their parents say are terribly vulnerable to each other, and very difficult for adults to manage. *Hold on to your kids.*

Neufeld lives in Canada, so perhaps that's why he's not well-known in America. But here in the United States we've had forty years of research confirming much of what Neufeld has to say, and yet none of us has heard of that work, either. Developmental psychologists have known since the 1970s that *authoritative parents*—parents who are warm *and* strict, who give their children the mental freedom to think whatever they want but not the physical freedom to do whatever they want—raise great kids. Children of authoritative parents do better in school than children of either permissive or authoritarian parents, and are much less likely to use drugs or get in trouble with the law. They are also more strongly oriented to adults in general than children raised by permissive parents.

I've come to believe that adolescents perform better in school if their parents are involved, and I do not mean involved in the ritual "Ethan, did you do your homework? Yes, Mom, I did" sort of way. (That was how I monitored Ethan from my high-rise office in New York City.) Adolescents perform *better* if their parents are *more* involved in the process, even when they behave in a manner that suggests otherwise. Neufeld advises that parents get in a teenager's space, "in a friendly way"—and even more so if they resist.

Well, that is exactly what I did with the SAT, though I had no idea what I was doing when I set out. I nestled my way into Ethan's space with a little bit of my fierce enthusiasm, and it turned out to be the elixir we needed.

MOTIVATING A TEENAGER

How to cultivate teenage drive is the $64,000 question, and while I am not a parenting expert, I do believe that the secret to motivating a teenager is the relationship. A shared experience can be a powerful agent of connection, and it is that connection that allows an adult to motivate an adolescent.

- **COLLECTING DANCE:** Developmental psychologist Gordon Neufeld explains the "collecting ritual" in his book *Hold On to Your Kids*. The collecting dance is akin to making a baby smile before picking it up. The same holds true for a teenager: you must catch the eye and establish a connection in order to be a source of motivation.

- **ENTHUSIASM:** Most teenagers are more interested in their friends than in their parents and the SAT. In fact, the more into their friends they are, the harder it will be to get their attention. A peer-oriented teenager will need more enthusiasm and initiative from the parent to become motivated than one who is oriented toward adults. Given Ethan's level of peer orientation at the time, I needed to deploy radical enthusiasm.

- **PARENTAL INVOLVEMENT:** Remain interested and involved, even if your teenager is resistant. Research shows that adolescents do better academically when parents are involved beyond monitoring homework.

- **INVITE THE CONNECTION:** The most potent source of motivation for teenagers is attention and interest in what they are doing. A shared project says that the child matters and is special. The relationship that results from this sustained proximity allows for the parent to act as a compass in the child's life and to activate motivation.

I should point out that I *don't* think it's necessary to take the SAT seven times in one year to light the fire. I did this because I wanted to, not because my children needed me to. I was thinking about Ethan, of course, but in the beginning I saw taking the SAT as the mental equivalent of running a marathon, which I had done in 2004.

Honestly, I'm not sure what level of parental engagement is necessary to be an effective motivator. What I do know is that if I managed, more or less by accident, to motivate my own teenage son to study hard for the test—and I still find it miraculous that I *did* manage to motivate my peer-oriented son—other parents can, too. Just going on instinct, I raised Ethan's motivation significantly—then found out about Neufeld and attachment theory after the fact.

The SAT is the last big milestone before a child leaves the nest for college, and that last year flies by fast. I'm pretty sure any level of warm and connected parental participation is a good thing and has the potential to be a powerful source of teenage motivation.

6

THE AFTER PARTY

Home Sweet Home

"How'd it go?"

When I arrived home after the test, Daisy greeted me at the door, more out of curiosity than enthusiasm. I staggered in at 1:30, thankful for not having strayed too far from home for my first SAT. I was in no condition to be driving.

I was ravenous for carbs. I wanted a Clifford the Big Red Dog–sized bowl of spaghetti, and I wanted somebody *else* to stand over the stove boiling noodles and heating up jars of marinara sauce. I *needed* comfort food, I *needed* to be taken care of, I *needed* to veg out on the couch— all of which was very un-me. Usually when I try to relax, I feel anxious because I can't stop thinking about all the things that need to get done. Not that day. Anything that required the use of my brain, or standing up instead of lying down, was simply not an option. Daisy came over and sat down, not quite sure what to make of me. *Are you my mother?*

"You're going to love it," I said, attempting to convince her that the SAT wasn't as bad as I looked. "You'll do great." But she wasn't buying it.

"How do you think you did?" she asked.

"I *think* I did well," I said (famous last words).

I hadn't expected to feel that way coming out of the test. I was just so relieved to have recognized anything at all on the test that I misinterpreted recognition as "doing well."

FAMILIARITY FOOLS THE MIND

Research tells us that most people are overconfident. A classic study from Sweden found that 93 percent of American subjects characterized themselves as better-than-average drivers, a statistical impossibility (69 percent of Swedish subjects felt the same).

Judging your own performance on the SAT is no different, and most test takers probably overestimate how well they've done. Overestimating your performance on tests (as opposed to driving) has to do specifically with the *feeling* of knowing something, which turns out to be highly unreliable. The feeling of knowing is not the same as knowing, and we think we know more than we do. Cognitive scientist Daniel Willingham draws the following distinctions:

- "Familiarity" is knowledge of having seen or experienced something, but it can be misleading and give the illusion that we know more than we do.
- Reading something can yield familiarity, but that knowledge is often shallow.
- Explaining something reveals deeper understanding, and when you explain a concept, you are more likely to remember it.
- "Recollections" have richer associations than "familiarity" and are more likely to be retrieved.
- Overlearning by a factor of 20 percent beyond the point of mastery is one strategy to avoid forgetting.

It took months for me to accept that I was an unreliable evaluator of my own test performance. I *always* thought I had done better than I had (except on one occasion where I significantly underestimated my performance). When it came to accurately predicting my scores, my optimistic outlook betrayed me.

After the first test, I decided to experiment to see how well I self-assessed. Before leaving the parking lot after each subsequent test, I'd jot down everything I could remember while it was fresh in my mind. Then I'd check my notes against the score report when it arrived in the mail a few weeks later to see how accurate I was, which turned out to be: *not very*.

For example:

NOTES AFTER TEST: Section 2, math—"I felt *strong*—answered 1–16, skipped one question. Pretty sure I got the rest right."

SCORE REPORT: I *did* in fact answer questions 1–16, skipping just one. However, I got five of the fifteen questions I answered wrong. Sixty-seven percent correct.

Ethan was no different. Months later, when he was up to bat, I tried the same experiment with him:

NOTES AFTER TEST: "There were questions about simile and personification. I don't remember seeing those on the practice tests before. But that's okay. I know what they are. I'm sure I got them right."

SCORE REPORT: Wrong on both counts.

This kind of thing was so typical that after a while we decided that *not* knowing how we did was a better sign than thinking we had done well.

Ethan and I are not alone. Exaggerated optimism is a common affliction; we overestimate our own performance and, by the same token, underestimate the performance of others.

Test to test, we usually saw improvement, just not as much as we anticipated—which made it all the more easy to rationalize. "At least we moved the ball somewhere," I'd say, "even if it wasn't as far as we thought we did."

The Water Cooler

The website College Confidential bills itself as "The World's Largest College Forum." CC, as I came to call it, is incredibly useful, though not *all* the observations posted on the website are correct. The website's visitors, high school students and their parents, produce most of the content, often stated with such authority that I always found myself assuming forum participants must be right and I must be wrong.

College Confidential has entire forums dedicated solely to the SAT, which is like catnip to the SAT-obsessed. Within hours of a test there would be dozens of comments—sometimes dozens about a single question alone. After each test, I'd race home to read the postmortems, at which point my confidence bubble would always let out a little air.

By early evening the conversation would usually split into three separate threads: reading, writing, and math. The trifurcation permitted an even more obsessive post-test experience.

God knows why I found the conversations about a test that was behind me inexhaustibly fascinating, but I did:

JUNIOR MEMBER: I thought the writing and math were pretty easy but some of the cr questions were tough. My prediction: 780 M 770 WR 730 CR.

NEW MEMBER: Section 4. It was like near impossible. Hopefully it was the experimental section.

JUNIOR MEMBER: Who else thinks the cursive is complete idiocy?

MEMBER: Do they really mean write in cursive?

MEMBER: Oh yeah, and I think the hexagon question was
                   36 btw not 61 . . . So if the curve is decent, I
                   can get 700 godwilling.

There were *always* post-test references to "the curve."

THE CURVE

The SAT is scored on a curve, which means that each test yields the
same relative number of 1200s, 1500s, 1800s, 2100s, and so on. To
keep the distribution of scores constant, raw scores change slightly
from one test to another. For instance, two incorrect answers on the
math section could be a 740 on one SAT but a 780 on another.

There is no way to game the curve. All of the items have been
tested and rated for level of difficulty. There is no way to predict
which tests will be slightly more or less difficult.

- Some SATs *are* harder than others, but the curve corrects for
  variations in difficulty.
- There is no advantage to taking an easier SAT. The curve ad-
  justs accordingly.
- There is no pattern as to which month is harder or easier.
- Relative test date popularity, in order (for 2011): October,
  June, November, May, December, March, January.
- Each test can be a mix of easy *and* hard sections—one test
  might include a hard math section, an easy writing section,
  and a medium critical reading section.

The moral of the story is: *Don't worry about the curve, worry
about learning math.*

I was usually too shy to jump into the after party myself. I preferred
to loiter on the sidelines where I could second-guess my performance in

private with a large bowl of spaghetti in my lap. It was like watching everyone else dance at the prom from the vantage point of the snack table.

There were always a few self-doubters like me, but as a general rule the commenters tended to be supremely confident. A few times I spotted references to math answers that had been stored in the memory of someone's calculator. Naturally, I assumed these answers must be correct given that whoever posted them (real names not used) had not only finished the math sections but had had the wherewithal to record the answers for posterity.

As Pollyannaish about my own abilities as I had discovered myself to be, my confidence was no match for the self-assurance on display in the forums, especially when it came to math. A lot of the College Confidential kids know their math the way I know a ladybug has spots. This is automaticity at its finest. Unlike me, these students don't have to *think* about such issues as:

- Is 1 a prime number?
- Is 0 an integer?
- How many parentheses do I use in the calculator to get the order of operations correct?

While I was squandering working memory on the basics, the math jocks at College Confidential were answering questions and recording the answers in their calculators for discussion and debate.

The Nutrition Label Problem

One test included a math question involving a nutrition label. Never having seen an American nutrition label before, the international students were distressed. They wrote (and posted) passionate letters to the College Board, asking that the question be nullified.

JUNIOR MEMBER: I scored a 2380 on the SAT in Oct. . . . This question is not a fair question to the international students.

NEW MEMBER: Knowing how to read nutrition charts has nothing to do with math. What if Indian or Korean students answered this question?

JUNIOR MEMBER: I do hope there will be a positive outcome for those who support nullifying the nutrition label problem.

One member claimed the question *had* in fact been nullified, though I was never able to verify this, and as far as I could tell from my score report the question seemed to have made the cut despite the ruckus.

TEST ERROR OR AMBIGUITY

College Board policy instructs test takers to continue testing if they encounter a test error or an ambiguous question, and to contact the Board after the test is over.

- Report the problem to the test center supervisor before leaving the test.
- Write to the College Board and explain the concern.
- Include the test question and test section.
- Communicate via e-mail, fax, or letter.
- Report the concern *before* the Wednesday after the test or it will not be considered.

International SAT takers are expected to compete on a level playing field with their American counterparts, and vice versa. But of course American students (along with test takers from other Anglophone countries) have a built-in advantage in reading and writing, while many international students, Asians especially, enter their high school years with a significant edge over their U.S. counterparts in math. The result is a scramble to improve skills via commercial test prep, a rite of passage today but a rarity when I was in high school.

BusinessWeek reports that in 2010 China's leading test-prep service (New Oriental, with a 90 percent market share) enrolled 200,000 students. In the same article, an associate dean at the University of Virginia reports that the average math score of UVa's 1,200 native Chinese applicants was 783, while the average math score for U.S. applicants was just 669: a 114-point difference. By way of comparison, the average SAT math score of all college-bound seniors that year was 514 (18 fewer points than in 2006).

The globalization of the college admissions process has paved the way for companies such as Steven Ma's ThinkTank Learning, founded in 2002 to prepare international students to take college entrance exams. According to the *New York Times*, by 2011 ThinkTank had grown into a $7 million college consulting firm whose clients pay tens or even hundreds of thousands of dollars to be molded into "well-rounded, socially conscious overachievers through a regimen often beginning as early as the year before entering high school." Mr. Ma claims to have distilled the college admissions process into an exact science. "We make unnatural stuff happen," he says.

The *New York Times* article ends with Li Manhong, a Beijing homemaker who convinced her husband to spend nearly $15,000 to hire ThinkTank Learning to prepare her son for admission to an American college. ThinkTank prepared him for the SAT, helped him pick internships and college courses, and so forth. "Whatever it takes to reach his maximum potential," Ms. Li said. "It's worth it."

Back at College Confidential, the forums were a constant reminder (lest I forget) that the SAT had morphed into an international arms race since I first took the test in 1982. I had no idea how Ethan would stack up against international competition, especially on the math, but I feared—*not well*.

Math was Ethan's strongest subject, but it was hard for me to see how, after years of slower-moving American math (in other countries all students take algebra in the eighth grade, not the ninth), he was going to be on a competitive footing with his peers in Europe and Asia. It's no secret that international students dominate STEM fields (science, technology, engineering, and mathematics). In 2011, foreign students earned more than 40 percent of all doctoral degrees in math and science in this country.

Meanwhile, back on the home front, I was grappling with my own SAT "issues" (especially in math), while at the same time attempting to convince Ethan that he was *not* the only kid on the planet whose mom wanted him to study for the SAT before his junior year. "No one else's mom makes them study for the SAT this early," he'd say.

It's always "everyone else," versus "me," according to my children.

Lord knows how I ever managed to maintain a house rule on video games (only on weekends), or why Ethan still believed dessert could only be served after schoolwork was finished. Somehow I made these rules stick. But trying to convince my son that there were throngs of international students vying for his slot in college seemed like a task requiring colossal levels of maternal energy.

7

SUPERSIZE ME: THE SKINNY ON THE SCORES

Second Thoughts

The moment of truth arrived on February 10 at five o'clock in the morning, two and a half weeks after the day I'd taken my first SAT. Over the course of those nineteen days my confidence had dwindled, and by the time the scores arrived I held out little hope of a good outcome.

I had grown discouraged reading the forums on College Confidential. Knowing there were thousands of posts relating to my test to comb through, I couldn't pry myself away even though I knew it was in my best interest to step away from the computer and spend my time more constructively. And lest you think I was the only crackpot obsessing after the fact, there were hundreds of thousands of "views" on those January SAT threads. I had company.

I read so many posts analyzing the same question-and-answer combinations over and over ad infinitum that by score day I could hardly remember which answers I had chosen when I took the test. The weeks of speculation and second-guessing had left me detached from my performance, and the scoring process felt random, as if I might just as well have scratched my answers off a lottery ticket or shaken a Magic 8 Ball.

My one wish: *Please, God, don't let it be worse than it was in high school.*

The College Board releases its scores in stages, each report adding further detail to the one before. It's a gift that keeps on giving. The first unveiling occurs nineteen days after the test, at eight in the morning, give or take. One time my scores showed up at two a.m. (and yes, I was awake, hitting the Refresh button at the start of each hour). On another occasion, the scores arrived a few days after they were supposed to, which, I won't lie, was torture. I learned about the delay from a message on the College Board website each and every time I logged on to confirm, again, that my scores were *still* delayed.

SCORE REPORTS

SAT scores are accessed by signing into "My SAT" on the College Board's website or by mail. Various score reports are available, and are issued in stages. Some are included with the test registration fee while others can be ordered at an additional cost.

- **SCORES ONLINE:** Free; available two and a half weeks after test date; score and percentile only.
- **ONLINE SCORE REPORT:** Free; four weeks after test date. Report includes number of questions correct, incorrect, or omitted; level of difficulty of each item; question type; and a copy of your essay.
- **SCORE REPORT TO HIGH SCHOOL:** Sent directly by the College Board if school code was provided during registration.
- **SCORES BY PHONE:** Costs extra.
- **QUESTION-AND-ANSWER SERVICE (QAS):** Test book and detailed answer report including both your answer and the correct answer. Sent by mail eight weeks after test date (meaning it often arrives after the *next* test date). Available: January, May, and October. Costs extra.

- **STUDENT ANSWER SERVICE (SAS):** List of question type, level of difficulty, whether answered correctly, incorrectly, or omitted. Sent by mail eight weeks after test. Does not include test book. Available: test dates for which QAS is not offered. Costs extra.
- **HAND-SCORE VERIFICATION:** Checked for No. 2 pencil, fully colored-in bubbles, complete eraser marks. Available up to five months after test date. Extra cost for the multiple choice, and an additional cost for the essay.

For specific costs related to the above, see the College Board website.

I was having second thoughts about telling everyone I would post my scores. Past the age of seventeen, no one shares SAT scores—not unless they're really high.

Take, for example, a discussion about the SAT in the comments on my friend Catherine's *Kitchen Table Math* site.

> STEVE H: Are you saying that a 'top math student' need not prepare for SAT math?
>
> GASSTATIONWITHOUTPUMPS: Yes, that is what I was saying. My son did no prep for the SAT when he took it in 6th grade and got a 720 on the math part. I'm quite sure that he'll do better on it when he takes it as a high schooler next year without doing any SAT prep. The math questions just aren't all that hard.

What was I thinking?

I'd upped the ante and now there was no way out. Why hadn't I given myself a loophole that would allow me to fail privately, like normal people? Mortification was imminent, I felt sure.

More than the issue of ego, I was worried about my kids. I still had a few good years left on the "Mom is smart" lease, and my word was still *the* word in our little house. My grown-up scores on the SAT should have had nothing to do with any of that, of course; millions of adolescent children listen every day to parents who were no great shakes in the SAT department themselves. Then again, those parents weren't posting their scores on the web.

Why hadn't I let sleeping dogs lie?

The night before those first scores came out, I hatched a loophole, just in case. My idea was to tell people it had *always* been the plan to share my January scores (the baseline!) *after* my March scores came back, an ever-so-slight backpedal. That way, we'd have a Point B for the sake of comparison. A single point of data wasn't interesting, I told myself; people want to see movement—from here to there—and I was sure my March scores would show upward mobility.

I was rationalizing, but really, it seemed like the right thing to do— *for the children.*

Decline and Fall

Somewhere in there I discovered a little-known scoring factoid that eased my anxiety somewhat: since I had taken the test, SAT scores had been "recentered." Meaning the College Board had moved the center score— *and* (the good news) they had moved it in a face-saving direction for any grown-up planning to post her high school scores on the web. A 500 on verbal, as the reading section was called in 1982, was now a 580. Math scores had changed much less dramatically, but those scores had gone up too, and a 500 on math was now 520. (When I told a friend with two teenagers what I'd found out, she said, "You mean all those parents bragging about their kids' high scores don't know the SAT added 100 points?") Thanks to recentering, everyone's scores had gone up, which meant people like me now had higher (equivalent) scores, too. They were posted on the College Board website in "SAT I Score Equivalent" tables.

It's like shopping at the Gap. Everyone gets to lose a few sizes without doing a thing.

THEY MOVED THE CENTER!

In 1995 the College Board recentered the SAT scores because 500 was no longer the middle. One side effect of recentering was an increase in the number of students achieving a perfect score of 1600. On the first recentered test in April 1995, 1 in 1,400 students earned a perfect score, as compared to 1 in 4,000 in 2011.

My SAT scores from 1982—and my same scores recentered, post-1995:

	ORIGINAL	RECENTERED	1982 AVERAGE	1982 AVERAGE (female)
VERBAL	410	490	504	499
MATH	480	510	493	473

The College Board's decision to recenter the scale followed a sixteen-year decline in scores that began in 1963 and finally ended in 1980. Verbal scores fell dramatically during those years, dropping from an average of 475 to 425. *Fifty points.* Average math scores dropped 30 points, from 500 to 470.

Over the next decade math scores climbed back up to a mean of 475, but verbal didn't budge—which meant that mean scores on verbal and math were now separated by 50 points.

Another problem: There was almost no one left at the top. Scores above 700 were few and far between. As a College Board report put it in 2002, the Board recognized "a clear need to repopulate the top end of the score scale, especially for SAT V [verbal]."

The decline in scores greatly distressed policy makers, educators, and parents, although people were of two minds as to whether the decline was real. One possibility—that the test had gotten harder—was eliminated by Harvard reading specialist Jeanne Chall, who found that the reading passages had actually become *easier* between 1947 and 1975.

The dominant school of thought seems to have been that scores had fallen simply because many more students were taking the test, diluting the talent pool. That more students were taking the test was certainly true: the test-taking population had mushroomed from 5 percent of graduating seniors before World War II to *over 50 percent* postwar, an enormous increase that brought many B and C students into the pool.

The problem with this analysis was that the huge increase in the number of students taking the test took place in the 1950s, not the 1960s, and average scores hadn't changed at all. Scores began their sixteen-year decline only *after* the test-taking population had stopped growing.

Moreover, if scores were falling because a throng of less talented students was bringing down the mean, the absolute number of high-scoring kids should have stayed the same. But it didn't. The total number of students scoring above 600—the head count, not the percent—dropped by more than a third. This was the heart of the Baby Boom era; the number of students had grown by 50 percent. And yet the raw number of students breaking 600 was falling.

Last but not least, these same students were doing much better on math than on verbal. Less talented students are usually less talented across the board; and you would expect math and verbal scores to drop by roughly the same amount if the decline was being caused by less capable students taking the test.

Instead, it looked like there was a problem specific to English classes. As it turned out, there was: the language in American textbooks had been dramatically simplified after World War I and then again after WWII. In textbooks published for grades four through eight, average sentence length dropped from twenty words to just fourteen, the equivalent of making sentences far less complex. Vocabulary was much simpler, too.

The first children to use the simpler texts were born in 1946. They started school in 1952 and, eleven years later, half of them took the SAT. Theirs were the first scores to drop. Ground zero.

High school books—especially high school English texts—were now below the level of the books seventh graders had read in the 1940s. Even the books in Advanced Placement English were junior-high level.

Which brings me to the aspect of the score decline most relevant to any parent reading this book. The decline in reading skills was real, but it didn't hit everyone equally. It seems to have affected only the *most capable* students in the country: the kids signing up to take the SAT. The SAT population is a self-selected, college-bound group whose academic performance is higher than that of the population that does not take the SAT. *This* was the group of students whose scores had fallen to Earth.

Meanwhile, what was happening to the skills of students who weren't planning to attend college and didn't take the SAT? One team of researchers used data from a twenty-year PSAT study, which used a representative national sample of high school students, to estimate what the average SAT score of *all* high school seniors would have been if they had taken the test. They found that the scores of *average* students hadn't changed at all. It was only the scores of the college-bound that had collapsed—in other words, decline at the top. There was even some evidence that within the SAT pool, the highest-scoring students saw the greatest score declines.

Simultaneously, college professors were witnessing a sharp decline in the skills of their students. Typical of their testimony was a 1991 article by Daniel J. Singal, a historian at Hobart and William Smith Colleges, that ran in *The Atlantic Monthly*. In it Singal cites the experience of a friend teaching at the University of Michigan. In the 1960s, Singal's friend had assigned his students one book a week. Now his students needed two to three weeks to get through a single book, and the books had to be easier, to boot.

To this day you can read articles in education and policy journals discussing the sixteen-year decline in scores. What you don't hear is parents—or the general public—lamenting the fall. Parents don't lament the decline in scores because they have no idea scores ever declined. The entire episode went down the memory hole when, in 1995, the College Board recentered scores using a complex statistical process explained in a handful of white papers you can download from its website. The score of 500 was restored to its traditional position as the mean in math and verbal (which had been rechristened "critical reading" the year before) and, overnight, everyone's scores went up. And people forgot.

People forgot because that statistical manipulation—shifting the entire scale higher—came with built-in consumer buy-in. Unconscious buy-in, no doubt, but that's the best kind. Unconscious biases in number processing are the reason Steve Jobs priced iTunes songs at ninety-nine cents instead of a dollar. Who *doesn't* want a higher SAT score—for nothing? It's like found money. I wish I'd known in high school that the College Board would, in effect, award me bonus points in the future. My 480 in math from high school sounds so much better as today's 510, even if it is the exact same score. I prefer being on the other side of the score mountain.

Loopholes

When my first scores from the January 2011 test finally arrived, they came as a bit of a surprise.

JANUARY SCORES

	MY SCORES	AVERAGE SCORES 2011
CRITICAL READING	**680** (93rd percentile)	**497** (female: **495**)
MATH	**510*** (48th percentile)	**514** (female: **500**)
WRITING	**610** (84th percentile)	**489** (female: **496**)
ESSAY	**9**	
TOTAL	**1800** (82nd percentile)	83rd percentile (female)

* Same math score as 1982.

Better than I had expected.

I could live with these scores, especially those percentiles. That was another thing: *When did they add percentiles to the score reports?* I wondered. I hadn't even noticed my percentile in 1982.

But what a fabulous loophole on the self-disclosure front.

Everyone called to ask "What'd you get?" and I'd say, nonchalantly, "Ninety-third percentile in reading," which sounds so much better than

610, somehow. Then I'd quickly change the subject so my caller wouldn't ask the obvious follow-up.

I soon discovered that most people will accept a percentile instead of the actual score. It's like American Express—it's accepted *almost* everywhere. Even if someone was thinking, *I asked what her scores were; why did she give me a percentile?* most of my friends were polite enough to leave it at that.

I did have one friend who was not satisfied by my answer, however.

"But what's your *score*?" she pressed after I told her "ninety-third percentile!"

"Well, my *percentiles*—" I started to explain.

"I don't care about your percentiles," she interrupted. "What's your score?"

She knew the percentile game—three of her kids had already run the SAT gauntlet. The first two were launched in college and she was working on number three, so "percentiles" were fresh in her mind. Not to mention, she's direct, which I like.

A week and a half later, when the College Board released the Online Score Report, I found a whole other dimension of loophole that made me feel even better. If you happen to live in a state where the average is *below* the national average, your percentile increases. Same score, higher percentile.

I had scored a 510 on the January math section—the exact same score as my recentered 1982 math score from high school. Thirty years without a math class and . . . exact same score. I'm not quite sure what to make of that.

A 510 was in the 48th percentile—*nationally.*

Ten days later, upon arrival of my score report, I discovered that a 510 in math ranked in the 53rd percentile in the state of New York, where I happen to live. I was in the bottom half of my country but the top half of my state!

My critical reading score increased to the *95th* percentile for my state, which felt great.

Poring over the reams of data I was collecting from the College Board,

I got stuck on "Will your score improve if you take the SAT again?" I was transfixed. According to the numbers, my chances of doing better on reading and writing on the next go-round weren't much higher than my chances of doing worse.

Worse.

I hadn't thought of that. I had just naturally assumed that if you worked hard and studied, you'd do better. Or, if the only real way to prepare for the test is to "take challenging courses, study hard, and read and write in and outside of the classroom"—as the College Board would have you believe—you'd do the same.

It hadn't occurred to me that I could do worse. But there it was. My reading score, 680, sounded to me like *lots of room to improve.* But according to the report, 47 percent of those with 680s scored higher on the next test while 45 percent scored lower. A remarkably consistent 8 percent stayed the same.

This made *no* sense to me.

I found much of the report mystifying, truth be told. Nevertheless, I was glad to have it, and felt certain that it would be terrifically helpful to my test-prep efforts if I understood it better.

Before 1958, the College Board didn't send SAT scores to students at all (scores were sent directly to colleges), let alone ply them with the bevy of score options and data reports available today. These days there are superscores and Score Choice, hand-scoring and score cancellation, the Student Answer Service, the Question-and-Answer Service—even a "test-optional" movement to ponder.

It's a lot.

Score Choice and Superscoring—What Does It All Mean?

I can't be the only person who's had to look up Score Choice and "super-scoring" a dozen times, can I? I can never remember which one is which, or whether you can do both.

Score Choice (per the College Board's explanation) is a feature that's offered to students to alleviate the stress of "test day." The thinking is that "choice" will ratchet down the stress because the student is allowed to choose whether to send that day's scores to colleges.

If a test taker bombs, he or she can wipe the slate clean, more or less (the scores exist in the College Board's database), and try again. The catch is that some schools (Yale, Cornell, and Georgetown, to name a few) have a non–Score Choice policy and require that *all* test scores be sent with the application. The College Board lists schools that require all scores be sent, but students opting for Score Choice are advised to confirm this on the websites of the schools they are applying to because school sites will have the most up-to-date information.

Critics of the SAT have accused the College Board of creating Score Choice as a maneuver to pick up market share lost to the ACT, which has a long-standing policy of allowing students to choose which scores to send and which to withhold (2010 was the first time in the history of the ACT that the number of high school seniors taking the test exceeded those taking the SAT). Clearly, the College Board has a financial incentive to offer Score Choice. After all, if you don't have to send your scores, you're incentivized to take (and pay for) the test more often.

Superscoring is what the colleges *do* with your Score Choice—to position themselves in the college rankings. You submit scores from test dates of your choosing, and the schools cherry-pick your best score from each section, creating a "superscore." Say you take the SAT three times and submit all three sets of scores. The college will extract your best math, writing, and reading scores from the three tests and combine them into one superscore. Colleges do *see* all submitted scores, of course, but it's as much in their interest as yours to use your best scores because superscoring raises the college's average SAT scores.

SCORE CHOICE AND SUPERSCORING: AN OVERVIEW

Score Choice allows students to choose which scores to send to colleges and scholarship programs. *Superscoring* is what the colleges do with submitted SAT scores; the schools combine the highest score per section into one SAT superscore for each student.

Score Choice:

- Score Choice is optional and must be *proactively* chosen by the student.
- All scores from an *entire* SAT test are sent. Individual sections from different tests cannot be selected for sending.
- Colleges will receive your SAT essay if you choose to send them your SAT scores.
- Colleges set their own policy regarding scores, but the College Board will not release scores without student consent.
- Score policies are listed on the College Board website but should be confirmed with schools for accuracy. Policies change.
- *Most* schools allow Score Choice; however, some don't, including Yale, Cornell, Georgetown, George Washington, and Tufts.
- For more info, go to collegeboard.com/scorechoice.

Superscoring:

- Admissions officials see all scores submitted and expect to see score variation.
- Most schools superscore (i.e., use the highest score per section from different SATs to come up with one "superscore" for a student).
- Colleges benefit by superscoring, which lets them position themselves more favorably in college rankings.

Test-Optional

"Test-optional"—leaving the decision to submit SAT scores to the applicant—appears to be a growing trend, not to mention a noble-sounding policy, since test-optional colleges convey the impression that they would like to diversify their applicant pool.

However, critics argue that test-optional colleges are simply gaming the system to gain status in the rankings, most notably the *U.S. News & World Report* ratings, which have created a frenzy among schools trying to move up in prestige. A test-optional policy means more applicants, which means more applicants to *reject*, which means a school is more "selective" as far as the rankings go. Test-optional also means the school's SAT average is artificially inflated because applicants who *do* submit scores have higher scores than applicants who don't—100 to 150 points higher, on average.

The other test-optional variable to be aware of is the issue of merit aid. Many test-optional schools still require standardized test scores to consider an applicant for merit aid.

All that said, if you happen to be one of the 180 students who scored in the 0 percentile on the SAT in 2011, test-optional is probably the way to go.

HIGHS AND LOWS—CLASS OF 2011

- Total testers (seniors): 1,647,123
- Total perfect scores (2400): 384 (approximately 1 in 4,000)
- Total worst scores (600): 180 (0 percentile)*

---

* Yes, it's true what you've heard: 200 *is* the lowest possible SAT score—per section.

8

PREPPING FOR THE SAT WITH THE MAKERS OF THE TEST

The Good Experience

During those nineteen days between taking that January 2011 test and receiving the scores, I did do *some* work.

I realized only too well that on the next test I wouldn't have the "getting a baseline" safety net, and the "Point B" loophole was contingent on upward mobility. Plus, I figured that giving out percentiles instead of scores was not a long-term strategy. Eventually, even my polite friends were going to want to hear the actual scores.

Sometimes, having your back to the wall provides the perfect motivation to finally begin. The next SAT was scheduled for March 12, not even two months after that first test. The tight deadline gave me just enough pressure to finally get going.

But first I had to recover from the brain trauma produced by four hours of extended, intensive focus on that first test. I actually felt cognitively impaired for about seventy-two hours, and I probably was.

After that, I was ready to choose my first test-prep method.

The question of where to begin was the problem (and, of course, the original conundrum that had launched the project in the first place). Advice poured in from every direction: "Kaplan doesn't work" . . . "try

The Princeton Review" . . . "hire the math teacher from our high school." There was so much advice it was mind-boggling, not to mention paralyzing.

So I went back to the beginning, to the very first piece of SAT advice I ever received, from my friend Mark Hurst, founder of a company called the Good Experience. Given that I was looking to have a good SAT experience, it seemed logical to start with Mark. Plus, he'd graduated from MIT, so I figured he was a reliable source. Obviously he'd done well on the SAT.

One day over lunch I said to Mark, "I want a redo. I think I can get a perfect score now—if I work hard. And I'm going to tell the whole world what works and what doesn't so no one else has to go through the stress of sorting through the millions of test-prep options."

He seemed excited about my idea and said he had the perfect plan for me. I sat at attention, riveted. I couldn't wait to hear about "the Good Experience SAT."

Mark laid out his method . . . very slowly.

"Get the College Board's Blue Book," he said.

"Uh-huh . . ."

"And do one . . . *full* . . . *timed* . . . *test* . . . every weekend."

"Okay . . ."

"And then spend the rest of the week going over all your wrong answers."

Pause.

That's it? Where's the "Good Experience" part?

Silence.

I hated it. A twenty-dollar paperback was not at all what I had in mind.

I was looking for something with complexity and subtlety: a secret sauce. The Path to Mastery simply had to be more intricate than a paperback (didn't it?). A multibillion-dollar industry is based on that assumption.

Mixed Messages

But after the barrage of advice from my friends and fellow parents, and my subsequent inability to make a decision about where to begin, I decided Mark's plan was as good a place as any to start, though I thought it could use a little zest.

I started with the College Board's website, to see what sort of advice they offered, but the more I read, the more confused I became:

Click: "Repeated studies show that test prep increases SAT scores by about the same amount as taking the test a second time."

Click (next page): "Affordable tools and strategies for success."

Same website, two different messages: "Test-prep doesn't work," . . . and, one click away, a pupu platter of test-prep options.

Huh . . .

THE COLLEGE BOARD'S TEST-PREP OPTIONS

Official College Board material, I eventually learned, should be the cornerstone of SAT test preparation.

Online Resources:

- **THE OFFICIAL SAT QUESTION OF THE DAY:** Free; SAT question arrives every morning via e-mail or mobile app. Run, don't walk.
- **THE OFFICIAL SAT PRACTICE TEST:** Free; can be taken (and scored) online or downloaded for hard-copy printout. There are two other official practice tests that I've linked to on my website: perfectscoreproject.com.
- **SAT SKILLS INSIGHT:** Free; intended to help students understand the skills tested on the SAT. I found it overly complicated and had trouble sustaining attention while trying to follow it.
- **THE OFFICIAL SAT ONLINE COURSE:** Costs more than the Blue Book, but worth every penny. Includes eighteen

lessons plus ten *more* practice SATs (different tests from those in the Blue Book), with auto essay grading. The value is in the extra practice tests. As for the robo essay grader: don't get your hopes up if you get a 12.

Paper Resources:

- **THE OFFICIAL SAT STUDY GUIDE, 2ND EDITION** (aka the Blue Book): Obtainable at a discount from retailers. Ten practice tests, access to solutions on the College Board's website, hundreds of pages of front matter that everyone ignores (includes concepts, tips, practice questions). Worth it!
- **THE OFFICIAL SAT STUDY GUIDE WITH DVD** (aka the *new* Blue Book): Obtainable at a discount from retailers; DVD includes an *extra* practice SAT and video explanations. Worth the extra money for one more practice test.

Call it what you will, this looked like test prep to me, even if it was presented under the guise of "familiarization with the material." So could I trust the College Board when they were talking out of both sides of their mouth? And was it a conflict of interest for the test makers to sell test *preparation*? The more I tried to figure out where they stood, the more confused I became. Did they believe test prep worked, or not?

I wanted results, not skepticism, and I didn't want to hear that the best way to prepare was to "do well in school," as the website put it. I wasn't in school. I wanted tips and tricks, or at the very least, a modicum of encouragement, some sort of promise that if I held up my end they'd meet me halfway.

It's what the macroeconomists call "expectations" when they talk about monetary policy. Tell people monetary policy is no panacea and you've just guaranteed that monetary policy will be no panacea. The College Board does the same thing—they ignore the huge element of psychology on test prep and instead throw a bucket of cold water on the idea that you can improve your scores.

Maybe it was a marketing strategy: undersell, overdeliver. I'd seen that used before. One time my son ordered sneakers from Zappos and the website said they'd be delivered in "three to five days," but those sneakers were on our doorstep when we got home—*that day*. Years later, we still talk about the shock and awe of that shoe delivery. *How did they get here so fast?*

The Story Behind the Story

In 1926, when the first exam was administered, the SAT was called the "Scholastic **Aptitude** Test" and was allegedly testing innate ability rather than academic achievement per se. (Hence the "studying doesn't work" dogma.)

The first crack in the veneer appeared in 1979, when the Federal Trade Commission (FTC) investigated Stanley Kaplan's claim that his SAT course could raise students' scores. Kaplan had been building an empire based on the premise that you *could* increase your SAT score. He'd started tutoring in the late 1930s from his parents' basement after being rejected by medical school (a disappointment he attributed to his Jewish heritage in that era of quotas).

Until the late 1970s, the College Board maintained its position: the SAT tested *innate* ability and could predict college success; therefore, studying for the test didn't work. Either you've got it, or you don't. But in 1979, the FTC concluded that test prep *could* improve SAT scores, which left the College Board in the awkward position of having to change its tune or face some difficult questions.

In 1978, under mounting pressure from the FTC, the College Board lifted the veil, just a little, by releasing the first practice SAT ever via a handbook that was intended to help students prepare for the test. Henceforth, the organization would allow students to examine old copies of the tests. Management even went so far as to invite Stanley Kaplan to be the keynote speaker at their annual conference, a high point of his life. He opened his speech by saying, "Never in my wildest dreams did I ever think I'd be speaking to you here today."

In the early 1980s, the College Board went into the test-prep business itself, initially by selling a book of past exams very much like the Blue Book of today. A decade later, the "A" in SAT morphed from "Aptitude" to "Assessment," before being dropped altogether, leaving the current "SAT" as an empty acronym.

Rock-Paper-Scissors

I'm an enthusiast. Once I commit, I embrace with gusto.

I was ready to try Mark's "good experience" method, but I thought it could use a little dressing up, to make it more "me." So I ordered everything that wasn't nailed down on the College Board's site—the Blue Book, the Online Course, even the official *Teacher's Guide*, which happens to be where I found my all-time favorite piece of test-prep advice: "Keep your attention focused on the test. Don't daydream."

I'd already sullied my Blue Book by hopscotching from problem to problem answering just the questions I liked. I needed a fresh copy to start the project, and so, while waiting for a new Blue Book to arrive in the mail, I spent the last days of January exploring the College Board's free offerings online.

Many are valuable. In particular, the full practice SAT exam is the filet mignon of any good test prep. *No one* should pass Go without taking advantage of that test. You can use it to get a baseline, or save it for later to build your skills and stamina before taking a real SAT. The College Board allows you to download the test and take it on paper or, alternatively, answer an online version that the computer will score for you.

I prefer my SATs on paper, which I assume is a better route for everyone given that the real test still takes place inside high schools with students using bubble sheets, No. 2 pencils, and old-fashioned paper.

I will admit, though, that I detest online learning, so if you like online learning you probably shouldn't go by me. My intense dislike of online learning—and online testing—always surprises me. I *love* computers; I love the SAT. Yet I hate the SAT on computers. For some reason I need a pencil or pen and paper to *feel* like something is sticking, and I don't feel the same hand-to-brain connection when I click buttons on a computer.

THE HAND BONE'S CONNECTED TO THE BRAIN BONE

Brain research continues to substantiate evidence that there *is* a connection between handwriting and the learning process, though, ironically, handwriting lessons have disappeared from schools. Most students today don't even know how to write in cursive.

- Handwriting stimulates brain activity and leads to increased language fluency.
- Handwriting is closely tied to learning to read.

That said, I put aside my personal bias and spent a few days clicking every button on the College Board's site while waiting for my new Blue Book, and I can honestly say that if online learning works for you, there are a plethora of exercises on the website that go way beyond that practice SAT.

There are also two additional free practice SATs on the College Board's site, but you won't find them easily because they're hidden. They were posted earlier and are so difficult to locate on the site that I finally posted the links on my homepage (see perfectscoreproject.com) so I could find them again without a lengthy sojourn in Search.

Which brings me to an important point: the College Board's site is so dense with information that it's often difficult to find the same thing twice. It can take what feels like hours of searching to find some critical link that feels like it should be right there, in plain view. So start bookmarking the important pages early on in the process. You'll save yourself hours of time and frustration.

Standardized Writing

The essay counts for one-third of the total writing score, though given that the essay is the only nonobjective part of the SAT, I'd give it slightly lower priority than the multiple-choice portion of the writing section (composed of forty-nine questions on grammar). It's possible to score a perfect 800 with a 10 (out of 12) points on the essay, and I've even heard of the occasional 9 resulting in a perfect writing score. The scoring formula changes slightly for each test.

The bottom line is that the more reliable strategy is to aim for no errors on the grammar questions rather than to shoot for a perfect 12 on the essay (which is not to say you shouldn't prepare for the essay—because you should).

The College Board's website offers free essay prompts. (A "prompt" is a topic. I don't know when English teachers stopped saying "topic" and started saying "prompt," but today "prompt" is the word.) Prompts from the most recent SAT are posted. Speaking from experience, the most effective way to prepare for the SAT essay is to practice writing SAT essays as often as possible.

Getting the timing down can be hard. The routine goes: esoteric prompt, twenty-five minutes, pressure, pressure—*write*. It's critical to go into the test with a few all-purpose examples (historical, literary, or biographical references) you can use with virtually any prompt, and make sure they are well rehearsed.

I've heard dozens of theories about the best way to get a good score: write about an esoteric poem . . . use three examples . . . historical and literary examples are better than personal ones . . . be passionate . . . it doesn't matter what you write about . . . and on and on. Based on all of the essays I read that year (*many*), I can't say I noticed any pattern to the examples at all (though the "personal story" essays seemed to be rare). I did notice that the essays scoring 11's and 12's were decorated with what I came to refer to by the end of the year as "the trimmings."

I'm referring to sophisticated vocabulary (I read one essay that used "ergo" twice and scored an 11), varied punctuation (colons, semicolons, dashes, parentheses), and metaphors. I do agree with the injunction to use historical or literary examples, not personal stories. The essay graders can be erratic, to say the least, so better to play it safe if you are hoping to score in the 10–11 zone.

12's are rare.

The prompts fall into predictable categories, though they're cloaked in enigmatic language that can be intimidating if you haven't practiced. The overarching themes come in size extra-wide: wisdom, choice, conflict, perfection, truth, suffering, ethics, sacrifice, technology, change, and so on. It seemed to me that nearly all novels kids read in high school English can be used to answer nearly all SAT prompts, so it isn't necessary to memorize dozens of different examples. Better to be well prepared with three or four versatile illustrations and leave it at that.

Of course, given that I'd been out of school for a few decades, I tended to use recent bestsellers as my examples because that's what I was reading. But I found that the same principle applied. *All novels fit all prompts.* I had no trouble using *The Battle Hymn of the Tiger Mother* and *It's Not About the Bike* for almost every essay I wrote no matter what the subject. On the other hand, I spent all year trying to work in one of my favorite books, *The Things They Carried*, without success. It wasn't until my final SAT that I managed to replace Lance Armstrong with Tim O'Brien.

Ethan used whatever book he happened to be reading in English at the time. He scored a 10 on his first test using *1984*, and an 11 on his second test with *One Flew over the Cuckoo's Nest*.

There *is* one exception to the all-novels-fit-all-prompts principle, and that is the technology prompt (some version of "Technology: Is it good or is it bad?"). I could never figure out how I was going to fit my books (or any books) into a five-paragraph essay on technology, and thankfully I was spared having to try. I did get the reality-TV prompt on my second test, which threw me, and everyone else, for a loop, but more on the reality-TV kerfuffle later.

A simple recipe for the essay exists that *should* earn you a 10 if you practice.

First, it's not necessary to read the "excerpt" that precedes the prompt. Save yourself that minute and jump straight to the "assignment" (aka the prompt). For the first two or three minutes, jot down your thoughts, then pretend you're on the debate team and try to convince the grader of your point of view. Do *not* waffle or attempt to be nuanced, and be specific and explicit with your examples. The prompts are so broad that it's fairly easy to be specific and explicit using pre-memorized examples from English class. Just adapt your examples to the particular essay you are writing. Answer the question directly and circle back to your thesis in every paragraph.

RECIPE FOR SUCCESS ON THE ESSAY

Paragraph 1:

- Line 1: Answer the question directly, yes or no. Basically, repeat back the prompt as a brief, declarative response.
- Line 2: Why you believe line 1.
- Line 3: Why you believe line 1 (give second reason).
- Line 4: End paragraph with general examples that you will elaborate on in the body of the essay, for example, "Compelling examples of this proposition can be found in Renaissance art and European literature."

Paragraph 2:

- Line 1: *Specific* example that supports your thesis.
- Lines 2–5: Describe example in detail. Be specific; don't generalize; circle back to the thesis (Line 1, Paragraph 1).

Paragraph 3:

- Line 1: Second example that illustrates your thesis (Line 1, Paragraph 1).
- Lines 2–5: Same formula as paragraph 2.

Paragraph 4:

- Conclusion: "While some might argue [counterargument], this argument loses force when one considers [examples from your essay]."
- Recap Line 1, Paragraph 1.
- Expand Line 1, Paragraph 1 (if possible).

There are sample essays and a grading scale on the College Board's website, which are worth a passing glance. But really, the best way to improve is to practice and get feedback. Feedback can come from an English teacher, a friend who's done well on the essay, a tutor, or, if you're really brave, the forums on College Confidential. Just be sure you can tolerate critiques from total strangers before going the College Confidential route, and that whoever is doling out the advice is familiar with "standardized writing" (as opposed to "creative writing," which is a completely different kettle of fish).

The Comfort Zone

I loved the writing section and would often default there rather than attempt to learn something new, like math. That way, I could rationalize and check "studied" off my to-do list without having to do any heavy lifting.

Ethan did the same.

Before the project began, I gave him a Barron's PSAT prep book and told him to spend thirty minutes a day working through it. We went back and forth (as we always do) until we finally agreed on twenty minutes, every day. I've learned to pad whatever it is I *really* want him to do so we have room to negotiate.

Then we did what we always do *next*.

"Did you do it?" I'd ask once a day, while juggling a dozen other things.

As deeply as I love my children, as much time as I spend obsessing about their well-being, in the day to day I can be distracted more often than I care to admit. Ethan and I probably have that in common.

"Yes, Mom," he'd say.

"How'd it go?" I'd ask.

"Good," he'd say.

"Do you have any questions?"

"Nope," he'd say. "I got them *all* right."

That should have been the tip-off. Time to stop multitasking and train *all* of my attention on Ethan. But I didn't. For me, it's easy to obsess, but hard to *focus*.

This went on for months (typical), until one day I asked a different question.

"What's a grid-in?"

Somehow "grid-ins" had crossed my radar, and I had been meaning to ask Ethan what they were.

"I don't know," he said, not even fazed enough to look up from whatever inane thingymabobber he happened to have been wasting his time on at that moment.

"Excuse me?"

I instantly recognized where this was headed. I grabbed his Barron's book from the dining-room table and started flipping through the pages. He'd left half the answers blank.

"Ethan!" I yelled. I couldn't believe I'd been duped, again.

"*What?*" he said, annoyed that I'd interrupted him.

"Why are half of your answers blank?"

I was furious, as much at myself as at Ethan.

It turned out he was doing the problems he knew how to do, and when I'd ask, "Did you do the workbook?" he thought that meant, "Did you practice the problems you *know* how to do?"

Not: "Did you practice the problems you know how to do *and* start learning how to do the problems you *don't* know how to do?" which was what I had actually meant. In fact, Ethan's take was completely reasonable. Practicing things you know and teaching yourself things you don't know (something Ethan was capable of in this instance) are two different things. I should have spelled it out.

But this was our familiar dance. Distracted parent, distracted teen; token asks and automated responses.

WHAT *IS* A GRID-IN?

Grid-ins are officially known as "Student-Produced Response Questions." *Student-produced response* means *not multiple choice*. In the grid-in section, students solve the problems as they would on a normal math test at school, then enter their answers in a grid by bubbling in digits, decimal points, or the forward slash to indicate a fraction. Be sure to review how to enter the answers before test day because there is more than one way to "grid-in" correctly. It can be confusing if you're not prepared.

- One in three math sections will be a grid-in (unless the test taker encounters an "experimental" math section, in which case there could be four math sections, two of which could be grid-ins).
- Eighteen questions make up the grid-in section.
- Two additional math sections contain sixteen and twenty questions each.
- Math questions appear in order of difficulty in each section.
- The grid-in section is slightly different. Questions 1–8 are multiple choice (in order of difficulty), and questions 9–18 are grid-in (in order of difficulty, starting with question 9 as the easiest).
- No points are deducted for a wrong grid-in answer (versus a quarter point deducted for wrong answers on multiple choice).

There was another lesson in the story about Ethan's selective approach to test prep, which brings me back to the reason why I had to buy myself a second Blue Book for the project.

I'd done exactly what Ethan had done. I had cherry-picked my way through the Blue Book, answering the questions I liked and skipping the rest.

You have to watch out for that because it *is* fun to do just the questions you like—and maybe reach just *slightly* out of your range but not too much. If the tension is just right, it's like doing the *New York Times* crossword puzzle on Monday and maybe on Tuesday through Thursday. But never on Saturday. The Saturday puzzle is no fun at all.

The danger in working on only the questions you like is that there are only a finite number of official SATs available, eleven of which are in the Blue Book. To prepare well you need fresh, untouched, complete tests, and once you've cherry-picked, as I did, a test can no longer be counted on as a means to accurately assess progress. Practice tests from the Blue Book should be saved and taken as full tests, just as Good Experience Mark recommended.

I'd picked through mine as if they were my own private box of assorted chocolates—just as Ethan had done with his Barron's book.

What I Wish I'd Known . . .

Unfortunately, there aren't enough Blue Books in the world to turn back the hands of time if you've already sullied yours, as I did mine. However, there *is* a Plan B.

PLAN B

Retaking practice SATs you've already taken once won't provide an accurate measure of your ability. You need to use fresh material, and fresh material is hard to come by. There is simply no substitute for authentic SATs, and only a limited number are available. If you run out of tests in the Blue Book and the free tests on the College Board's website, try the following alternatives before turning to imitation tests.

- **THE SAT ONLINE COURSE:** Includes ten *more* official practice tests. It costs more than the Blue Book, but it's worth the price for those ten extra tests.
- **THE RED BOOK:** The Red Book is the Blue Book's predecessor (before the Red Book, there was a Green Book). It includes ten practice pre-2005 SATs. Not a perfect solution because these tests don't include the writing section, have analogies (which are no longer on the test), and have a Column A/Column B math section (which no longer exists), but it *is* official material and better to study from than most of the tests created by imitators. (Out-of-print editions are available from online retailers for a reasonable price.)

So don't touch the tests in the Blue Book until you've got a plan in place. Then start your Blue Book on page 1 and continue from there—that is to say, read the first 376 pages.

Most people do exactly what I did: skip to page 377, where the practice tests begin. But those first 376 pages are worth, at the very least, a cursory glance, if only to gain insight into the minds of the test makers.

I did review those pages, after a fashion. I whooshed through them as if I were in an Evelyn Wood speed-reading course instead of doing what I should have been doing, which was picking them clean like a turkey bone at a Thanksgiving dinner. There are valuable clues and tips in those pages, including one essential reference, *on page 11*, to the fact that the College Board has posted solutions to every single Blue Book question online. *Solutions*, not just *answers*, which is all they provide in the book.

It took a good six months before I discovered that the College Board had online solutions for the tests in the Blue Book, and at the time, I believe I knew just one other person who was aware of their existence. (You're not supposed to skip those pages!)

Plan A

If you have fresh Blue Book tests, save them for endurance training and skill building within the context of a timed exam. Take as many as possible under full-test, timed conditions, and then study the questions you got wrong over the next week or two, just like Good Experience Mark said. The real heavy lifting happens in those two weeks. It's essential to understand the solutions to the questions you missed so well that you can explain the answer to your teacher's teacher.

While understanding the solution for every problem is critical, it is *not* necessary to use the College Board's solutions if they don't work for you. I often found them confusing, especially for grammar. A College Board solution might say something like "It avoids the comma-splice error of the other options by turning the first independent clause into an appositive," which made me feel like Charlie Brown listening to the teacher: "*Mwa mwa mwa . . .* other options *. . . mwa mwa mwa.*"

I'd never heard of an appositive, or a comma splice, or an independent clause before this project—at age forty-six, in 2011. I'm pretty sure I was never taught grammar in school (unless I've forgotten, which is possible). I've been under the impression that grammar lessons went the way of cursive handwriting, sentence diagramming, and math drills—i.e., out to pasture at some point during the 1970s.

Of course, as a publishing professional I had been using independent clauses and appositives (and not using comma splices) for years. I knew what these things were; I just didn't know what they were called. Once I learned the terminology (not essential, but I wanted to), I found it helpful. Finally, I could organize the mental closet—and understand the College Board grammar solutions.

Rest assured, though, that if the College Board solutions don't work for you, there is a wide world of alternative options right at your fingertips.

Start, for example, with the Google machine and type in the exact words of any SAT question in the Blue Book. Dozens of solutions will appear on your screen (though some may arrive in foreign languages, especially for the critical reading questions). And if you don't understand any of those solutions, there are people (and by "people," I mean total strangers) who are available to answer your questions online, round the clock. I realize this must sound far-fetched, but it's true. Go to the forums on College Confidential and post a question asking for the solution to any SAT question, and someone—probably *many* someones—will answer your question so fast it will feel like they've been waiting there all day just to help you.

SOLUTIONS FOR THE BLUE BOOK PRACTICE TESTS

There are almost as many sources for Blue Book "solutions" as there are methods for test prep. Here are the ones I found most helpful:

- **TUTOR TED'S SAT SOLUTIONS MANUAL:** Math solutions only, and easy to understand; became a trusted source.

- **THE ULTIMATE SAT SUPPLEMENT FROM KLASS TUTORING:** Solutions for *every* problem in the Blue Book (i.e., all three sections). Klass's reading and writing solutions are better than the math.

- **KHAN ACADEMY:** Video math solutions. Videos feature Sal Khan narrating SAT math solutions as he writes the problem in steps on a digital blackboard. Can be frustrating to navigate, though the explanations are great and free (khanacademy.org).

- **PWN THE SAT Q & A:** Solutions for all three sections. Students can ask questions and get back thorough, clear, and prompt solutions (free) from a 2400-scoring tutor (qa.pwnthesat.com).

Vocabulary

To squeeze every drop of value from the Blue Book, use it as a source of vocabulary words to study from. After a test, go through it with a highlighter and mark every word you can't define, even if you got the question right. Then make a homemade flash card that includes *all* definitions and a sentence you've written yourself.

Yes, I realize this is a lot of work, and yes, I realize there are pre-printed "SAT vocabulary flash cards," SAT vocabulary lists, SAT computer programs, and SAT phone apps. But I'm pretty sure the words stick better with *homemade* flash cards. It took many months for me to convince Ethan of this, but eventually he agreed with me (or at least he complied with less grumbling).

The College Board has been testing the exact same words on the SAT for decades. I noticed about one curveball word per test, but other than that, it seemed to be the same words, over and over. If you pick through the practice tests in the Blue Book, you should be solid as far as vocabulary is concerned.

I heard about people studying thousands of words for the test, and I would never dissuade anyone from learning *more* vocabulary—but I'm just not sure it's necessary *for the test*. The SAT is a "reasoning" test. You aren't expected to know every word in the dictionary; you are expected to be able to reason your way to the answer using what you do know.

After Ethan would finish taking a practice test, I'd have him go through it with a highlighter and mark every word he couldn't define (even those from the reading passages). This usually resulted in about fifteen words. Then I would go through his test and pepper him with questions about words he *hadn't* marked, which usually doubled his list. Next came the homemade flash cards and my repeated attempts to have him *use* these words as frequently as possible. "Put them in your papers," I'd say. "Highlight them in your books when you see one." Eventually he got into the habit, and by the end he was pointing out "SAT words" everywhere. He'd nudge me in movies or call them out when he heard them on TV shows, and he always seemed excited to recognize a word in the wild. It reminded me of when he first learned the alphabet on *Sesame Street*; he'd squeal with delight every time he spotted a letter from the show when we were out in public.

Vocabulary testing (in the form of Sentence Completion items) makes up about one-third of the critical reading section, but a strong vocabulary is essential for the reading passages, too. The reading sections include "words in context" questions, and the passages themselves often require a strong understanding of sophisticated and nuanced vocabulary to understand the gist of the passage or a question.

The words tend to fall into predictable categories—"unoriginal" (pedestrian, banal, hackneyed), "to make better" (ameliorate, alleviate, mitigate), "to praise" (tout, revere, laud)—making it easy to study the words by group, which I've seen people recommend—that and studying word roots, which also makes sense (although Ethan and I didn't try either one).

Taking the test, we both found it helpful to cross out the wrong answer choices—that is, to physically cross out the wrong answers so they were removed from our field of vision—as well as to come up with our own word choices before looking at the answers. I often found my own word or a synonym of my word in one of the answers.

The bottom line is that more is better when it comes to vocabulary and the SAT. But in the name of efficiency, start with words on the tests in the Blue Book.

THE MIGHTY VOCAB TOOLS

Knowing all the words in the English language (over one million) is not necessary for the SAT. Knowing the words that appear over and over again on the test, as well as how to reason with language (often a process of elimination), *is* necessary. Be methodical, make flash cards (even if you use other methods), keep lists of words, and practice using the words every chance you get.

Helpful Resources:

- **DIRECT HITS:** An excellent series of books that group SAT words by category and uses them in a pop culture context (e.g., "One of the most *presumptuous* moments in recent memory occurred during the 2009 MTV Video Music Awards . . ."). Start with the Core Vocabulary edition.
- **THE CRITICAL READER:** No one knows the critical reading section of the SAT like Erica Meltzer. Look up Top SAT Words on her website, thecriticalreader.com.
- **WORDNIK:** Free online dictionary and thesaurus that compiles definitions from different sources and shows words in context with examples from across the web. Allows user to maintain personal word lists, a feature I loved. Go to wordnik.com.
- **WORD-NERD:** Based on the psychology of memory, Word-Nerd organizes the 1,500 most commonly tested SAT words into groups organized by theme ("SmartSets"). Offers extensive quizzes and tests for practice at word-nerd.com. Subscription levels and prices vary.

In the beginning, vocabulary was Ethan's least favorite part of the SAT, which baffled me because it seemed like low-hanging fruit. We had many a battle. At first, he categorically refused to study *any* words, even declaring he'd rather get a lower critical reading score than study. I tried everything I could think of to motivate him, including pointing out that a lower reading score might jeopardize his chances for merit aid, to which Ethan responded that he'd rather sign up for ROTC than study SAT words.

"You would rather go to *war* than study vocabulary?" I asked.

"Yup," he said, "I would."

I wanted to throttle him.

One day I made beautiful charts and graphs out of his scores on practice tests. I drew one line to illustrate his current scores and another to show his hypothetical, vocab error–free *potential* scores. "You'd be turning some heads without those vocabulary mistakes," I said.

He was unmoved. "Why would you spend your time like that?" he asked. "Are you a procrastinator?"

Yes. I am. A *productive* procrastinator.

A month or so later Ethan and I went on his first college tour. Late on the last day of the trip, a cold and drab New England afternoon, we were tired and more than ready to be home. We'd had a great time, but I'd crammed one too many schools into the itinerary. As we slogged our way to the end, trailing behind the last of five student campus guides in just three days, we passed a sad-looking 1950s card table the ROTC chapter had set up to answer prospective students' questions. I didn't have to say a word. In one split second Ethan changed his tune about studying vocabulary. If I had only known which buttons to push, I never would have wasted my time on those charts.

The oldest child is like a first pancake—you never get it right.

It's a Wonderful Life

I love arts and crafts.

The day my new Blue Book arrived, I was moved by the creative spirit to change the book *just a little*. Given that I'd already ruined my chance to use the book the way it was intended, I thought, "Why *not* be whimsical and make the Blue Book a little more 'me'?"

So I cut up all the pages and pieced them back together the way *I* liked them: by category. Linear function problems, all in one place. Right triangle problems, all in one place. Misplaced modifier questions, all in one place.

Then I digitally scanned my newly organized book so I could print off sheets of like problems: all right triangle problems, for instance, or just the dangling modifiers, and so on. There were resources to help me categorize—*PWN the SAT Math Guide* and *The Ultimate Guide to SAT Grammar*—to name two. And when I was done, I printed out my brand-new Blue Book, by category.

It was months before the true fruits of my labor were realized. Ethan was in the thick of it, studying for *his* SAT, when we had a Hallmark moment. He was in the dining room correcting his practice test from the day before and was frustrated by all the mistakes he'd made on the function problems (who isn't, right?).

And just then, a lightbulb went off and I remembered my Blue Book project of a few months earlier. I searched my computer for "Functions," and the most coherent, logical, and *useful* document I'd ever seen appeared at my fingertips—function problems of every sort, from tables and graphs to nested functions and word problems. It was magnificent, if you're into this kind of thing, which I *was*, and Ethan now was, too, apparently.

I printed out the document and handed him the first sheets, which consisted of about eight function problems. He looked up when he saw them, wide-eyed and incredulous, so I ran back to the printer and got more—maybe twenty in the next batch—and brought those over, too. He'd already started to work on the first ones, and dare I say, I saw a glimmer of delight in his eye.

When I laid that second batch on the table, he looked up and smiled with such love and tenderness, becoming, for an instant, the same little boy who'd first looked up at me and said "Mama" so many years before, and right then he uttered the magic words without so much as realizing what he was saying. He raised his head and said, "You're the best SAT mom in the whole world"—just like that, in slow motion.

We both realized in that one instant what I'd done.

Sometimes you can't see the forest for the trees, but at that moment we both did. Some moms show their love through food. Ethan always says, "Castalucci's mom makes the best meatballs I've ever had" (translation: they're made with such love. Can you do that?). And Carolyn, his friend Philip's mom, "makes the *best* salads," and grills steak like he's "never tasted before" (translation: can you at least try to do that?). And

Sam's mom "brings peanut butter and jelly sandwiches to *every single game*—for the whole team." (Some moms go to every single game.)

My love showed differently. My love was delivered in the form of test prep for the SAT—function problems specifically, on that day. And I had triangles, and dangling modifiers, and faulty parallelism, too—you name it, I had it. I could serve it up fast, like a short-order cook.

In that moment, Ethan and I both realized that my homemade worksheets *were* the meatballs in our house that year. Mother love gets expressed in all kinds of strange ways.

9

AN ABSOLUTELY FABULOUS MONTH OF MATH

Bad Things Come in Threes

February was all College Board all the time, and I didn't feel ready to move on when March began. But I had to. That was the plan: a method a month.

I *hate* change.

I scoured my January score report, scrutinizing each morsel of data, probing for clues as to which way next. I fixated on my "Chances of Improvement," looking for where I had the highest chances of score gain, and with that in mind I decided to devote the entire month of March to math.

SAT No. 2 was in twelve days, so I figured I could make the most headway if I focused on just *one* section instead of all three at the same time. I *loved* the math sections—more than the other two, which was strange given that I was better at reading and writing. The math felt like fun, while reading and writing were arduous. Technically, both the writing and the reading sections were easier for me than the math. But they were far more mentally fatiguing.

I also had an inkling that I was secretly *good* at math, despite all the evidence to the contrary. My theory was that I'd been an underachiever in school. I'd thrown in the towel too soon when the going got tough in tenth-grade geometry.

I wanted another chance to test my potential.

I researched the best SAT math books and decided to begin with *Dr. John Chung's SAT Math*. Catherine had been working her way through Chung's book when all of a sudden she *and* Chris took a fifty-point score leap. They'd made no gains for many months, and then suddenly she was finishing the math sections with enough time to go back and check her bubbles. Chris said it felt like he'd jumped over a wall.

Of course, there was no way those score jumps could be attributed to Dr. Chung's book because (a) the spike occurred just as Catherine started the book, and no one becomes an expert overnight, and (b) Chris wasn't using the book at all. Nevertheless, "power spike" and "Dr. Chung" had become connected in my mind.

Plus, the reader reviews were *so* passionate it was hard to refuse: "I have been using SAT books for many years," ... "I was really desperate to learn and aim high on the SAT," ... "*Dr. Chung's SAT Math* has increased my score greatly."

When the book arrived, I could hardly wait to begin. The volume itself was robust and hearty—as big as the Blue Book, but solely devoted to math: six hundred pages' worth. It was like a box of Lucky Charms with just the marshmallows.

On the opening page is a greeting to students from Dr. Chung:

> Achieving a perfect score on any math exam is quite simple.
> Though this may sound clichéd, all it takes is practice ...
> Since 1992, I have personally helped more than 50 students
> each year achieve perfect scores on the SAT math ... I hope
> this book helps you as much as it has helped my students.

He had me at hello. I was ready to spend quality time with the doctor right up to the point where I actually *tried* one of his mock tests, at which point I realized something was very wrong. The problems were terrifically hard—even the first few, which I mistakenly assumed would be on the easier end of the spectrum, as they are in the Blue Book. I pushed myself to keep at it, but Dr. Chung was altogether too hard for me. I could solve only five out of twenty problems a section.

The questions were like trick birthday candles—they *looked* normal, but something was different. After a few tests, I got it: Dr. Chung is for people who are *already* good at math.

I put Dr. Chung on my bookshelf and went back to the drawing board.

The dilemma: should I buy a math book or an *SAT* math book?

I had a little over a week until SAT No. 2.

IS IT MATH OR IS IT *SAT MATH*?

"SAT math" is like a puzzle, which is why it's fun. The harder problems are designed to activate wrong associations and smoke out students whose approach to problem solving is too procedural. The test rewards students who can break routine and can spot a shortcut.

- Standard math techniques taught in school can often take too much time on the SAT, though it's essential to have basic math down cold.
- Nearly all students need to learn new techniques to solve "SAT math" problems fast enough to finish the test.
- "SAT math" is often about perception ("find the hidden right triangle") and spotting clever shortcuts to problems that can easily be solved using the traditional but more time-consuming methods.

I decided to take the "regular math" fork in the road this time, figuring I'd better start with the basics. I ordered a book called *Practical Math: Success in 20 Minutes a Day*, which was more my speed (i.e., remedial-ish), though I will add that the editors' claim of twenty minutes a day was only valid for the first three or four chapters. After that, the practice sheets required more and more time to finish until, by week's end, I was up to about forty-five minutes a day. That's when I got stuck.

There was *one* little math problem I couldn't figure out. I'd been able to do the whole chapter, getting every other problem right, except for that one puzzler whose answer made no sense to me at all. I asked Ethan for help—he was *way* beyond this level at school—but the answer didn't make sense to him either. I kept at it for days, not wanting to give up again like I had in tenth grade. I wanted to build a solid foundation this time, which meant I *couldn't* move forward until I understood this particular answer.

Catherine, my go-to math friend, was away on vacation, so I left urgent messages for her to call me as soon as she got home. When she called, a day or two later, I went right over with my book to get help. She took out some scratch paper, spent about thirty seconds, then said, "The answer in the book is wrong," as if it were no big deal.

That possibility hadn't even occurred to me. I'd squandered so much time on that one little problem—how could it be wrong? Math books aren't *wrong*. I was shaken.

I put the book on the shelf next to Dr. Chung's. Then I went hunting again.

My next selection was Rong Yang's *A-Plus Notes for Beginning Algebra*, which seemed like an excellent choice, since this one volume alone contained eighteen thousand problems. I needed eighteen thousand problems.

When the package arrived the next day my first thought was that the book was suspiciously thin given the number of problems it boasted. Dr. Chung's book was three times the size.

I was excited to start, and the exercises *did* look just my speed, and yes, it did appear that the book contained eighteen thousand problems.

What it did not contain, however, was white space—as in no white space at all, anywhere in the book. The problems were jammed together so tightly my eyes crossed and my head hurt and everything looked fuzzy. I gave it my all, but by day's end I was forced to concede that I couldn't work under these conditions. So Rong Yang's book went to the shelf of dejected math books that don't work for me—right between Dr. Chung and *20 Minutes a Day*.

A Mighty Effort

I ordered more and more books, desperate to find *the one*, but my shelf of rejects bulged ever wider until I had to move the forsaken books to a larger space downstairs, and then ultimately, when they outgrew that room too, to the big bookshelf in the sky. I'd agonize each time I had to decide which one to sacrifice, like this was Sophie's choice.

I *love* my books.

The local library used to take orphaned books, but apparently they've run out of space too. A sign in front says "We Don't Take Books," though one time I ignored it and left a full box on the doorstep when no one was looking. I felt like Miriam sending baby Moses down the river, hoping someone would find him. I hoped my books would be found by a teenager in need of test prep.

I had wasted so much time on all the wrong choices that my anxiety level was soaring. I only had a few days left until the next SAT when Catherine recommended *The New Math SAT Game Plan* by Philip Keller because it had a scoring strategy she thought sounded right.

I'll cut to the chase: it *is* right, and I discovered soon after I bought the book that *all* the SAT cognoscenti agree on this math strategy, though they package it up a little differently. If you want to do well on the math section, you'll save yourself a lot of time by accepting this method from the get-go instead of resisting like I did.

The following is a condensed version of the strategy.

THE GAME PLAN

The SAT awards one point for each right answer, and deducts a quarter point for each wrong answer. There's no deduction for questions you skip. Naturally the quarter-point deduction leads to a great deal of speculation about whether guessing is ever a good idea.

The answer is: it depends. Philip Keller (*The New Math SAT Game Plan*) tells you exactly when to guess, and when not to guess, based on your current baseline score.

Keller also explains why the quarter-point deduction means that most test takers should *deliberately* work too slowly to finish the test. The reason to slow down is that everyone makes more mistakes when they rush, and on the SAT mistakes are costly. Your score will be higher if you leave the hard problems blank and get 100 percent of the problems you *can* do right—you can score well above a 700 (about 740, on average) intentionally skipping one question per section if you get everything else right.

The strategy:

- Choose a target score 100 points higher than you achieved on your most recent test.
- Decide which questions to *skip* based on your target score. Math questions appear in order of difficulty, and Keller tells you exactly which questions to answer (Answer Zone) and which to skip (Skip Zone) according to their sequence on the test.
- *Only* answer questions in your Answer Zone. Any questions not in your Answer Zone are in your Skip Zone, and that's what you do. Skip them.
- Only guess if you're in your Answer Zone. *No guessing on Skip Zone problems.*
- Grid-in strategy: Only answer grid-ins if they are in your Answer Zone. You do not lose points for wrong grid-in answers but you do lose time.

The rest of the book is filled with shortcuts for solving SAT math problems faster than you can solve them using traditional methods. Keller says there's "a little bit of high school math, much of which can be avoided," and that the test is biased against the "good student" who does things the way he or she was taught in school. "The SAT is biased in favor of the non-conformist," he writes, which is a nicer way of saying "the kid who cuts corners." Keller gives examples of high school algebra problems solved twice: once using the familiar method and a second time using the nonconformist approach (i.e., the shortcut). The school method might take two to three minutes, the shortcut under a minute. On a twenty-five-minute test, that differential can have a huge impact. He says most of his students reach their 100-point score gain in a few weeks; then they raise their goal by *another* 50 points. (Keller's son scored a 2400 the year after the project.)

I couldn't argue with Phil Keller's arithmetic. The problem was that *I hated the idea of skipping questions*, even if they *were* hard. I preferred to tackle the math section like it was an apple orchard, grabbing as much fruit as possible. Keller's strategy was so *methodical* and required such discipline that it didn't seem humanly possible (are there really people who can decide *not* to answer certain questions before the test—and then follow through on that?). Not to mention it required aiming for *less than perfect,* which was akin to calling what I was doing "The Higher Score Project."

There was *another* strategy in the book that I found more intriguing. It was actually a tip, but I thought of it as a strategy. It wasn't highlighted on the front cover, but hidden a few pages in on a page titled "Memo: About Calculators," where Keller described all the calculator options: basic, advanced, and the Monster (aka the TI-89). Apparently, the Monster does the algebra for you. (You see where this is going, right?)

I should have paused for a moment and thought, *Now Debbie, why isn't everyone acing the SAT if there's a calculator that does the work for you?* But before I had finished reading the page, I had one on order, after which I finished reading the page and learned that the TI-89 is "so intimidating" that many students don't know what to do after they turn it on. ("You press the 'Home' button.")

I'll spare you the hours of agony I spent trying to learn how to use the Monster. I read two different instruction manuals and finally hired a high school student to give me calculator lessons, thinking I could master the thing before test day. Unfortunately, I didn't.

If there's a moral to this story, it's that I should have spent my time learning algebra, not the Monster. The other very important lesson is that you should *never* (ever) take the SAT with a calculator you're not familiar with. You'd be better off without one, which for all intents and purposes was the state in which I took my second test. I had a calculator, but I didn't know how to use it.

Catherine had a similar calculator calamity, which I hate to admit was partly my fault. Four days before she took the SAT, I told her about the *math frac* function on the TI-84. I said Mike, the math tutor we both trusted with our children's SAT lives, said you have to have *math frac*.

The trouble was, she'd been practicing for years with the much-lower-tech TI-36 and could pretty much touch-type the thing. But the math-frac button seemed like such a must-have once I learned about it that I convinced her *she* needed one too, so she asked her husband to pick one up on his way home from work, which he did—a day or two later.

Not a great idea.

On test day she used the TI-84 on her first math section and tripped over every problem because she couldn't remember where the Enter key was, or how to do square roots, exponents, and such. She squandered so much precious working memory trying to remember where the calculator buttons were instead of solving the math problems that she switched back to her old (trusty) calculator for the rest of the test. Things went smoothly after that, but she still refers to the incident as "death by calculator."

Given that two grown women who should have known better than to use a new calculator on test day *both used a new calculator on test day,* the lesson bears repeating: **use the calculator with which you are most practiced and comfortable**. Automaticity—knowing your calculator so well you don't have to think about how to use it—trumps fancy tricks.

Despite my calculator fiasco, which was a self-inflicted debacle, I returned to *The New Math SAT Game Plan* all year long. It doesn't replace the Blue Book (in fact, Keller refers you to the Blue Book—a good sign), but it is a terrifically helpful supplement.

AVOIDING CARELESS MATH ERRORS

- Always use the calculator, even for the easy questions. (Or maybe especially for the easy questions. Some test takers report making more "dumb mistakes" on the easy problems than on the hard ones.)
- Know *all* basic math facts like the back of your hand. (What's the first prime number? Hint: not 1.)
- Don't get stuck on a question. *Always be aware of the time.*
- Don't be thrown by complicated-*looking* questions (e.g., know exponent rules by heart).
- Always be on the lookout for special right triangles. They're everywhere.
- Practice bubbling the grid-ins. There is more than one way to do it, and you don't want to have to think twice on test day.
- "Not drawn to scale" means *not drawn to scale.*
- Read every single word of the questions and answers. Don't make a "one-word" mistake.

Paint by Numbers

The other book I spent a fair amount of time with between those first two SATs was a gift from an author, Dr. Tahir Yaqoob. He'd seen on my blog that I was having trouble with math and wanted to help. Dr. Yaqoob is an astrophysicist who trains postdoctoral researchers, and I loved his book so much I probably read it two or three times in one week. The book is called *What Can I Do to Help My Child with Math When I Don't Know Any Myself?*, and the fact that I happened to drift way off course as a result of reading it is no reflection on Dr. Yaqoob, because his advice is excellent.

Somehow, Dr. Yaqoob's instructions passed through my brain and came out the other side a remix, never quite achieving the intended effect. For example, he recommends creating a "wall sheet" to commit hard-to-remember math facts to long-term memory, providing precise instructions in great detail. "Take a piece of paper that has dimensions of 8.5 inches by 11 inches (or approximately 22 cm by 28 cm)," he writes, then advises using "small neat handwriting," and *not* using "complete sentences."

Well, I couldn't wait to get started. I had all sorts of visions as to how I might improve upon Dr. Yaqoob's "wall sheet" idea.

I opened a fresh set of markers and started with one cabinet in the kitchen. I decorated it with theorems and formulas I didn't want to forget, and when I was done with *that* cabinet, I decided to try another because I was having so much fun. And really, how could it *not* help to be surrounded by math while I was cooking and washing the dishes?

After adorning my second cabinet, I decided to crank up the music and make a project out of it. My cabinets were looking so beautiful by that point that I climbed onto the counter so I could decorate every nook and cranny of white space. (There are *a lot* of math facts to remember for the SAT, especially if it's been decades since your last math class.) And as I sang along with the music, decorating my kitchen cabinets with math facts, I had a vision. It came to me, in a flash: I would start an "SAT wallpaper" business when the project was over. It seemed like such a no-brainer.

I invited my friend Jen over to get her take on the viability of this idea. Her son, Sam, was a junior at the time, so who better to ask than my target market, a mom in the midst of her child's SAT test prep. She also happens to be a colorist who graduated from the Rhode Island School of Design around the same time I went to Bennington.

I led her to the kitchen and unveiled my masterpiece as if it were a fresco I'd been working on for years. She stood back, assessing my work, though not immediately expressing an opinion. I'd certainly brought movement to the math facts, there was no doubt about that, and in my opinion, *my* math was so much more interesting than the usual textbook math. *My* ratios were pumpkin colored, and my sequence problems were sea-foam green. I'd colored mean, median, and mode in shades of saffron, sycamore, and silver sage, and I'd included every single type of function problem, too, in burnt sienna, coral, and terra-cotta.

"What do you think?" I finally asked. I couldn't stand it another second—I needed to hear what she thought.

"It's amazing," she said.

I knew it, I thought. "Everyone's going to want this for their junior year, right?" I said, confident I had a million-dollar idea here.

"I don't know," she said hesitantly, which surprised me. "I'm not sure everyone's as *into* it as you are."

Excuse me?

"But *I* love it," she qualified. "Especially what you've done with the angles over there." She pointed to the parallelograms in the upper right corner. "They're gorgeous."

A Very *Special Right Triangle*

That night I washed the dishes and admired my colorful renditions of the math rules, trying to use the wall as a memory aid just like Dr. Yaqoob recommended. I was sure there'd be a payoff in my score for the March SAT, now just a few days away.

I took a step back to admire the full view of the wall . . . and spotted a blemish.

There was a faint, delicate, and minuscule—even elfin—yet unmistakable defacement. I moved in closer to examine the flaw, and as it came into focus I realized it was Ethan's distinctive chicken scratch. He's a lefty with handwriting so illegible school authorities classified it as a disability. I always tell him he'd make a great doctor.

I couldn't *believe* he'd had the nerve—without asking me first. I stepped in closer to see what he'd done, and from a few inches away I could see that he'd drawn a microscopic special right triangle and marked the sides and angles: 30° = x, 60° = x√3, 90° = 2x.

"Ethan!" I yelled upstairs from the kitchen. "What did you do to my wall?"

He ran downstairs to explain.

"How could you?" I asked.

"But you wrote it wrong," he said. "I wanted to fix it for you."

Oh, I felt so ashamed at how mad I'd gotten at him. He'd only wanted to help (even if it did detract from the design).

I thanked him and apologized. Then I asked if he'd check the rest of my walls, which he did, hurriedly, before announcing that the special right triangle was my only mistake. I couldn't tell whether he was giving me an honest answer or just avoiding further trouble (and if it was the latter, I didn't blame him). I could never trust my wall after that. It felt unsafe, like the *20 Minutes a Day* math book with the one wrong answer in the back.

I'm not sure this was the type of "memory jogger" Dr. Yaqoob had in mind, though it was quite a lot of fun.

WORKING WITH WHAT YOU'VE GOT: A REALITY TV PROMPT

Knee-Deep in the River of Teens

I took my second SAT on March 12 at a public school in Dobbs Ferry, just down the street from the private school where I'd taken the first test seven weeks before. If I were writing the difference as an old SAT analogy, it would go like this:

> PRIVATE SCHOOL : COUNTRY CLUB ::
> Public school : Multiplex cinema

The line in March was much longer than the one in January. January was manicured; March was messy. January was single file; March was clustered. January was Park Avenue; March was Times Square. A lot of the girls had on flannel pajama bottoms at the March test, like they'd just rolled out of bed for the SAT.

"Separate rooms," yelled a proctor from the check-in desk. "We've got another set of twins over here." She gestured to another proctor who was walking the line. I never got to the bottom of *why* they needed to separate the twins.

This time there were kids just ahead of me in the line who I knew from my district. The first one I spotted was a girl I'd known since she was in preschool. She'd been in the same class as Ethan, and I had just seen her a few months before at a party with her mother, where we talked about the SAT. I had told her all about my idea: seven SATs, the perfect score, blah blah blah. She didn't say hello to me in the line, though, or even acknowledge me, for that matter. We were spaced just a few people away and I couldn't quite get her to make eye contact, which felt intentional on her part, so I followed her lead and didn't say hello either.

A few minutes later, I saw my friend Jennifer's son, Sam. They'd lived two doors down from me for ten years and I saw him almost every day, but Sam wouldn't make eye contact either, even though he was standing just two feet away. Then I realized, *Ohhhh, it's a thing*—some teenage code that stipulates, "Don't say hi to parents." Apparently it's embarrassing, which made no sense to me, but I played along.

After the test I walked outside and heard someone yelling my name—loudly and brazenly. I scanned the parking lot to see who could be calling me with such abandon. It was a grown-up (of course)—Lisa DiMona, a literary agent I'd known from my book-publishing days. She was waving her arms from the car window and shouting for me like there was nothing awkward about it—not a shame in the world.

"How was it?" she hollered from across the lot.

"It was great," I yelled back. "I loved it."

Thank God my kids weren't there to tell me how embarrassing I was.

Guess Who's Coming to Dinner?

That night I had dinner at Sam's house—yes, the same Sam who'd ignored me at the test that morning. Without his posse, Sam was friendly and uninhibited. I guess it's okay to communicate with adults in the privacy of your own home. Sam is smart—*whip* smart. In fact, he'd scored higher that day than I had. He's also one of the popular kids, and I was pretty sure he wasn't home studying all the time—or, if he were, he'd never admit it to a living soul. But I don't think he was.

Over dinner, I got right into the morning's test, asking him this and that, comparing answers, doing the whole post-test recap (that's half the fun of the SAT, for me). And let me tell you, Sam responded with enthusiasm. He was genuinely animated about the test—not at all the kid I'd seen in line that morning.

And, of course, the more excited he became, the more questions I asked. There were sparks flying from both ends. He was egging me on . . . whack . . . whack . . . whack . . . And we went back and forth, dredging up all the details for a good long time over dinner. I got so into the conversation that I guess I forgot where I was—or maybe I forgot *who* I was—because I blurted out a stupid question without even so much as a second thought, and then the good times were over, fast, with one big *thunk*.

"It was so much fun," I said. "Right?"

Silence.

Uh-oh. Very awkward moment.

The SAT's not fun. It's hard, it's arduous, it's unpleasant. At least, that's what he'd had his mom believing.

He was exposed.

We all knew he liked it. You could *feel* how much he'd liked it, listening to him enthuse at the dinner table. Of course he thought it was fun, like trying for a top score in a video game—but did I really need to point that out to everyone at the dinner table?

His poor mother; I could feel her pain.

She was exhausted from all the pushing and prodding she'd had to do every step of the way up that mountain, and she thought Sam hated the whole thing. She'd bought his "woe is me" story and had just assumed this was her lot in life: to goad, remind, keep track of test dates, and spend enormous quantities of mental energy trying to galvanize her son.

It was the same story back at my house: the mom herding cats so everything gets done while the kids whine, evade, and complain. "I have so much work. . . ." "But I did that already. . . ." "I said I'll turn it off in a minute. . . ." ". . . in five minutes . . ." The grooves are well worn.

It's exhausting trying to be the frontal lobes of an entire family.

Reality Check

Having gotten us into this conversational impasse, I felt a certain responsibility to get us back out. "How'd you answer the essay question?" I asked Sam. "That was so weird, right?"

THE SAT ESSAY

The essay was introduced in 2005 as part of the new writing section. It counts for 30 percent of the total writing score. The essay prompt includes a short paragraph from an authentic text (a previously published passage not written specifically for the test) and asks students to consider the issue at hand.

- The essay is scored "holistically" by two independent graders on a scale of 1 to 6, which means you get one score from each grader based on an overall impression of your essay's quality, as opposed to a set of scores on grammar, thesis, development, and so on.
- If the two graders' scores differ by a point, a third grader scores the essay as well.
- Essay graders are high school teachers and college faculty members who hold a bachelor's degree or higher.
- Graders cannot work in the test-prep industry, and they go through extensive training.
- Graders read the essay once and spend two to three minutes per essay.

The question that day was about reality TV, and it sparked outrage and made front-page headlines across the country. The text excerpt and prompt read as follows:

Reality television programs, which feature real people en-
gaged in real activities rather than professional actors performing scripted scenes, are increasingly popular. These
shows depict ordinary people competing in everything
from singing and dancing to losing weight, or just living
their everyday lives. Most people believe that the reality these shows portray is authentic, but they are being
misled. How authentic can these shows be when produc-
ers design challenges for the participants and then editors
alter filmed scenes?

Assignment: Do people benefit from forms of entertain-
ment that show so-called reality, or are such forms of en-
tertainment harmful?

The universal indignation was astounding. People complained that
the essay question was "culturally insensitive," arguing that it assumed
students are watching reality television. "I'm proud my son doesn't watch
television," one father told a national newspaper. "I guess the kids who
watch crap TV did well," said a school official.

The Daily Dialogue

The essay has been a bone of contention since long before that infamous
reality-TV prompt. From the moment the essay was introduced there
was widespread concern that it would perpetuate formulaic, dumbed-
down writing. Les Perelman, a former director of undergraduate writing at MIT, found something worse: a direct correlation between word
length and score regardless of essay quality. Longer essays with more
sophisticated vocabulary received higher scores even if the writer's facts
were all wrong. Dr. Perelman revealed his findings at a national writing
conference.

LES PERELMAN'S SAT ESSAY WRITING TIPS

Dr. Perelman advises preparing four examples before the test and including a lot of details, even if they are inaccurate and don't fit the prompt. According to Dr. Perelman, "Details count; factual accuracy doesn't."

- Prepare two historical biographies and two works of literature as examples.
- Ignore the short reading (the excerpt) and respond to the specific prompt.
- Fill both pages. Length matters.
- Take one side. Don't equivocate.
- Write a five-paragraph essay with a topic sentence as the first sentence of each paragraph.
- Use big words such as "plethora" and "myriad."
- Insert a quotation in the concluding paragraph.

Subsequent studies designed to refute Perelman's findings ended up confirming them instead. Essay length actually *is* the best predictor of score, and there is, in fact, an advantage to using literary and historical examples as opposed to personal stories. In one study, of the essays that scored a perfect 12, only 22 percent used a personal example. Even the College Board's own results indicate a correlation between essay length and score, though its researchers say the figure isn't as high as critics maintain. They do concede that "essay assessments have lower reliability than multiple-choice tests."

Pretty much everyone in SAT-land thought the reality-TV prompt was below the belt. Personally, I thought it was more unexpected than unfair. The essay is intended to be a rhetorical exercise, and what you think about a particular issue is supposed to be irrelevant.

I'd never watched reality TV in my life, so I took a leap of faith and discussed memoirs as a form of art. Then again, I only scored a 9, though somehow I doubt my score was the result of the topic. I didn't know about the essay recipe at the time.

There was also talk that the reality-TV prompt was the College Board's attempt to mimic the ACT's essay prompts, which tend to be more pedestrian than their SAT equivalents, and are written in colloquial terms about topics relevant to high school students:

> In your opinion, should high school be extended to five years?

> In your opinion, should high schools adopt dress codes for students?

> In your opinion, should teenagers be required to maintain a C average in school before receiving a driver's license?

In 2010, for the first time, the number of high school seniors taking the ACT exceeded those taking the SAT, so perhaps it *was* an attempt by the College Board to imitate the competition, though ironically, many students find the ACT prompts to be *harder* because they ask specifically about everyday high school issues and are more challenging to support with literary and historical examples.

The reality-TV prompt on the March SAT made headlines and drew tears, but it also offered the perfect segue out of that uncomfortable moment when Sam's delight in the SAT was exposed for what it was. We quickly covered it up with extraneous conversation about how a person *might* answer the question without ever having watched the shows—and regardless of whether the prompt was or was not fair, it did provide a welcome respite from our dinner dilemma that evening.

BIG-BOX TEST PREP:
KAPLAN, INC.

Progress, Not Perfection

On March 31, I logged on to the College Board's website at the crack of dawn to check my scores. Typing in my name and password, I felt like a person who had chosen *Door Number Three*, not someone who had turned in a test performance she could be held accountable for. My scores felt inadvertent . . . random, even. One tutor told me she's seen the "maybe-I-nailed-it-this-time" syndrome before, and it's usually a bad sign. She says the "jackpot" phenomenon occurs when students haven't studied as hard as they think they have. Apparently, she can spot the score day "crash and burn" from miles away.

I still considered myself lucky, so I felt hopeful.

MARCH SCORES		
	Jan. 22	Mar. 12
CRITICAL READING	680	690
MATH	510	530
WRITING	610	690
ESSAY	9	9

Disappointing . . . not what I was hoping for.

As far as I could tell, one of two things must have occurred: my good luck was on a temporary hiatus, or this SAT thing was going to need a lot more elbow grease than I'd anticipated.

It took about a minute before the rationalizations crept in and began to take root. *At least I didn't go in the wrong direction . . . It wasn't my fault (I'm not a good tester) . . . I did my best . . . These things happen.* And of course, the percentiles went a long way toward soothing my bruised ego.

THANK *GOD* FOR PERCENTILES

	NY State Percentile	National Percentile
CRITICAL READING	**95th**	**94th**
MATH	**59th**	**54th**
WRITING	**95th**	**96th**

A percentile feels so much better than a score, right?

I made a video for friends and family. They were keeping track of my progress, like I was a science project and they wanted to know: had there been growth? "I know a lot more math than what you see in my score," I told the camera, "and I'm sure that my hard work is going to be reflected in my *May* scores."

Almost everyone was encouraging, which helped.

I did have one grumpy viewer (that I know of): my cousin's third husband, a mathematician who had expressed interest in helping me with math at the beginning of the project. He didn't seem too impressed by the updates. "Stop making videos and get back to work," he'd write. Which was probably good advice.

Founding Father

I knew I wanted to go big-box brand name next—Kaplan or The Princeton Review—but I didn't have a clue what the difference was. I started my research with Stanley Kaplan's memoir, *Test Pilot*, and it took about five pages for me to decide: *He's my guy.* Stanley was so earnest and enthusiastic, not to mention that his integrity sang from every page. I would have moved the moon to have Stanley himself as my own personal tutor, but he died in 2009.

I *loved* his attitude.

When he was rejected by medical school, he didn't cry. "I still had a flourishing tutoring business," he wrote. And when he was first introduced to the SAT in 1946, he said, "It was love at first sight."

Stanley H. Kaplan believed students could improve their Scholastic Aptitude Test scores through study and practice, a radical belief in his day. The SAT was designed to test innate ability, not knowledge or skill, and in claiming he could raise students' SAT scores, Stanley was saying he could raise IQ—and he was charging for his services. He was attacked as a quack and a snake-oil salesman who preyed on students' hopes and fears, and was so universally condemned that some of his students registered for his courses under false names. But Stanley stood up for what he believed and withstood accusations that lasted for decades. Finally, in 1975, the Federal Trade Commission investigated the company's advertising, marketing, and sales practices and, three years later, concluded that Stanley was telling the truth. Scores could be raised with study, and Stanley's courses had helped his students raise theirs.

Stanley was devoted—he was a man on a mission. He wanted every one of his students to enjoy learning as much as he loved teaching.

"To say you can't improve scores is to say you can't improve students, and I disagree with that," he told the *New York Times*.

Every page in his book inspired me. Kaplan would stay up past midnight writing new questions for his students to use the next day, and he would drill students on math facts and vocabulary with passion and commitment. He was a traditional teacher who believed preparing for the SAT meant going heavy on the basics: lots of math, reading comprehension, and vocabulary.

"When parents asked me when a student should begin preparing for admissions tests," he wrote, "I always answered, 'in kindergarten.'"

For decades, the "A" in SAT stood for "aptitude," and were it not for Stanley H. Kaplan we might still believe that the SAT reveals immutable intelligence, something fixed, like eye color.

I committed to Kaplan before finishing the book.

A Tale of Two Times

What I didn't know then was that the Kaplan, Inc., of 2011 bore little resemblance to the company Stanley described in the book I'd just read. He sold the business to the *Washington Post* in 1984, though he stayed at the helm for ten more years before passing the torch to "younger talent," Jonathan Grayer, a twenty-nine-year-old Harvard grad.

Grayer was aggressive. "Revenues rose by 8 percent in 1994 and 11 percent in 1995," wrote Stanley. Under Grayer's leadership, Kaplan, Inc., underwent a decade-long makeover, morphing into an almost unrecognizable version of its former self. By the year 2000, the company was sprouting shoots in every direction, venturing into businesses that went far beyond test prep. Kaplan, Inc., invested in loan centers and job fairs, career services, computer consulting, Kaplan book publishing, Kaplan universities, and a law school.

By the time I got to Kaplan, Inc., in 2011, the company had blown up like Violet, that girl in *Willy Wonka* who turns into a blueberry and has to be carried off and juiced by the Oompa-Loompas.

Think of it like this:

STANLEY KAPLAN : KAPLAN, INC. ::
The Jackson 5 : The Neverland years

(I hate to keep using these old SAT analogies, but they convey so much, with so little.)

The First *Wolf at the Door*

Kaplan's first real competitor was The Princeton Review. Its founder, John Katzman, started the company in 1981 from his parents' New York City apartment, positioning himself as a maverick on the side of the students and leaving Kaplan to look like a crypt keeper by comparison. Katzman called the SAT a sham and said he could teach students how to *beat* the test instead of studying for it—and really, who wants to do crusty old worksheets if there's some new scrappy guy teaching everyone else how to crack the test like it's a puzzle?

RESULTS: KAPLAN VS. THE PRINCETON REVIEW

The authors of the *Fiske Guide to Colleges* conducted one of the largest independent studies of SAT preparation in 2003, which resulted in the following findings:

- Practice tests were the single most crucial element cited by high scorers.
- Kaplan students achieved an average combined score increase of 12 points above those who didn't take *any* test-prep course.
- The Princeton Review students scored 26 points *below* the non-prep average.

The Princeton Review took aim at Kaplan in advertising campaigns: "First he lost his students . . . then he lost his mind," they taunted. It was all-out guerrilla warfare, with The Princeton Review even going so far as to register Kaplan.com before Kaplan, Inc., thought to do so. When unsuspecting students would arrive at the site, they'd find The Princeton Review instead of Kaplan, provoking them with trash-talk taglines such as "Stanley's a wimp" and "Friends don't let friends take Kaplan." When Kaplan lawyers discovered the prank, The Princeton Review offered to relinquish the domain in exchange for a case of beer. Kaplan declined and went to court instead.

The rivalry cut much deeper than the mocking. This was about laying claim to market share in a nascent industry. The Princeton Review was innovative in a way that Kaplan wasn't, launching a line of books and software products and staking out territory all through the 1980s while Kaplan, Inc., rested on its reputation as "the gold standard."

By the time Grayer took the helm in the mid-1990s, Kaplan, Inc., was playing catch-up not only with its nemesis but with many other rivals as well.

By 2011, test prep had ballooned into a $4.5 *billion* industry with hundreds of thousands of SAT options, from brand names like Kaplan and The Princeton Review to millions of smaller chains and franchises. The test-prep industry is unregulated, so the barrier to entry is as high as the price of a shingle proclaiming its owner to be a great tutor.

Getting into college had become more competitive than ever, high school graduation rates were on the rise, and the economy had failed to recover from the financial crisis, driving some of the unemployed back to school. With *U.S. News* rankings emphasizing how high the SAT score averages were at colleges, naturally I assumed both The Princeton Review and Kaplan, Inc., would be thriving.

Wrong.

Buyer's Remorse

One of the many (many) things I didn't realize when I began the project was that both Kaplan and The Princeton Review were struggling financially. (Who would have thunk, given the test-prep landscape at the time, which was booming.)

"Princeton Review Inc. has been bleeding red ink," reported *The Wall Street Journal* in 2012, and Kaplan wasn't doing much better, dragged down by a squeeze on federal student loans, which put a dent in the margins of their higher education division. The government had begun scrutinizing loans for "online degrees" because in many cases they weren't worth more than the paper they were printed on, and students were saddled with debt they couldn't repay.

And while I *was* still committed to *Stanley* Kaplan, I did have a hunch right off the bat that Kaplan, Inc., wasn't "it."

Have you ever ordered something in a restaurant and a few minutes later you see a dish at the next table that looks better, but it's too late to switch because the waitress already put in your order? That's what I felt like as soon as I hit the "I'll take it" button on the Kaplan website.

I had a case of buyer's remorse.

A click or two later I stumbled onto *another* website—one without any bells and whistles or fancy mix-and-match packages like the ones on the Kaplan site, where I'd just plunked down a few hundred dollars for an online course. This *other* website was plain-Jane: just a funny-looking cross-eyed elephant for the logo (now there's a more stylish Viking helmet in its place) and lots and lots of math worksheets. It was also filled with insider factoids about the SAT and a timeline highlighting the test's history and evolution. On the About page I found a note saying that *all the worksheets were free*, as long as the site's creator, Erik Jacobsen, PhD, was given attribution.

The site was *Erik the Red*, and I sensed authenticity from the second I hit that homepage.

Instantly, I wanted to exchange my Kaplan package for *Erik the Red*'s worksheets. The problem was, I'd already committed to Stanley for the month of April and I had to stick with my method-a-month plan or I'd never know what was what in the end.

The Package

"The package" was a decision that required *way* too much contemplation.

Kaplan private tutor packages ran as high as several thousand dollars, and there was no way I was going to spend that kind of money on a tutor without a solid recommendation from a reliable source, which I couldn't find. Then there were the Kaplan classes, but they didn't work because (a) classes took place at undoable times (dinner hour and weekends, when there was usually someone in need of chauffeuring); and (b) the price, at just under $1,000, was daunting. Without a reference, I was hesitant.

I *was* able to locate a few people with positive things to say about Kaplan, though the most recent review was a decade old, which felt like a thousand years ago. So that whittled my Kaplan choices down to the online options and the books—still a paralyzing number to choose from. I'm sure I logged on to kaptest.com a good half a dozen times, trying to decide *which one*, but each time I left the site undecided and overwhelmed.

The barely perceptible differences among the options combined with all the Kaplan jargon made me short-circuit every time: Complete SAT Prep, Prep Trio, Classroom Anywhere, Adaptive Online Instruction with "Smart Track," customized plans, cutting-edge, nine hours, two proctored tests, videos, self-paced, fifteen tests, SAT on Demand, etc. I finally decided to try the free "SAT Quizbank" (online) before committing real money, and then go from there.

So how did that go?

There's really no way to say this diplomatically, so I'm just going to put it out there: it was excruciating, from the signup process to the seemingly infinite number of "customize your questions" boxes that had to be checked off before getting to answer a single Quizbank question. I was worn out before I even started. I was also determined, because it was already April 1, and I was supposed to have *started* my new method that day, not still be trying to figure out which Kaplan test-prep option to use.

When I finally did make it to the questions—it was now ten p.m.—I discovered that the typeface was so jumbled and the spacing so weird I could barely decipher the text. Compare:

SAT formatting:

The students <u>have discovered</u> that <u>they</u> can address issues more
                   A   B

effectively <u>through</u> letter-writing campaigns <u>and not</u> through
          C   D
public demonstrations. <u>No errors.</u>
                          E

Kaplan Quizbank formatting:

<table>
<tr><td></td><td><u>have discovered</u></td><td></td><td><u>they</u></td><td></td></tr>
<tr><td>The students</td><td>A</td><td>that</td><td>B</td><td>can address issues</td></tr>
<tr><td></td><td><u>through</u></td><td></td><td></td><td><u>and not</u></td></tr>
<tr><td>more effectively</td><td>C</td><td>letter-writing campaigns</td><td></td><td>D</td></tr>
<tr><td></td><td></td><td><u>No errors.</u></td><td></td><td></td></tr>
<tr><td>through public demonstrations.</td><td></td><td>E</td><td></td><td></td></tr>
</table>

I plowed ahead, bouncing my eyes up and down across each sentence and developing a roaring case of digital eyestrain in the process. When I was finally finished with the section, I hit Submit to see the answers and get my score, and—I was greeted by a faceful of spam.

"Funny Pictures!!!"

"Penile Enlargements!"

"UFOs!"

The site had been hacked, and I did not feel sympathetic. I was now three long hours into my first online experience with Kaplan, and staring at Funny Pictures!!! and Penile Enlargements! instead of my answers just reinforced my case against online learning.

Books would *never* betray a girl like that.

There was one positive take-away from the experience: it clarified *which* online Kaplan course I should pay for (the least expensive, whichever one that was), and that's how I ended up choosing Kaplan's "SAT on Demand" online course.

I hated every minute of the course, and my misery had nothing to do with being from the wrong generation, as people told me every time I complained about online learning. The (online) diagnostic

SAT was absolute drudgery, and I say this as a person who loves the SAT.

The timed essay came first, as it does on the real test. I had never practiced writing a timed SAT essay before, and I felt nervous and extremely pressed for time. I raced along, typing my essay into the window, and managed to finish just under the twenty-five-minute limit. Then I pressed Submit.

My essay vanished.

I hadn't saved a copy, of course, since I was typing directly into the Kaplan website. So the whole thing was just *gone*.

I paused the test, opened a Word document, and tried to reconstruct what I'd written from memory. Then I cut and pasted my new remembered version into the Kaplan window.

This time, the essay stuck.

The rest of the test was just as trying. The questions were hard to read, the website was beyond glitchy, and it took me two or three tries to get through the entire test. By then my focus was shot.

When I was finally finished, it took a full *hour* to submit my answers. I would click Submit and be sent to a far corner of the Kaplan site, where I found myself staring at a page that had nothing to do with "SAT on Demand" or the answers I was trying to submit. I'd have to find my way back to my test answers (which were still there, thankfully, though I couldn't get to them just by pressing the Back arrow in my browser) and press Submit again—and get sent back to the same distant page I'd been sent to on the previous try. This went on for an hour.

Imagine my relief when, heading into hour two, I hit Submit—and suddenly, miraculously, my answers went through. *Finally.* Three days into the diagnostic test, I would have my *diagnostic score.*

I scanned the screen, looking for the scores, and . . . nothing.

Just a notice saying my score report would be delivered in five days (which turned into ten, but who's counting). I was incredibly frustrated. April would be halfway over before I was finished with the Kaplan preliminaries.

WHAT'S WRONG WITH KAPLAN'S "SAT ON DEMAND"?

My issues included, but were by no means limited to, the following:

- Typos (lots and lots of them).
- Major spacing problems throughout the website, making questions hard to read—for example, Error ID questions with the underlined words raised a quarter inch above the rest of the sentence.
- Illegible critical reading passages. Imagine a fiftieth-generation photocopy on the low ink setting.
- A disappearing essay after I hit the Submit button. Having typed my essay directly into the online course without saving it elsewhere, this was particularly dispiriting.
- Five days to receive a "diagnostic report," though in my case it turned out to be twice that amount of time.

The part that really got my goat, though, was that Kaplan was robbing me of the joy. As strange as I know it sounds, I loved studying for the SAT. It was fun. It was more than fun: it was satisfying. I was learning the things I should have learned in school but didn't, and I felt happy.

All of those feelings evaporated on the Kaplan website. The course material was as glitchy and unreadable as the diagnostic test, with the added frustration of a whole new design flaw: the score reports didn't include the questions or the answers, just the correct letter choices. All you learned from the scoring was that you'd put down A, C, and E for questions 8, 9, and 15 when the correct answers were B, A, and B, and that was it. Math practice without the answers.

After I'd spent ten days arm wrestling the Kaplan website and losing, I felt something akin to road rage. I was having urges to toss my computer out the window when I officially called it quits and decided to spend the rest of the month studying from the Kaplan *books*—of which there were at least a dozen options. I was only too happy to pick three (one from each level), and commit:

1. **KAPLAN SAT STRATEGIES FOR SUPER BUSY STUDENTS:** It didn't say anywhere that this was the "SAT lite" edition, but I gathered from the Captain Underpants–looking design that they weren't targeting future Rhodes Scholars. Adding to the "lite" impression was talk of "two- to four-week preparation" (read: not for the go-getters), and then there were tips for those who had even less time than two to four weeks and were cramming.

2. **KAPLAN SAT STRATEGIES, PRACTICE & REVIEW:** This appeared to be the mid-level option, though, again, that impression was based on the packaging rather than anything stated directly. This was the thickest volume of the three, suggesting to me that it was Kaplan's anchor book.

3. **KAPLAN SAT 2400: ADVANCED PREP FOR ADVANCED STUDENTS:** The promise of this one was clear: "master the questions that most people get wrong."

The Kaplan books were such a welcome relief after all that online anguish that I dove in with gusto, which, looking back, was a rookie mistake. I should have been more discerning after the online experience, but I'm an enthusiast by nature and I projected onto the books everything I wanted them to be (and more): they were my homemade worksheets from Stanley—every bit as enjoyable as I'd imagined while reading his memoir. I didn't finish all three books in April, though I did complete a good portion of each, and I can say from the bottom of my heart that I *loved* every second of working with them.

They all had the same "Kaplan Method," which became familiar and comforting, and they were formatted beautifully with tips in shaded bubbles in the margins, and plenty of white space in which to work the problems. I was committed and steadfast in my efforts and worked my way through those books with love and devotion. And I was absolutely sure that my scores were going to reflect my effort.

My first inkling that something was amiss came a few days before the May 7 SAT. I wanted to get a read before test day on how I was doing in relation to the *real* test after all the work with Kaplan. So I broke out my Blue Book and tried a math section—after which I scored it, instantly, by myself—and that's when I realized something had gone awry.

First of all, the Blue Book felt "funny," like it was off somehow. Then, when I tallied up my score and saw it had dropped by *30 percent*, I started to panic.

I tried another section, but that one felt weird, too. All of the questions in the Blue Book felt . . . unfamiliar. I couldn't find any Blue Book questions that would work with the new tricks I'd learned from Kaplan.

Oh God—I'd gotten so used to the Kaplan questions that it had never occurred to me they might mess with my performance on a *real* SAT. They certainly *looked* like real questions—maybe ever so slightly different—but how could "slightly different" be such a big deal?

After I scored my second Blue Book section and confirmed the score decrease, I came unglued. There was less than one week until my third SAT and I felt almost hysterical.

I'm almost ashamed to air the dirty laundry of my Kaplan experience given my admiration for Stanley, but the truth is that Kaplan circa 2011 probably didn't have much in common with those homemade worksheets.

THE GOOD, THE BAD, AND THE DOWNRIGHT WRONG

Not *all* Kaplan advice was "bad" or "wrong." In fact, some of it was good. The problem was that I couldn't distinguish what was accurate from what wasn't. To give you some idea of the tips I learned from the Kaplan books that led me astray:

- **KAPLAN "TIP"**: Questions in the writing section are *not* in order of difficulty. **REALITY:** Not true! There are forty-nine multiple-choice questions in the writing section. Forty-three are listed in order of difficulty. Only six questions—in the

Improving Paragraphs section—are not sequenced in order of difficulty.

- **KAPLAN "TIP"**: "No error" (E) in the writing section is correct one in five times. **REALITY**: Poorly worded advice for students who take it to mean that the E answers are evenly distributed throughout the test so you won't see two correct E's in a row. In fact, the tests do sometimes have two correct E's in a row, occasionally even three in a row.

- **KAPLAN "TIP"**: *Listen* for a mistake in the writing section. **REALITY**: If you have a good ear, this can work for easy and medium questions, but the hard questions are intentionally designed so that most test takers *can't* "hear" the error. Either that or they *do* hear an error in a sentence that is awkwardly written but grammatically correct. One tutor told me she refers to these questions as "Is it weird or is it wrong?"

- **KAPLAN "TIP"**: Move around the math section. **REALITY**: The most effective math score strategy is to work carefully through easy and medium questions, making sure you get all of those questions right. Skip all of the hard questions until you've practiced solving them to the point where they are no longer hard for you.

- **KAPLAN "TIP"**: Use a calculator selectively. **REALITY**: Better to use a calculator even on easy questions to avoid calculation errors, which are more likely to occur under test pressure.

My *Algebro*

I sent out desperate smoke signals on Twitter about my Kaplan-induced score decline, and a stranger named "PWN the SAT" responded to my sad little squeaks.

"Let's get you moving on the right track ☺," he tweeted back.

I had no idea who this guy was, but his Twitter handle made me smile: Your Algebro.

"When and where?" I tapped.

"Tomorrow morning works," he said. "Let's make it happen."

When he called the next morning, I knew three things about the man with whom I was speaking:

1. He had an SAT advice blog called *PWN the SAT* that was decorated with LOLCAT images, which hit my funny bone. Most test-prep websites are decidedly *un*funny.
2. He scored a 2400, if the screenshot of the score report on his About page was to be believed. (I'm now sure: it's legit.)
3. His real name was Mike McClenathan, which I learned from caller ID when he phoned.

We spoke for hours that day—so long, in fact, that we each went through full battery charges on a few phones. I felt like the dim-witted William Hurt character in the movie *Broadcast News* with PWN playing Holly Hunter, the brainy producer who whispered the news through his ear bud. I was just so *relieved* to have my brain scrubbed clean of all that month's contaminants that when the call was over, I felt refreshed—and back to square one, which I chose to view as a "30 percent increase" rather than the alternative.

LESSONS FROM THE CALL

On the phone that day, PWN the SAT clarified my misconceptions, taught me some math, and showed me a few "SAT shortcuts" for the math section. He guided me through his diagnostic drill, which he uses to highlight techniques. He also told me about his "technique guide" for the Blue Book, which he'd put together so students would know when to use which strategy on official College Board material.

- **CLARIFICATION**: Kaplan advises starting with answer choice C while another book advises beginning with choice E.

PWN explained that starting with choice C *only* works with the "Backsolve" technique because SAT math answers are listed in numerical order from smallest to largest. "Backsolve" means plugging the multiple-choice answers into the problem one by one to see which one is right. By starting with choice C, the middle number, you save time because if C is wrong, you presumably know whether the correct answer has to be larger or smaller than C, leaving you only two other choices that could be right.

- **PATTERNS:** The SAT is full of patterns, and the more you can identify them, the better you'll do. PWN showed me some clues (e.g., √2 and √3 indicate that the problem probably involves right triangles, even if you don't see them).

- **PLUG IN NUMBERS:** Pick numbers to try in the problem whenever you see variables in the question *and* in the multiple-choice answers. Keep numbers as small as possible, but don't use 0 or 1. Start with 100 for percent questions and try 60 for angles.

The Magic Link

By the time PWN and I hung up that day, I'd been fully deprogrammed. I'd also learned another detail: he lived close by, with his girlfriend. I wanted to know more—who *was* PWN? So I sent him a text message inviting him for dinner. I invited Catherine and Chris as well, in case I needed backup.

For some reason, I was assuming that PWN must be unattractive (grown-up gamer, anonymous on the web, perfect SAT scores, LOL-CATS . . .).

I was wrong.

PWN is cute. I'd say he's in his early thirties, a little indie rock with shoulder-length wavy brown hair. And on a delightful-dinner-guest scale of 1 to 10, he's an 11.

I learned everything I could about him that night over dinner. PWN grew up in Connecticut, the oldest of three boys; his father was a mail carrier, his mother an interior decorator. He graduated valedictorian of his high school class (by a tiny margin, he emphasized) and then went to Brown. For about a decade after college he had worked for a prestigious SAT test-prep company, but he had recently left the industry to go to grad school.

His website, PWN the SAT, was his way of trying to level the playing field for students who couldn't afford test prep. He had never intended to set up an independent tutoring business and had chosen to be anonymous on the site because he wanted to be irreverent and didn't want people to Google his name and find him cursing out math problems on the Internet. He also didn't want people to think he was *selling* his tutoring services, because he wasn't. He was (and is) conflicted about the industry.

But I had a vision that night that he was going to tutor—even if it was just a business with one student.

It came to me as clear as a bell when I walked him out to his car after dinner. I noticed a sticker on the back window that was so familiar—but I couldn't quite place it.

"What is that?" I asked.

"It's a Transformer," he said (proudly), and then it all came back.

Ethan loved Transformers. I used to call them "boy dolls," because that's the closest I could come to understanding the appeal those scary little figurines held for my son. No question—PWN was the perfect person to help me connect the dots between "fun" and "SAT" for Ethan. PWN would be our connector.

I was sure the sticker was a sign from above: *Do what you have to do*—move the sun, the moon, and the stars—*but get that guy.* It took a few months to convince PWN that this was his calling, but eventually he came around, and I was right: PWN was our magic link.

12

WHICH WAY NEXT? ADVENTURES IN WONDERLAND

ALICE: *And how many hours a day did you do lessons?*
THE MOCK TURTLE: *Ten hours the first day, nine the next, and so on.*
ALICE: *What a curious plan!*
THE GRYPHON: *That's the reason they're called lessons, because they lessen from day to day.*

It's Always Something

I took my third SAT on May 7, 2011, at Ardsley High School. Although the school was just a few miles away from where I lived, I didn't know a soul in the district, so there would be no *We don't say hi* moments, like last time. But there was a different flavor of awkward along the lines of: "Who *are* you and why are you late?"

I was late because I was confused. The Ardsley check-in process included assigned rooms, which I hadn't encountered at the first two test sites, where everyone took the test together in the same room. I wasn't prepared for that curveball and hadn't left myself enough time to decipher the layout of a high school I'd never seen before. It was only SAT No. 3 and already I'd become blasé.

It turned out that the kids I saw crowded around the front door when

I walked into the school that morning were checking for their room numbers. That's what those sheets of paper on the wall were for.

I totally missed that cue.

Inside the building I took a seat in the auditorium, which was filling rapidly with students—who, unbeknownst to me, had checked their room numbers and were now awaiting further instructions. I was awaiting the test. When the school principal announced that it was time to go to our testing rooms, I wasn't concerned. I did what I'd done the other two times I'd taken the SAT: I followed along with the crowd.

It was a trek. Ardsley High School is one of those buildings that began life as a long skinny rectangle with a parking lot out front and then, as the years went by and the community grew, accumulated new wings, gymnasiums, self-contained cafeterias, whole new buildings (and whole new parking lots), and glassed-in walkways for passage from one era in the school's history to another. The layout made no sense at all, especially in the dark. None of the hallways were lit, and after a few twists and turns in the dim light I started to feel like Alice down the rabbit hole.

Finally we rounded a corner and there before us was a well-lit hall dotted with two lines of classroom desks, each stationed immediately adjacent to a classroom door. I was the only person surprised to see this. Not breaking stride, my fellow test takers entered the hall, sorted themselves by room number, and lined up beside the desks to check in.

This was the first moment I understood that the kids knew something I didn't: *where they were supposed to be.*

It was an archetypal exam dream, only real. I panicked.

"What do I do?" I asked the first proctor I found roaming the halls.

She told me about the room lists outside the front door and gave me a complicated set of directions back to the parking lot that included multiple "bear lefts" and "when you get to the restroom keep walkings." I probably couldn't have remembered them on a good day, let alone a day when so much of my working memory was being consumed by thoughts of missing half the essay section.

I pushed on, bearing left and walking past restrooms until I had no idea where I was or where the proctor was, either. Now I was speed-walking down the wide, dark halls looking for someone—anyone—who could get me out of there.

Finally I spotted a girl up ahead, standing in front of her locker. "Help!" I said.

The locker girl gave me a second set of directions, shorter than the first, and this time I made my way to the front doors, retrieved my room assignment, and hustled back to the testing classrooms, the last one in. Not an effective strategy when trying to "blend in." I was happy this wasn't happening in Dobbs Ferry.

By the time I got there, nearly every seat in the room was occupied by a quiet student having his or her calculator inspected by the proctor, a mid-thirtyish, suburban, Teva-wearing, English teacher–looking guy.

A name card indicated that my desk was front and center. All the desks had name cards that day; it was the one and only time in seven SATs that I would encounter assigned seating.

I sat down and took out my calculator for inspection.

A few months later I learned that "adult testers" are supposed to be seated front and center, or be sequestered in a private room "where they can be more closely monitored." I'm still not sure whether my assigned seat that day was intentional or just a coincidence, though it did make me realize that I liked sitting in the front row, which minimized the visual distraction of kids yawning and stretching in the seats ahead of me.

Apart from my lost-in-the-funhouse entrance, SAT No. 3 was notably . . . *unnotable*. I remember not knowing the definition of the word "mawkish," which is now high on my list of rarely used words to nonchalantly weave into casual conversation—and I remember thinking about PWN's essay advice from our marathon call the day before. "Pretend you're on the debate team and convince me," he'd said. "Pick a side and stick. Don't waffle."

Got it.

	MAY SCORES		
	Jan. 22	Mar. 12	May 7
CRITICAL READING	680	690	690
MATH	510	530	530
WRITING	610	690	700
ESSAY	9	9	10

Notably unnotable, right?

My first two essays were better written (in my humble opinion) and used more sophisticated examples than essay number three, but I waffled on the first two (ever so *slightly*). Rule number one for the SAT writing section: no waffling. To score a 10, you have to be direct and unequivocal.

So, for essay number three, I did exactly as PWN advised: I picked a side and I stuck. The question asked whether rules and limitations contribute to a person's happiness, and I said, "Yes." I didn't use a single literary or historical reference, and I blathered on (rather boringly) about children being in need of boundaries. I was firm.

Essay number three was pretty bad, I thought, but apparently it's better to be bad and unequivocal than good and of two minds, even when you support your *on the one hand, on the other hand* paragraphs with compelling examples from literature and history. Okay, lesson learned. I can play that game now that I know the rules.

What's Grockit?

My original plan for May was to test out Grockit, an online "game" that prepares students for the SAT and other standardized tests. I'd read about Grockit in *The Wall Street Journal* when I first came up with my plan. At the time, it was the hot new thing on the test-prep scene, having just raised almost $20 million in venture capital. The *Journal* article used words like "leveling up" and "multi-player games" to describe the company. Since those were words I'd heard coming from Ethan's room, I figured there was no way he couldn't love it, even if gaming wasn't my thing.

"What do you think of the idea of an SAT video game?" I asked him one day as I attempted to set up a Grockit account for myself.

"I hate it," he said, unequivocally. "I don't like good-for-you video games."

Oh, what does he know.

He was going to love it, and I was prepared to put aside my own distaste for online learning and video games to make sure Grockit was up to snuff for my firstborn cub. I believed a good online learning experience was out there somewhere; I just hadn't found the right one. Grockit seemed like a worthy candidate: state-of-the-art technology, gaming, adaptive learning (none of which appealed to me, of course), and a peer-to-peer aspect, which actually did sound interesting.

Part of Grockit's philosophy is that students learn best when they explain concepts to others, which was in line with everything I'd read about how people learn, so I was up for trying—until I attempted to sign up, at which point my willingness to keep an open mind diminished with each error message:

> There was a problem processing your order. Please check the information below and try again . . . Incorrect email and password combination . . . We're sorry, but something went wrong . . . Before contacting us, please see our frequently asked questions.

After two days of this, I was so angry I wanted revenge, not test prep. I do not handle wasted time well, especially when it's computer related. I will say this, though: Grockit customer service was extremely helpful. They took full responsibility for the problem and a very nice man got me signed up and logged on—but by then it was too late for me to put aside my feelings and give it a fair shot. I know my limitations.

I thanked the man from customer service and said it was probably best for me to put it off for a month. I promised I'd be back and I did try again later, briefly, but it wasn't my cup of tea (as my mother would say).

What Is *Test Prep?*

So if not Grockit, then *what?*

The Princeton Review? Gruber? Kumon? (Did Kumon even have test prep?) Did I need to learn the fundamentals, or strategy, or both? A class? A course? A book? Alone? Online? With friends? A teacher? A tutor? How *do* they teach critical reading in a group setting?

And what *is* test prep, anyway?

I ruled out SAT classes as an option because it would have taken wild horses to drag Ethan to a test-prep class after school or on weekends, and I didn't have nearly that kind of energy. It would have been easier to homeschool. Ethan *can* be self-directed—when he's interested—but I seemed to have little influence over the rationing of time he spent on his interests. I was thrilled that he'd recently developed an obsession with health and working out, but I'd be lying if I didn't admit that I would have preferred for him to spread a little bit of that love onto his school-work and the SAT.

I'd also started to realize that I needed to clarify and define what I meant by "score increase." According to the College Board, just taking the SAT for a second time is as effective as test prep. A 2009 analysis showed that test-prep courses had "minimal impact"—about 10 to 20 points in math and 5 to 10 points in critical reading.

That was not *at all* what I had in mind.

From what I could tell, most test-prep companies made claims of score gains much higher than 5 to 20 points, though it's surprisingly hard to pin down an actual number. Were we talking 50 points or 150? Personally, I was envisioning a 250-point increase in math, but was that even possible on a regimen of test prep alone? Or did I need remediation, too? (And how embarrassing would *that* be?)

I was doing much better in the writing section: I had hit 700 without having learned a lick of grammar, just answering everything by ear.

But could I get to 800 by ear?

Or did I need to learn what a dangling modifier actually was instead of counting on the danglers in the grammar section to jump out at me. Of course, most of the time the danglers *did* jump out at me, and that raised another question: what did it mean to "know" grammar, anyway? I seemed to know quite a lot of grammar although I didn't know what any of it was called, and I couldn't explain what I knew to anyone else.

I was having an existential SAT crisis.

Discernment

So here I was, five months in and back to square one: confused, confronting too many options, and feeling overwhelmed and borderline frantic. I flipped through the books on my shelves—The Princeton Review, Gruber, Barron's—figuring I must have learned *something* to help me discern the one true path, and in fact I actually had begun to develop a feel for the test and the best way to go about preparing for it. What I had not developed, though, was confidence in my ability to tell good from bad. The more I studied all the different "tips," the more confused I became.

KAPLAN: Start with C . . . GRUBER: Start with E (ME: *Why?*).

KAPLAN: Move around the section, just pick the *right* answer (ME: *Duh . . .*).

THE PRINCETON REVIEW: Work slowly through the first two-thirds of a section and skip the hard questions at the end if you're below the 700 bar. (ME: *There's no way I'm going into an SAT planning to skip questions.* That was against nature as far as I was concerned, even if it did turn out to be good advice.)

KAPLAN: Questions in the writing section are *not* ordered by level of difficulty (this, I eventually learned, is inaccurate).

THE PRINCETON REVIEW: Writing questions *are* in order of difficulty, with the exception of "Improving the Paragraph" questions (this *is* accurate, but with respect to all these tips, how *does* one know who is right and who is wrong?).

KAPLAN: *Listen* for the errors in the writing section. If you *hear* a mistake, your work is done. (**ME:** Depends on how good your ear is and *what* score you're aiming for.)

THE PRINCETON REVIEW: Do *not* base answers to grammar questions on what *sounds* right. This is the *worst* way to go.

Running the gauntlet of tips (which I don't recommend) will leave you *begging* for standardized advice. Take the issue of guessing. If you don't know the answer, is it better to guess or skip the question? I would never have imagined this to be such a complicated issue, but it can be.

The SAT isn't like school; you don't get partial credit for showing your work. On all but the ten grid-in questions (in math), you gain 1 point for a right answer and lose a quarter point for a wrong answer.

At least with the grid-ins, it would seem that you might as well guess because you've got nothing to lose. Except that's not exactly true. You've got *time* to lose, and time is a precious commodity on the SAT, not to be squandered on questions for which you have no idea of the answer, even in the grid-in section (or so some experts advise). Philip Keller (*The New Math SAT Game Plan*) clarifies the theory: "The SAT is not an all-night casino, where you can keep betting for as long as you can stay awake, hoping to parlay some slight perceived advantage into a big take-home payoff." The reason you don't want to guess on every question is that "getting things wrong is a WASTE OF TIME!" but "If you are working in your Answer Zone and you have already spent time on the question, GO FOR IT!"

The stock advice for guessing is: if you can eliminate one answer, then go for it. But that advice works only if you actually guess *randomly* among the four remaining answers, which you very likely do not. The human brain is not a random number generator, and answer sets always include red herrings that seem right to an awful lot of test takers.

My strategy was to eliminate two wrong answers and then guess. If I couldn't eliminate two answers, I left the question blank.

I tracked all my guesses on practice sections and most of my guesses on test day, and found that I guessed right quite a bit more often than chance. That should have given me an advantage, but I had trouble staying the course. I was an answer switcher, and not just on guesses. Even on questions I had answered confidently, if I had time left at the end of a section to go back and check my work, I would change my answer as often as not. Most of the time (I tracked answer switching, too) I changed from a right answer to a wrong one. My seeming talent for guessing was neutralized by my penchant for second-guessing.

Once I discovered the damage I was doing via answer switching, I established a policy: I could change an answer *only* if I could consciously point to a specific reason for changing.

No switching based on gut feelings.

GUESSING

Unfortunately, when it comes to the issue of guessing, the experts are not much help.

- **THE COLLEGE BOARD:** Try making an educated guess.
- **KAPLAN:** If you can whittle down the choices to two, your chances just increased from 20 percent to 50 percent.
- **THE PRINCETON REVIEW:** If you can eliminate one incorrect choice on the multiple-choice questions, guess.
- **GRUBER:** It's okay to guess . . . it doesn't make a difference.
- **FISKE:** Never leave a question blank.
- *PWN THE SAT MATH GUIDE:* If you have read a question and thought about it for more than five seconds, you should *not* leave it blank.

- **BARRON'S:** It pays to guess.
- **ERICA MELTZER (*THE ULTIMATE GUIDE TO SAT GRAM-MAR*):** Not all guesses are created equal: (1) wild guesses—don't do it; (2) gut-feeling guesses: do it; (3) educated guesses: definitely do it.

Of course, the best strategy is to know the material so well that you minimize guesswork as much as possible.

One thing is certain: no matter what guessing rule you use—or, for that matter, what bubbling or calculator strategies—it's got to be extremely well rehearsed. The helter-skelter approach is a terrible method (speaking from firsthand experience). You need to figure out what works for you, then practice it to the point of automaticity, and stick with the plan.

Since it sometimes felt as if there were as many opinions on these issues as there were alternatives for test prep (many hundreds of thousands), I was dying for someone I could trust to just tell me what to do.

It was *too much*.

As time went on, though, I began to see patterns in the advice, at first subconsciously, but soon the different strands became clear. I began to create a roster in my head of the "SAT Cognoscenti"—experts I thought of as the real deal, whose advice I trusted.

If you're a parent (or a high school junior), not an expert on the SAT, and you didn't take seven SATs in one year, telling the good from the bad is a formidable challenge.

Looking back through the lens of experience, I see that all the big commercial test-prep companies offered some advice that was good, and some that was not.

When it came to strategy, for instance, The Princeton Review's approach was closest to what worked for me, though there were significant yet subtle flaws in the advice:

1. The Princeton Review does not point students back to *official* College Board material. Instead, all Princeton Review materials refer students to other Princeton Review material, which means unofficial practice tests. Those felt off-key to me, and they *were* off-key. Good test prep, in my experience, is *supplementary* to the Blue Book. It consistently leads students back to the mother ship.

2. The Princeton Review does not address the issue of whether a student has the fundamental skills to follow its advice. Test-prep materials take as a given that students can do high school math and comprehend an author's meaning. These assumptions may sound reasonable, but ask a high school student to tell you what the main idea is in a *New York Times* opinion piece and listen to what he or she says. This does bring up a critical issue: should SAT test prep teach foundational skills or test-taking strategy?

The Princeton Review is strategy based, which will get most students (including me) only so far. Students in search of *significant* score gains should nail down content knowledge and skills first. Find your weaknesses, address them, and *build speed*.

GOOD VS. BAD ADVICE: THE TELLTALE SIGNS

Hard test prep does not necessarily mean "good" test prep—but how on earth can the average layperson distinguish?

Signs of Good *Test Prep:*

- Refers back to Blue Book. Helps student interpret the Blue Book.
- Written by an SAT expert. (Don't assume PhD signals "SAT mastery." Maybe, but maybe not.)
- Recommends official material for diagnostic SAT, and full official practice tests as part of test preparation.
- Has a goal-setting strategy: for sections that are in "order of

difficulty," you should strive for mastery of questions inside a goal zone before attempting harder questions. Put simply: you should leave hard questions blank if you haven't mastered the easy ones.

- Addresses issue of fundamental skills *and* test strategy. Exception: test prep aimed solely at high achievers.

Signs of Bad *Test Prep:*

- Mock SAT used for "diagnostic test." Unofficial SATs can be intentionally harder than a real test to inflate score gains. Or mock tests can be unintentionally inaccurate and give faulty readings. There *are* exceptions (though rare). See Chapter 20 for one example.

- Branded advice (e.g., "the Kaplan Method" or "Gruber Critical Thinking Strategy"). From what I could tell, branded advice tended to be "off," or at the very least, suspicious. Upselling (e.g., "More Great Titles from . . .") would fall into the same category (i.e., suspicious).

- Author not an SAT expert. For example, the author bio of one Kaplan SAT book read: "has written over a dozen books, covered a presidential campaign for a national news organization, and edited a magazine." No mention of SAT credentials, and while this author is definitely an accomplished individual, an SAT-specific background is a safer bet.

- Money-back guarantees. They're usually misleading.

The Imitators

Why do mock tests seem so *off*?

Can't the imitators just swap out a few pronoun antecedents and switch some numbers around to create a structural match with the Blue Book tests?

Is it really *that* hard to approximate the SAT?

With three SATs behind me, and apparently no closer to identifying a test-prep method that worked, I began to wonder what it was that made the original-formula SAT questions so "special." What I learned was that each and every official SAT question has passed through a rigorous process, which includes vetting by multiple committees of experienced educators and pretesting in the field via the experimental section. Only items that survive this process make it onto the test. Think: the SAT Olympics.

A College Board booklet called *How the SAT Is Made* explains in minute detail the two-year-long "rigorous and thoroughly researched process" that questions go through to finally make it onto a real SAT. The process involves reviews by *dozens* of consultants, multiple revisions, sensitivity checks, and rounds of statistical analysis. After reading about all the hoops these questions go through, you can see why they're so difficult to imitate.

HOW THE SAT IS MADE

Every SAT question goes through a meticulous two-year process of review that includes statistical analysis, editing, and proofreading for starters. Among the many criteria are:

- **LEVEL OF DIFFICULTY:** Each question appears in an experimental section and is reevaluated afterward. A question is judged easy if 85 percent of students answered it correctly.

- **ETHNIC/RACIAL AND GENDER PERFORMANCE:** Questions are checked to confirm that there is no difference in performance by race or gender when test takers are matched by ability.

- **CONTEXT:** Questions are evaluated on the assembled test to see how they all fit together.

- **ABILITY:** All questions must allow the testers to distinguish between a high and low scorer.

In particular, the College Board goes to great lengths to make sure questions contain no "disconcerting references": no stereotyping, no symbols, phrases, or examples that might potentially offend any group. As *How the SAT Is Made* puts it: "Even the generic 'he' is unacceptable unless used in historical or quoted material."

Questions are also tested in the context of a complete section to see how well they fit within the group of items, then the group as a whole gets tested on a test—*then* the whole test is reviewed by a College Board "policy committee."

After seeing the level of rigor invested in each question, it's clear why the SAT is so difficult to mimic. Each question is a corporate effort; one person can't do it.

Why is it detrimental to prepare for the test using only non–College Board material and practicing on non–College Board tests? Think of it this way: you wouldn't train for a tennis match by practicing on a squash court. Or for a squash match by practicing on a tennis court. You train for a tennis match by playing tennis on a tennis court, and you train for the SAT by taking real SAT tests written by the College Board because only the College Board has the resources to write a real SAT test.

Which is why the best methods of test prep don't replace the Blue Book—and don't *try* to replace the Blue Book. The best test-prep materials are supplemental; they explain and elaborate the sample tests in the Blue Book. Some even include lists of every question in the College Board book organized according to type and solution.

Often, the imitators make the mistake of hiring question writers who fall into one of two categories:

1. Those who know a lot about their subjects but not a lot about the SAT. Frequently, they're specialists with PhDs, which leads to questions that are hard but not well attuned to the way the SAT has changed over the years.
2. Those who know a lot about the SAT but not a lot about their subjects. These individuals don't have the level of technical knowledge to precisely deconstruct the Blue Book questions,

and if you don't know how the questions are constructed you can't reproduce them accurately. Material generated by those writers who are deficient in subject knowledge often comes with advice like "listen for the mistake."

WHAT'S WRONG WITH UNOFFICIAL MATERIAL?

Most commercial test-prep services are unreliable. The industry has essentially no quality control because the only people evaluating its product are short-term customers who lack sufficient familiarity with the test to make discriminating judgments.

Common ways in which unofficial test-prep material can fall short:

- **IT GIVES MISGUIDED ADVICE ABOUT THE CONCEPTS THAT ARE TESTED.** Some test-prep materials omit concepts that are tested *all the time*, while others cover topics that are never tested on the SAT at all (e.g., "who versus whom" is not tested on the SAT, though "who" and "whom" are sometimes underlined in questions).
- **IT GETS THE LEVEL OF DIFFICULTY WRONG.** Some non–College Board materials are too hard, some are too easy, and some miss the mark altogether in the language they use (the words are either out-of-date or too figurative).
- **IT'S ARBITRARILY TRICKY.** The SAT is tricky, but it is never arbitrary.

The SAT is a *reasoning* test; the questions possess a degree of subtlety that forces students to use logic and contextual clues to arrive at an answer. Imitators often miss that point, conveying the sense that finding the right answer is simply a matter of figuring out which answers to eliminate. Another area where the imitators fall short is in the creation of critical reading passages. Because many potential passages are under copyright, a test-prep company must decide whether to spend money purchasing rights to passages or use material that has passed out of copyright—which means using material substantially older, on average, than the passages on the test. Copyright protection lasts for the life of the author plus seventy years for works published since 1978. Because writers used more complicated sentence structures in the nineteenth and early part of the twentieth centuries, reading passages in big-box materials (Barron's, The Princeton Review, etc.) can be well above the level of the most difficult material appearing on a real SAT.

An even worse sin on the imitators' part may be writing the passages themselves. If the passages are too straightforward, they can give the student a false sense of mastery. Finding out your test-prep materials were too easy is not a welcome discovery on test day.

A Fork in the Road

The more I explored the commercial test-prep options, the more discouraged I became—discouraged because neither my reading nor my math score had budged in five months of intensive prep, and the 100-point jump in my writing score could have come (and I'm sure did come) from any of the options I tried. I was proficient in prose grammar going in, and picking up the grammar used in more academic writing (which is what is tested in the writing section) had been easy.

So, almost halfway into the year, I found myself at a crossroads. Did I want to continue vetting commercial test-prep methods, or did I want to go for a perfect SAT score?

Well, that was a no-brainer—I wanted the perfect score. That being the case, one thing was very clear: I was way behind the eight ball.

So now what?

I called Catherine in a panic, because she always knows what to do.

"My plan is a bust," I said. "*What do I do?*"

"Well," she said, "let me think about this."

Pause . . .

"*I* know," she said. "Call that mom who left the comment on your blog."

The mom to whom Catherine was referring was a tutor named Stacey Howe-Lott, from Seattle. I'd been asking everyone I knew to put me in touch with people who had *dramatically* improved their SAT scores. I'd even written a blog post asking the world. Stacey had left a comment to say that she'd boosted her own math score from the 45th percentile to the 93rd.

That's it, I thought—*the perfect plan. I'll get in touch with Stacey, the high-scoring mom, and ask her what to do.*

13

TO TUTOR OR
NOT TO TUTOR

And the Winner Is . . . Another Mom

S tacey Howe-Lott was the biggest score raiser I was able to locate. I
found her while hunting down score raisers after a close call with
despair, contemplating the possibility that I might spend a year
prepping for the SAT and end up with the 10-to-20-point gain in math
and the 5-to-10-point gain in critical reading that the College Board
said I could expect.

Certain that an entire test-prep industry could not be founded on
such slim gains, I sent a query to the world via my blog, asking for stories
of big score improvements. Ethan had started receiving test-prep flyers in
the mail that were making big promises:

> *Dear Ethan,*
>
> *Did you know that the SAT is the single largest factor in your
> college admissions decision that you can still control? Many Revo-
> lution students have increased their scores by 200, 300 and even
> 500 points! . . . We're so confident . . . that we offer a Money
> Back Guarantee.*

Was there any truth to a pitch like that? I wanted to talk to the big gainers, so I wrote a blog post and asked the world to please send them my way. And *voilà*—Stacey Howe-Lott appeared in a comment on my blog.

"I raised my math score by 220 points," she wrote.

She'd proven the tiny-score predictions wrong by a factor of 10.

Needless to say, I wanted what *she* had, so I e-mailed to ask if we could talk. When we connected I had so many questions: How'd you do it? When'd you start? How long did it take? What *exactly* did you do? I picked her brain for hours. She was so generous, patient, and nurturing, sharing every detail without any hesitation. "Start from the beginning," I said, "and tell me the whole story."

Stacey's a mom (like me), and she loves charts and graphs (*just* like me), and she had discovered the joy of the SAT long after high school (definitely like me). How many other moms in their forties have discovered they love the SAT? I believe Stacey and I belong to a very small group—a micro-niche, if you don't mind the marketing terminology. The kicker was discovering we both loved the exact same SAT books (and that our favorites weren't the big boys everyone thinks of).

Stacey had begun her journey after the birth of her daughter a few years before. She'd earned a degree in English and a master's degree in education, and she loves to teach. She was afraid her brain was shrinking from all that laundry and cooing, so she went to the bookstore in search of mental stimulation and brought home a Kaplan SAT book to study during nap time. She liked it. She thought the problems were fun, like logic puzzles.

She moved from Kaplan to the Blue Book and then through stacks of guides before deciding on her favorites: *The New Math SAT Game Plan* by Philip Keller, *Outsmarting the SAT* by Elizabeth King, and *The Ultimate Guide to SAT Grammar* by Erica Meltzer. We were peas in a pod—those were *my* favorites too.

Stacey sang math lullabies while rocking the baby to sleep and relentlessly tracked down the explanations to every problem she didn't understand, and began taking an *official* SAT once a year to keep her proficiency evergreen. Over time she defied the odds and raised her math score by *a few hundred points*. (I love saying that.) Her most recent scores were:

> Writing: 750 (98th percentile)
> Critical Reading: 800 (99th percentile)[*]
> Math: 670 (89th percentile)

IF SHE COULD DO IT ALL OVER AGAIN

Stacey spent three and a half years' worth of nap times raising her scores by a few hundred points, but if she were to do it all over again knowing what she knows now, here's what she'd do differently:

- Hire a tutor for a few hours to put her on the right track. She wasted a lot of time and money on bad materials, bad strategy, and bad advice. A trusted guide would have saved her time, energy, and frustration.
- Keep obsessive records to track what she learned and what she still needed to learn.
- Target *precisely* the right amount of material she needed to know for the test, rather than casting her net as wide as she did when she began.

Eventually Stacey began to tutor for a few of the national test-prep chains, but she was disenchanted with their approach. They taught every student the same way at the same pace, which wasn't Stacey's experience of how people learn, nor was it a good use of time. She was sure there must be a better way, so she created one.

Interestingly—given the failure of my first two online test-prep experiences—she had developed an *online learning experience*. But

---

[*] There is no "100th percentile," according to the College Board's definition of percentiles.

Stacey's online tutoring was nothing like the ones I'd tried. Stacey teaches her students from home using Skype and an online whiteboard. She also uses Google apps to create detailed reports that target *very precisely* each student's particular learning gaps.

In theory, the College Board and the test-prep chains provide individual reports, but the reports are so broad they're not much use in planning further study. The College Board might identify a need for further work in geometry, or report that you "answered 60 percent of the exponent questions correctly," but that's about it. No further detail.

As for the test-prep chains, they break down the material into subcategories but don't give feedback in terms of question difficulty level, nor do they take your target score into account.

Stacey's reports dig *way* deeper.

She has categorized all 1,700 Blue Book problems, so she can pinpoint a student's weaknesses and have him or her work on skills as specific as, say, *medium-difficulty problems finding the slope of a perpendicular line*. Being able to pinpoint each student's practice needs so precisely allows her to be more efficient and effective.

She has also identified which topics are common on the test and which are less so, which allows her to start her students working on the problems they absolutely *must* master before moving on to questions they are much less likely to encounter on test day.

This is the kind of fine-grained effort and analysis that goes into the making of a great tutor. That's not to say that all superior tutors make use of deep-dive charts and graphs the way Stacey does, but they do all have a few traits in common.

QUALITIES OF A GREAT TUTOR

- A *great* tutor *loves* to teach.
- A *great* tutor knows the SAT like the back of his or her hand—and the subject matter inside out too.

- A *great* tutor understands that quality is more important than quantity. He or she knows, for example, that it's useless to take full practice tests over and over if core concepts haven't been mastered.
- A *great* tutor customizes his or her approach and strategy. Every student has different background knowledge, talents, interests, anxiety levels, and so on.
- A *great* tutor offers instruction that is both content *and* strategy based. Tips and tricks alone will only get you so far.
- A *great* tutor is adept at assessing a student's skill level, motivation, and goals.
- A *great* tutor works primarily with College Board materials.
- A *great* tutor recognizes the signs of test anxiety, which aren't always obvious.
- A *great* tutor can, upon request, supply plenty of references attesting to the quality of his or her work.

The Cost of Hope

Some students need the focus and attention a tutor provides, while really bright, self-motivated students with solid fundamental skills can do great studying on their own. If your child is one of the former, a great tutor does not have to be prohibitively expensive. Many excellent tutors have sliding scales and are willing to be flexible if a student is enthusiastic and in need of financial aid.

Bottom line: you never know about a price accommodation unless you ask (but don't ask for a discount unless you really need it and are willing to put in the effort and do your part too).

The College Board study finding minimal score gains from test prep did distinguish between types of test preparation, pointing out that students who'd had "coaching" showed the largest gains. The authors made the point, though, that not all coaching is created equal: quality makes a difference.

So how much will a good SAT coach cost you?

I've seen prices vary from $15 to well over $900 (yes, that's *per hour*). So don't assume that finding a great tutor is insurmountable or exorbitant. Often, what is required is simply adding a little elbow grease to the hunt and the willingness to ask.

Honoring the Great Mother

Halfway into my conversation with Stacey Howe-Lott I was ready to get started. She had what I wanted: a huge score gain that beat the odds.

"When can we start?" I asked.

The very next day Stacey and I began working together—the most enjoyable four weeks I'd spent in quite some time. She focused me—and boy, did I need *focus*—and she honed right in on my problem areas and gave me assignments that she returned with beautiful charts coded in ski-slope symbols that showed my progress. Charts that show progress are highly motivating, and I *loved* receiving guidance from a kind and warm mother who knew what she was talking about.

FIVE GREAT TIPS FROM STACEY HOWE-LOTT

1. In the sentence completion section, write your own answers in the blanks before looking at the multiple-choice options. Then see if one of the answer choices matches your word (or words). You'll usually see a synonym, and that is the answer.

2. Cross out wrong answers. Put a line through them to get them out of your line of vision.

3. Circle words signaling contradiction ("not," "although," "to the contrary," "nevertheless," etc.) to help you remember to look for the *opposite* of the idea being conveyed (e.g., "While early experiences are not solely responsible for _____ an individual's personality, they do set pathways that can either be changed or _____ by later experiences").

> 4. Draw pictures to help yourself see the answers to the math problems.
>
> 5. Medium questions have medium answers. *Easy answers to hard questions are wrong.*

Stacey and I met twice a week on Skype, and she taught me math in all sorts of non-mathy ways (which I very much appreciated). She had all kinds of different teaching techniques, so if one didn't stick she'd break out another—mnemonics, cute little drawings of flowers with square roots on their bottoms, that sort of thing.

By the end of our month, I was so sad to say good-bye. She'd set the bar high and I was counting my blessings. I knew how lucky I'd been to find her. Not everyone lands Dumbledore on the first try.

How can you be as lucky in finding a great tutor? Do a lot of searching, using everything from school recommendations to suggestions from friends to online sources—and once you find a candidate remember to (1) ask the hard questions, (2) check *all* the references, (3) factor in the baseline and goals of the referrer versus your own starting point and target, and (4) be wary of inflated score claims. Boasts such as "600 points in five weeks" should be a red flag.

FIVE ESSENTIAL QUESTIONS TO ASK
A POTENTIAL TUTOR

1. Do you customize your approach and, if so, how?

2. What's your average score gain per student? Many tutors won't answer this question because there are so many variables that it's almost not fair to ask. That said, an excessive "*average* score gain" (e.g., 200 points in a month) should be a red flag.

3. How long do you advise students to prepare for the SAT and how much will it cost? The right answer will be individual and will depend on where the student begins and what the goal is.

4. What test-prep materials do you use? (If it's not official College Board material, be wary.)

5. How much homework will there be between sessions? (A great tutor will have students do as much work as possible off the clock.)

Joy to the World

I finished working with Stacey at the beginning of June, a few days before my fourth SAT, which I took at the public high school in Ossining, New York. I was sure I had made progress.

Thankfully, the test agreed with me.

	JUNE SCORES			
	Jan. 22	Mar. 12	May 7	June 4
CRITICAL READING	**680**	**690**	**690**	**720**
MATH	**510**	**530**	**530**	**570**
WRITING	**610**	**690**	**700**	**610**
ESSAY	**9**	**9**	**10**	**9**

I had jumped to a 720 in critical reading, which put me in the 97th percentile. Ooooh-weee—did that feel good! I liked being on the other side of the 700 mountain. I felt as though I was with my people now—the really good readers.

I dipped back into the 600s on the writing section, scoring a 9 on my essay (again). I hadn't practiced between the May and June SATs, which was a mistake. Stacey and I covered a lot of territory, but we never got to the essay.

The prompt that day: Does every achievement bring with it new challenges? Let's just say nothing came to mind and leave it at that—my effort that morning really is that embarrassing.

I'd prefer to discuss the math.

Hallefrickinlujah!

Finally, a little action. Those 40 extra points were like motivational rocket fuel—570 put me in the 66th percentile and felt so close to a 600 it seemed I could almost reach out and grab it.

My June scores always make me think of something my daughter, Daisy, says. She's a worker like her mama, and she always tells me, "Mom, it's really hard to do well in *every* subject at the same time."

She's right.

14

KUMON: GET 'EM WHILE THEY'RE MUNCHKINS

You may give them your love, but not your thoughts.
For they have their own thoughts.

—*KAHLIL GIBRAN*

Blind Spots

On the way to my grandmother's funeral I made a wrong turn. It was late morning in the foothills of Arizona and the roads were wide and empty. Ethan sat in the front seat and Daisy in back, and the car was quiet—no music or fighting. I pulled over to turn the car around.

This was not a complicated maneuver.

I remember every detail in slow motion. I placed my arm on the passenger seat and turned to look through the rear window, then I backed up the car. That step completed, I looked forward, shifted into "drive," and pushed the gas pedal just a little—very *slowly*. And then . . .

BOOM! Just like that, I drove right into a stop sign.

It appeared out of thin air and I knocked it down, flat on its back. I was shaken. This made *no* sense. I was driving slowly and paying close attention. I am *positive* that stop sign wasn't there the second before I hit it. Even now, my memory sets off phantom "metal crunching" sensations. It was jarring—discordant.

There was a moment of silence—a stunned noiselessness—and then both kids started jabbering in unison: *"Mom . . . why did you do that?"* As though I'd driven the car into a stop sign on purpose.

"Because I didn't see it!" I said. "That's why."

I was trying to make sense of it myself. How could I have missed that sign? It was directly in front of me.

I got out of the car to assess the damage. Thankfully, there was none. The kids and I tried to lift the sign back up, but it was too heavy even for the three of us, which surprised me. Who knew stop signs were so heavy? So we got back in the car and drove on into the desert to my grandma's funeral, *almost* as if nothing had happened, except that the kids pecked at me for days: "How could you *not* see that stop sign?"

I don't know.

I have seen this sort of thing before, though, in friends as well as in myself: big blind spots, literal or metaphorical, like felt patches that block the light and make otherwise competent people miss the neon signs directly in front of them. They're concentrating—but they're looking in the wrong direction. One dad I know devoted entire years' worth of springs and summers to coaching his son into an all-star pitcher. When the son got to high school, he quit the team out of the clear blue sky and joined a band, leaving his bewildered father to wonder how he could have missed all the signs.

The Gaps

School was out for the summer and the SAT was on hiatus till fall. The four months until my next SAT in October felt like forever, and it seemed as good a time as any to work on my math fundamentals. I was a little rusty. *More* than rusty. In the math section, the devil is in the details, and the details were killing me.

> *Factors, multiples, divisors? (I remembered the words but not what they stood for—what were they again?)*

Are whole numbers the same thing as digits?

Is 0 a digit?

Are integers the same thing as digits and whole numbers?

Can they be negative?

Can negative digits be prime whole numbers?

And when, exactly, do you use reciprocals? (I could never remember.)

How do you find the greatest common factor and is that the same thing as the greatest common multiple? (I couldn't remember that, either.)

Last but not least, when did they invent prime factorization?

I had no memory at all of prime factorization, not even a fuzzy one, which tells you everything you need to know about the effectiveness of my math education as a child.

Learning was the easy part . . . it was *remembering* that was hard. I *loved* the math section; it was my favorite by far of the three. But the intricacies of grade-school arithmetic were going to be the death of me.

Take, for example:

What is the sum of four times the largest negative integer
and the smallest positive integer?

In one simple problem, you have to instantly remember the negative integers, the positive integers, and—for me at least—which direction on the number line makes a negative integer larger and a positive integer smaller; then you have to perform addition and multiplication of nega-tive and positive integers (that part I could do).

You *can* work SAT problems by pausing to remember what the terms mean, or what steps a procedure entails, but you're not going to hit 800 relying on conscious memory. I doubt you can even break 600 relying on conscious memory, in fact. SAT math is a test of speed as much as reasoning, and there is no time to stop and run a memory search. You have to know what the words mean the moment you read them, and you have to know how to do the procedures the moment you decide which ones to use. Your math knowledge has to be *ingrained*.

If your math knowledge is not ingrained, getting to automaticity may take more work than you imagine. I was always surprised by how much more practice it took to make things stick than I thought it would.

UNDERSTANDING IS REMEMBERING IN DISGUISE

Cognitive scientist Daniel Willingham, author of *Why Don't Students Like School?*, researches learning, memory, and K–12 education. Willingham explains that studying hard does not protect against forgetting, but *continued practice* does.

The virtues of drilling, according to Willingham:

- Extended practice is essential for proficiency at a mental task.
- Continued practice beyond mastery enables more advanced learning.
- Basic skills practice should continue in the context of more advanced skills.
- Mental processes can become automatized only through repeated practice.
- Automaticity takes *lots of practice*.
- Practice makes memory long-lasting and protects against forgetting.

I was having such a hard time getting the math to stick that I started to think maybe I had dyscalculia, a math disability that sounded like dyslexia for math. It was distressing (not to mention frustrating) to understand a concept perfectly well and then not remember it on a timed test—or maybe it's more accurate to say not remember it *fast enough*, with the clock ticking, because I scored much better on the untimed tests I took at home. In fact, under time-and-a-half conditions, I scored significantly higher.

I called Catherine to see what she thought. "I think I have a math disability," I said. As I uttered those words, the answer dawned on me: it *had* to be the bug spray.

Every fall I saturate my house with insecticide from top to bottom when the stinkbugs arrive, like clockwork, on September 27. For a few days, the bugs take over my house. They fly around and terrorize me—I am deathly afraid of them for some reason—and so I go to war with cans of poison because there is absolutely no other way to get rid of them. Then I spend the rest of the year worrying I've given myself early Alzheimer's or cancer from all the noxious toxins I'd doused my house in over the course of those few days.

"*No*," Catherine said. "It's not you. You're having the '*All math looks alike*' problem. Have you read Wickelgren?"

Um, no.

She forwarded me a blog post she'd written summarizing Wickelgren's explanation of "associative interference," which explained why remembering what you've learned in math is so hard. "It's the similarity between the facts," she wrote. "That is, the fact that 3 + 5 = 8 is not so different from 3 + 5 = 9; they both contain pluses and they both contain single-digit numbers. The facts overlap in the brain, creating a blur that makes it easy to confuse them. In cognitive psychology, this 'blur' is called associative interference. It's like static on the radio."

"So what's the cure?" I asked.

"Kumon," she said. She and her son Chris had done Kumon together a few years back.

What Exactly Is *Kumon?* (And Why Isn't That Little Guy Smiling *on Their Logo?*)

Kumon is the world's largest after-school math and reading "enrichment" program. It emphasizes old-fashioned, nuts-and-bolts worksheets that you do at home, moving through them at your own pace. The Kumon worksheets are the meat-and-potatoes practice they used to do in school before the 1960s, when worksheets and speed drills went out of fashion. Today timed practice is condemned as "Drill and Kill."

I think of the worksheets as caulking. They seal up the cracks in knowledge that open up over your years in math class. Maybe one year it was a bad math teacher, so you didn't learn everything covered in class; the next year there was a case of mono; then a sports concussion here or there—and, years later, you arrive at the SAT not even realizing you're shaky on polynomials. You've taken all the classes, but you haven't learned all the content.

Almost everyone has math gaps, except the kids who do Kumon. Kumon kids are solid gold because they do twenty minutes a day of math worksheets, regardless of what's going on in school. That's all it is—twenty minutes a day—but you have to stick with it through the more difficult levels, which can be harder than it sounds.

Kumon has its own sequential program. You work your way up by mastering each level. No judging. No grades. Students complete all the worksheets in a level, a few pages a day, and graduate to the next level by passing a timed test with no more than a few answers wrong.

If a student does not pass the timed test, he or she continues working in that level. Speed—not just accuracy—is a fundamental Kumon criterion for mastery.

It's not "test prep," it's *sealant.*

The more I learned about Kumon the more perfect it sounded: Twenty minutes a day? Unshakable mastery? What could be better?

I'll *tell* you what could be better: my children doing the program along with me. They had gaps just like me, and I had tender visions of the three of us correcting each other's Kumon worksheets with red pens over cornflakes and muffins every morning.

The Halcyon Days of Summer

On my first visit to Kumon, I flung myself headlong into a wide and gaping blind spot, trailing my children along behind me.

I missed all the warning signals. And because the ensuing collision was psychic, not physical, the after-effects cut much deeper than the fender bender in the desert. My children and I did not move on quickly or easily.

I still find it hard to talk about. For months afterward, an innocuous "how are you?" from a person I passed on the street could open the faucets and I'd start to cry, and then we'd have an awkward moment where the person wouldn't know what to say because "how are you?" is a rhetorical question. Everyone knows that.

I started to think I should call ahead on my cell phone if I saw someone I knew walking toward me and warn them. *"Don't ask 'how are you?'—okay?"* I went through the classic stages of grief: denial, anger, bargaining, depression . . .

My little chickadees had grown into surly teenagers while I wasn't looking, and I missed their sweet selves. I had been too busy keeping all the balls in the air to notice that they were no longer the bottomless pits of love and devotion they had been when they were little. Their teenage feelings for me seemed altogether different, less like love and more like entitlement, and secrecy. Both of my children seemed driven by an urgent need to dismantle my authority while at the same time both still clearly needed—and expected—my care. There were days when I felt they hated me.

I was caught completely off guard, without a road map to show the way back. I had no framework, no intuition, to help me deal with my newly disrespectful children, or to understand what had happened.

In fact, I had lost my children to their friends, who had replaced me as the indispensable source of attention, love, and authority in their lives—my children answered to other children, not to me. But I didn't understand this at the time, nor did I know that it was critical for their well-being for me to reclaim my place as their respected mother. I would not have known how to do so even if I'd had the insight.

Our little family broke that day at Kumon, and it was excruciating.

The Kumon center by my house is teensy-weensy, not nearly big enough to accommodate the intensity of emotion radiating from the three of us when we walked in that day. It had been a frustrating morning: failed attempts to complete essential errands and chores, and too much time spent in the car on a summer day. But looking back, I can see that my biggest mistake was thinking my children would cheerfully cooperate with my plan for the three of us to do math together over the summer. I had failed to understand that I was no longer their north star.

Maybe I should have just required compliance, if a Kumon summer for my kids was that important to me—but it wasn't. I had brought my children to Kumon for the bonding experience; the worksheets were mostly for me.

Jennifer, the store owner, greeted us when we arrived. You've never met a sweeter, more evenhanded woman. She's always got swarms of cute little munchkins tugging and poking at her with questions about their worksheets, and she is unflappable.

I was grateful to see a friendly adult, but my timing walking through that door was dreadful. The tension in the car had grown more palpable with each thankless errand we tried to check off our list, and my kids were smoking mad. Now they were supposed to do math.

Jennifer gave each of us a placement test to determine our Kumon levels. Ethan, who has always been good at math, puffed up like a peacock and overestimated his abilities—to prove he didn't need any *caulking* over the summer—which, of course, made him even angrier when he couldn't do the problems. Daisy and I chose the same level, which started out easy but got hard fast. Soon, Daisy was fuming. By that point both kids were being openly disrespectful to me and borderline rude to Jennifer, which was very out of character. Ethan and Daisy had always had nice manners around adults.

I should have stopped before that diagnostic test and said, "You know what, guys? You're right! This is a terrible idea. Let's get out of here."

But that's not what I did. Instead, I made a rookie teenage parenting blunder. I asked Jennifer to please excuse us, then took my kids outside and *offered to pay them each $100 to do Kumon with me.*

I'm embarrassed to admit that today.

Their answer was no. Not for love or money would my children do math with me that summer.

The fight that ensued was wounding and harsh. I was furious at the way they had treated me, and they were furious that I hadn't noticed (or cared) that this wasn't their idea of fun on a summer day.

By the end of the day both children had left my house and moved in with their father, who was generally of the opinion that I pushed too hard and expected too much. When we spoke, he said he was giving the kids a "respite."

I did push, and I did expect a lot, but I didn't know how else to move my children forward. They were both bright and capable, but they had little interest in anything academic and I had no savings for college, which was looming. *Somebody had to push.*

So I pushed. I didn't know any other way.

That day, when Ethan and Daisy moved out, I felt that I'd lost my children, and my children had lost their futures.

The Idiot Box

I hadn't lost my children, and my children hadn't lost their futures, but without that summer's rupture in our relationship and the events that followed, I don't know that I would have found my way.

The kids returned home after a few days, but the standoff lasted half the summer. Everyone dug in their heels. I wanted appreciative children—or at least children who could be reasonably polite while doing something they didn't want to do—not bratty adolescents. They made it clear that they wanted a different mother.

Ironically, it was now time for Ethan to begin studying for the SAT in earnest, and we were barely speaking. I was sorely tempted to scrap the whole project and say, "Fine, do it yourself. I don't care." I felt such heartache.

I called Catherine and sobbed. "What should I do?"

"Do something fun," Catherine said. "Watch a funny TV show together."

"I don't have a TV," I sobbed.

Silence.

"You don't have a TV?"

"No."

I'd donated our TV to charity a few months before, on a whim. It hadn't crossed my mind that my kids would care because I didn't recall ever seeing them watch TV. Truth be told, I didn't really know people still watched TV shows on TV sets. I thought everyone watched movies on laptops in their bedrooms.

Catherine had grown up on a farm in Illinois, where her family had one TV set that got four stations. Every Saturday and Sunday night, she said, the whole family watched their favorite shows together. Then once or twice during the week, when the kids were home watching reruns after school, Catherine's mother would march into the living room looking put out, deliver her stock line about how she would *never understand* people sitting around *staring* at the *idiot box*, and snap off the set. Catherine said that was fun, too.

"That's what families *do*," Catherine said. "They watch stupid TV shows together and they laugh, then the parents tell the kids they're watching too much TV, so go play outside or read a book."

I had no idea television was an essential ingredient of happy families! I made an immediate purchase of a big-screen television and stuck it in the middle of the living room, where you'd have to trip over it not to notice.

When Daisy saw the television her eyes lit up.

"Want to watch *Gilmore Girls*?" I asked.

Later I heard her whispering to her friends on the phone. "She bought a TV," I heard my daughter say. Apparently I'd developed something of a reputation. "I know," she continued after a pause. "I can't believe it, either."

And with that, our lives began to change.

Catherine was right. TV shows *are* a great way to stay connected with teenagers who are trying to push you away, a shared experience and a gift that keeps on giving. After the show you get to keep laughing and making references to this or that scene or character.

Our favorite TV shows always have a character who reminds us of my own mother.

Rising to the Occasion

A few weeks later I mustered the nerve to go back to Kumon—*alone*. The learning center was teeming with adorable children who all looked so cheerful about the prospect of improving their academic skills over the summer. Jennifer greeted me with her signature smile and we shared a slightly awkward moment about "the incident."

"I think it's the logo," I said. "Why isn't that little guy smiling?"

"It's a thinking man's face," she explained.

I've never quite seen the little Kumon guy that way, but it worked as an icebreaker and allowed us to move on. "I'm going to do it alone," I said to Jennifer. *Yolo*, as Daisy would say that summer.

I'd tested into third-grade math, which was just fine because naturally I assumed I'd blow right through that and get to the "SAT math" before long. I even asked for a double dose of worksheets, which she gave me, though with an air of hesitation that should have given me pause. I walked out of the store that day with my worksheets in hand, passing the parents who were waiting for their nice, *compliant* children who still lived in their house and hadn't rejected them to go live with the parent they liked better. I smiled and pretended I was there to pick up supplies for *my* nice, compliant children, whom I'd left at home for some reason.

The Kumon worksheets were harder than they looked, especially Level D, long division. Level D is where kids fall off the Kumon cliff, and I can see why. It actually hurt my brain. You have to divide big numbers, like 53,493 divided by 541, super fast with no mistakes.

Seriously, Level D hurts.

At the time, I was running on fumes thanks to lack of sleep, and it was nothing short of a miracle that I could think straight at all. Jennifer said to do the worksheets "first thing in the morning," which sounded manageable until I'd get so jammed up I'd skip a few days. Then I'd lie awake at night feeling anxious about the stacked-up worksheets until I couldn't bear the guilt anymore and would finally get out of bed at one or two in the morning to catch up on a few days' worth . . . which only made things worse *because it was one or two in the morning.*

As it turned out, I had to repeat Level D. "Too many mistakes," I was told.

"How long till the polynomials?" I'd always ask Jennifer when I'd swing by to pick up more sheets. "Not for a *long* time," Jennifer would say, unwaveringly cheerful.

A Little Kumon History

"The Kumon Method" was conceived in 1954 by a high school math teacher named Toru Kumon, who founded the company in Osaka, Japan.

He came home from work one day to find his wife upset because she'd discovered a crumpled math test in their second-grade son Takeshi's backpack. Mrs. Kumon told her husband he needed to help their son with math, so Mr. Kumon wrote homemade worksheets for him, and Takeshi improved. Word spread about the worksheets and neighbors started asking if *their* kids could have some, too.

Cut to 2012. *Entrepreneur* magazine ranked Kumon the number one education franchise for the eleventh consecutive year. The same company that ignited a rebellion in my own children had *exceeded* industry expectations, growing by 13 percent in that year alone. Takeshi's worksheets are the basis of a worldwide operation now, with nearly 25,000 Kumon Centers instructing 4.3 million students.

Kumon is not a quick fix, but it is the real deal. I wish I'd known about it the first time I found a crumpled math test in Ethan's backpack. (Catherine told me the crumpled math test in the backpack was a turning point in her family's life.) Who knew the crumpled math test is a universal experience, transcending generations and continents?

A Whole New Day

Over the next year Ethan . . . matured. His grades went up, and though he was loyal to his old friends, he began to make new friends, too. He was becoming friendly with the academic kids.

I always chalk the change up to the college tour we took that February, but I was changing, too.

After Ethan was home again, we watched a TV show together every night before bed. We'd pick a series and watch it straight through, one episode each night. *30 Rock*, *Parks and Recreation*, *Arrested Development*, *Portlandia*.

We've just started *South Park*, which is hilarious.

The following summer Ethan asked, unprompted, to sign up for Kumon because he wanted to "brush up" for calculus in the fall. So I got to see what it felt like to hang out in the waiting room with the parents of the compliant children who were serious about their studies. One day I overheard Ethan asking Jennifer, "Are you *sure* I'll be ready for my math class?" Now *he* was the one worried about gaps.

"Yes," she said in her trademark tone, soothing, confident, and unruffled.

It was a whole new day.

15

IQ AND THE SAT

How Long Till the Polynomials?

I wound up repeating Level D twice. It was a bitter pill. I consoled myself with stories of triumph over obstacles, and I tried to see failure as an essential step in the process.

As to failure being part of the process, I found research to back me up. "If you want to increase your intelligence, you have to challenge yourself," I read in Daniel Willingham's book. "That means taking on tasks that are a bit beyond your reach, and that means you may very well fail, at least the first time around."

This was my third time around, but who was counting.

I wanted the fraction worksheets, the ones I saw the munchkins doing. Enough with long division. The three-digit divisors and the five-digit dividends were killing me. Pages and pages of 78,721 and 59,016 divided by 813 and 536—*nooooo*. I forged ahead, but I seemed to be developing neither speed nor accuracy.

"What's the trick?" I asked as I handed Jennifer my worksheets, speckled with red error marks.

"Practice," she said.

"Nothing's wrong with your brain," she added. "Just practice."

Starting Level D for the third time, I found this inconceivable. *I must have a math disability*, I thought, though the more I looked into dyscalculia the less sure I was because I didn't seem to fit the profile.

Proficiency was another story. I wasn't fast, and I wasn't accurate. Or, rather, I wasn't both at the same time. You need both to be proficient.

Speed and accuracy take sustained practice (like Jennifer said), even when a skill seems to come naturally. Some of us have to practice more than others, but there's no getting around it for anyone. And while it is certainly *possible* to be bad at math, without sustained practice there's no way to know whether you could be good at math if you tried. For most people, "I'm not good at math" means "I haven't practiced."

But that's not the way Americans tend to think. We see talent as inborn—God-given—and if we've just flunked Level D for the second time, our go-to explanation is "I'm bad at math."

In Asian countries they see things differently. Asians believe intelligence is malleable: if you work hard, your intelligence increases. (Hence Kumon.) That puts the responsibility for success in math back in the hands of the student, which can be empowering or exhausting depending on how you look at it.

THE EFFECTS OF GENDER AND CULTURE

The overall SAT score average has dipped 20 points over the last six years, though Asian scores (which include those achieved by Asians, Asian Americans, and Pacific Islanders) have risen 41 points during that same time frame. Sian Beilock discusses the role of gender and culture on test performance in her book *Choke*:

- Female SAT math scores were on average 33 points lower than male scores in 2012.
- SAT math scores underpredict female grades in university-level math classes compared to those of their male counterparts.

- White men do worse on SAT math when reminded before they take the test that Asians are good at math.
- Boys are more likely than girls to use shortcuts on SAT math problems.

Jennifer was right. I needed more practice. I also needed to make some headway on the SAT, and most of the math you use on the SAT happens in levels E through K, so I *really* needed to get to E. But Levels E, F, G, H, I, J, and K all depend on Levels A, B, C, and D, so the only way around D was through it.

"Hit me again," I said. "I'm in."

Kumon is not test prep, but if you do Kumon you'll most likely raise your score. On the other hand, while Kumon worksheets teach all the skills tested on the SAT, they don't teach the Blue Book per se, and I would not advise relying on Kumon alone.

It's never too late to start a Kumon program, and it can only help, especially if a student has a nice long runway and is willing to put in an extra twenty to thirty minutes a day. The assignments are timed so that students are accustomed to managing time constraints (i.e., testing conditions) and the worksheets reinforce skills through daily repetition, locking in knowledge that may have been covered in school but is shallow rather than deep.

Kumon offers both math and reading instruction, though it's known for the math.

Mind-set

One day after yoga, a man in the class told me he'd read my blog and thought what I was doing was interesting. We chatted for a while and I learned that his name was Dr. Adam Stein. He was a psychologist in town.

"I might be able to help you," he said.

A more logical person might have asked, "*How* might you be able to help me, and with *what*, exactly?" But I love the free-fall sensation of saying yes to something that sounds interesting without knowing what I'm agreeing to. It's an adventure. I never know where fate will take me.

"Great! When?" I said. I couldn't wait to find out what his specialty was. I had visions of finally crushing those Level D worksheets.

He mentioned a computer-based working memory training program he used with some of his patients to improve attention. At the mention of the word "computer," I balked. "Uh, that doesn't work for me," I said. "I can't focus on a computer—I've tried."

He wasn't trying to sell me, though. He said studies showed that memory training can work on children, but research hadn't verified whether adults could benefit, too. He also said he himself was doing memory training and thought he'd seen positive effects. He even rattled off a sequence of thirteen numbers backward. I was impressed.

A few days later, he showed me the office where he kept his memory-training computer and suggested I give it a try. He shut the door and I was alone in the room—no windows or anything on the walls, just a desk with a computer. I felt hermetically sealed *and I loved it*. I'd never felt so focused in all my life. Who knew how comforting a distraction-free zone could be? I didn't, though now that I did, I wanted one.

"I want the room," I said as I walked out.

Picking My Brain

I met with Dr. Stein once a week for a good part of the summer. After the first visit, he suggested we do neuropsych testing to see what was going on up there.

"Can you cure me?" I asked.

"That's such a Western view," he said. "This is about understanding yourself better."

Hmmm . . . not according to Jennifer. Jennifer says it's about "practice."

The testing was much more extensive than I'd ever imagined. There were IQ and achievement tests, and attention and memory screenings. I took Wechslers and Woodcock-Johnsons and everything in between. I was tested like I'd never been tested before, and I thought it was a blast. Some days Dr. Stein tested me for an hour or two, and other days we had sessions that lasted three to four hours, which was mentally fatiguing but still fun. And yes, I do realize it's odd to love testing as much as I do.

But maybe not so strange. Imagine working on, in succession, a Rubik's Cube, a crossword puzzle, one of those *Highlights* "What's Wrong with This Picture?" exercises, and sudoku—it was like that. What is not to love? The doctor read stories to me that I had to repeat back at certain time intervals, and gave me math tests that were sort of like Kumon. There were word associations and color tests, and tests that involved repeating this and that, backward. It was mental gymnastics.

When all was said and done, I learned a lot about myself.

For one thing, I take directions much more to heart than most people do. During one test, Dr. Stein would show me an image, then take it away and show me a second image with slight changes and ask whether items in the second image had been in the first one, too. The directions instructed test takers not to answer yes unless they were sure.

I interpreted the word "sure" to mean *I would stake my life on it,* where most people interpret "sure" to mean *I am reasonably confident my answer is correct.* I would say things like "I *think* the picture of the cat was there, but I'm not 1,000 percent *sure,*" and then I'd end up answering "no" because I wasn't 1,000 percent sure, thus depressing my score. I did this question after question. After the test was over, Dr. Stein told me that as the test went on he'd actually started rooting for me to get a couple of answers right. I obviously *knew* I was seeing the cat picture for the second time, he said.

That finding was a revelation, and since the testing I see it in my life all the time. Whenever I have to fill out long, complicated forms (think FAFSA, the financial aid form for college), I spend hours going over and over every answer, making sure what I've put down is exactly right. I perseverate. On *forms.*

Either that, or there is a Little Miss Perfect lurking inside me somewhere who is hoping for a gold star for "Best Direction Follower." Incidentally, this is not a useful trait for SAT math. Boys use more flexible approaches, while girls tend to be more conventional, which can eat up more time.

"I aced that Rubik's Cube test, right?" I asked.

Wrong.

I had done well, but I was slow. Apparently, I'm a slow processer. Or slow-ish. I didn't get my percentiles from Dr. Stein, so I don't know how slow. All I know is that I tested as having low(ish) working memory combined with slow(ish) processing speed, a combination Dr. Stein told me was classic ADHD.

Apart from the attention-deficit profile, the headline news was that I had a huge disparity between verbal and visual recall. Very high on verbal and so low on visual that I was borderline impaired.

In one visual recall test, the tester starts by giving you a page with three simple images: a triangle, a circle, a square, say. You look at the image, then the tester takes it away and you draw it from memory. The target images grow more complex as you go along.

I couldn't do it. Even with the easiest images, I felt a kind of panic when Dr. Stein removed the image; I could feel it dissolving in my mind's eye.

My very low score on visual recall explained a lot: my lifelong tendency to get lost, my fear of driving an unfamiliar route, even my problems with cut-and-paste in Microsoft Word. Whenever I move a sentence or a paragraph, I forget what it says as soon as I hit Cut. I have to paste the text into a separate document so I can see it while I'm finding the place in my text I'm moving it to.

Poor visual recall probably explains the stop sign in Arizona, too. At the time, I assumed that I had somehow managed not to see a stop sign standing directly in front of me. What probably happened was that I saw it *and then forgot.* Out of sight, out of mind.

The one silver lining in the bad news about my visual recall was that I found out I needed glasses. After looking at my scores, Dr. Stein insisted I see an optometrist, who told me I needed reading glasses. The reading and writing sections were noticeably easier as soon as I filled the prescription.

My performance on the verbal tests was a completely different story than the visual testing. After one of the writing tests, the doctor said, "*Wow!* I've never seen anyone write like that. *You were fast!*"

I was.

I could remember the most intricate story lines, too. One test begins with a simple story line: *John got up and ate breakfast,* maybe. You retell the story from memory.

Then *John gets up, eats breakfast, and reads the newspaper.* After you hear a very intricate story, you retell it over and over, at specific intervals that the doctor is keeping track of. And you must remember as many details as possible with each telling. I could easily remember all the twists and turns after I *heard* the story. For me, stories stick.

People with high verbal ability are apparently good at remembering stories and vocabulary words, which describes me to a T. No wonder I loved SAT vocabulary so much—I was good at it!

So was it worthwhile to have my IQ checked, and do I recommend it to others? Yes and no. IQ testing is obviously not necessary for SAT prep, though it was fun making sense of myself after all these years.

The risk in learning your IQ, of course, is that you might experience the number as a ceiling—a limit—not just a single data point in a range.

The truth is that practice improves performance on almost every task, for almost everyone, no matter what your IQ.

Is the SAT an IQ Test?

I'm going to lob an observation into this discussion that will make people queasy.

In my sessions with Dr. Stein, I noticed a suspicious amount of overlap between the IQ testing I did and the SAT, which left me with the disturbing sense that we've all been duped into taking a national IQ test to get into college. I felt woozy at the thought that I'd been tossing around my SAT scores as though they were no more consequential than a dress size when I should have been guarding them tightly, as I would an IQ score. (Ultimately I decided not to publish my IQ. IQ scores are way too fraught.)

IQ scores feel private because they leave the impression that they're a fixed number—immutable. By contrast, everyone thinks you can improve an SAT score to some degree.

The IQ tests weren't identical to the SAT, more like first cousins. Which makes sense when you consider their origins: both the SAT and the army IQ tests were developed by Carl Brigham. The "A" in SAT originally stood for "aptitude" and the test was intended to measure a student's innate ability. It wasn't supposed to assess the knowledge he or she had learned in school.

The tests are so close that there are equations for converting SAT scores into IQ estimates, and SAT scores are used at times as an IQ shortcut. Scores from some years are accepted as a qualification for membership in "high IQ" societies and are also used by some programs for gifted children.

In the end, I came to think of IQ and SAT tests as measuring something both important and malleable. IQ is a range, not a number, and I want my children and me to be at the top of our ranges, not the middle or the bottom. It's also obvious the tests can be wrong. While my adult scores on SAT reading and writing are highly correlated with my adult IQ, my teenage SAT scores and my adult math scores look like those of different people.

At the end of the testing, Dr. Stein suggested a five-week regimen of Cogmed, a working memory training program that uses computer exercises to improve attention and complex reasoning skills. According to the Cogmed literature, eight out of ten people who have completed the experience show "significant lasting results."

I was game.

There were eight different memory exercises to complete, on a schedule of five days a week for five weeks in all. The program would automatically select which six exercises were to be completed. It was like a combination video game/IQ test and involved clicking numbers, cubes, or letters in various orders—forward and backward. Some exercises involved listening, others were just visual. The regimen took a little over forty minutes to complete, and required *extreme* focus (so much so that footsteps two floors above me would throw me off my game and I'd make mistakes).

I *hated* the Cogmed routine at first, which I told Dr. Stein, whereupon he showed me tricks such as "chunking" and "patterns," which made it easier. Surprisingly, I started to crave the computer exercises after the first week, and at my next appointment I asked the doctor for a double dose. He said no, explaining that the test was much more mentally fatiguing than I realized. Weirdly, after the session in which he explained the fatiguing properties of the test, I hit a mental wall on my way back home. My brain went *kaput*—I'm done. It was scary. I couldn't string a simple sentence together. When I got home, I dimmed the lights and told Ethan not to utter a word because I couldn't bear to hear a sound without my brain hurting. Very strange.

I had the next two days off (the regimen called for two days off per week), and when I returned my Cogmed Index points took a huge leap. Suddenly I could click six or seven numbers backward when just two days before I could only click four. The program synched up with the doctor's computer and he would e-mail feedback: "What happened on the cube? Were you getting distracted, interrupted, fatigued?" And when he saw progress, his e-mails were so encouraging, it was impossible *not* to be egged on and want to try even harder. "Your training looks fantastic! You are pacing yourself well. Your index is steadily improving. Maximizing success and minimizing consecutive failures!"

By the end of my third week, I was up 25 points, which was the average improvement after the *full*, five-week course.

Naturally, I assumed this would translate into SAT score improvement.

I finished the full course of Cogmed having improved by 27 index points (2 points more than the average gain), but the only positive effect I was feeling was appreciation for the forty extra minutes I now had to myself each day. I kept asking Dr. Stein, "When will I feel it?" and he kept answering, "Everyone's different."

DOES MEMORY TRAINING MAKE YOU SMARTER?

Cogmed is one of the many commercially available memory-training programs that are intended to improve attention. Some studies have reported an increase in fluid intelligence (inductive and deductive reasoning) as a result of Cogmed-type training, though the findings have been inconsistent.

- People do get better at what they practice, but there is scant evidence that the practiced skill transfers to other tasks. Practicing crosswords won't help you with sudoku.
- Some findings support the effectiveness of memory training for working memory.
- Studies have shown benefits in *some* children (not all), but there is no evidence that it's been effective in adults.
- Claims of increased intelligence through memory training have been inconclusive.

By that point, I was only too happy to consider the illusion of forty extra minutes in my day to be a positive effect of memory training. I was worn down. Between Cogmed and Kumon and my recalcitrant children, who were going to be the death of me (or the end of the project), I felt impaired. Stress is *very bad* for clear thinking.

It must have showed because four different people e-mailed me the same article one day: "DO YOU SUFFER FROM DECISION FATIGUE?"

I still wasn't improving in Kumon, which was exasperating and eventually led me to postpone (not to be confused with "quit") Kumon until after I finished the project, at which point I planned to return and stick with it until I got my certificate for Level O calculus along with the rest of the munchkins.

I finished my work with Dr. Stein at the same time I wrapped up with Kumon. It was the end of the summer and time to figure out what to do next before I took my fifth SAT in October.

16

LOVE IT AND IT WILL LOVE YOU BACK

The Critical Reader

L ate one night I received an e-mail.

"Dear Debbie," it said. "I just stumbled across your blog, and I thought that you might be interested in looking at mine."

I clicked on the link and there it was: the blog I'd spent weeks trying to find again after forgetting to bookmark it.

I'd discovered it late one night when I should have been sleeping. I'd come upon the blog after falling deep down an Internet rabbit hole I couldn't climb back out of, and I'd loved it from the very first click because it felt legit for the verbal sections in the same way that *Erik the Red*'s site felt real for the math. But I could never find it again because I'd been in such a haze the first time I saw it.

Let's start with this: I *love* that she says "*the verbal*" instead of "critical reading" and "writing" like everyone else. It's retro. That's what we said back in the day—"*the verbal.*"

"I'm so happy," I wrote back. "I'm sick as a dog and it's the middle of the night, but *I'm so happy to find you.*"

I spent the next three days scouring every nook and cranny of her website. Then I signed up to receive more as soon as she wrote it. I felt as though I were sitting at the chef's table in the kitchen of a fine restaurant, learning the secrets from a master chef. I wanted to know every single thing she knew about the SAT verbal sections, and as far as I was concerned she couldn't write it fast enough, so I invited her over for dinner. I wanted more of what she had—*whoever* she was.

She was Erica Meltzer, a verbal tutor originally from Brookline, Massachusetts, but now living in New York City who'd graduated from Wellesley College. Verbal was her specialty. I invited a few others from the tribe of those of us willing to admit that we *like* the SAT. We're a niche, a subculture, and what we lack in tally we make up for with passion. There was PWN the SAT, the tutor who'd saved me from near catastrophe the day before my third SAT, and my friend Catherine, who'd introduced me to the idea of standardized testing as an activity of leisure. That was everyone I could think of within a sixty-mile radius, though I'm sure there must have been others—I just didn't know them.

Catherine resigned from the tribe a few months later. She took her first real SAT in decades and decided she didn't like it under official testing conditions, though she definitely liked having a proctor. For a couple of months afterward, every time I happened to catch her on an unproductive day, she would say, "I need a proctor." She'd had fun doing Blue Book sections at home with Chris (mostly the math because that's what they were working on), but the endurance required by a full-length test was a shock to her system. The SAT had grown an hour longer since the last time she took it in high school, and taking the new one was like running a marathon and finding out at mile 18 that it's now 26.2 miles and not 22, like the last time you ran it. That's a painful difference.

Soul Food

My SAT dinner party was like a tea party, but with Blue Books instead of crumpets. It took place on a warm summer night on my back deck. Generally speaking, I'm not much of a cook, but that night I was *on*—probably because I made the food with love (that's the secret sauce for all good things). I grilled salmon with fresh herbs, cooked fluffy rice pilaf, and made a salad out of summer corn and local heirloom tomatoes. Crisp summer wine flowed as we enthused about the SAT, free for once from the self-consciousness that comes from having such a quirky—and unpopular—passion.

We were four well-fed grown-ups, sitting around a dinner table for hours, shooting the breeze about nothing other than the SAT. No shame, no covering up, no camouflaging—just unbridled enthusiasm. We could let loose that night without friends and family nudging us to say we were *boring* them.

Erica was everything I'd hoped she might be, and more. She was a verbal savant—but "normal" and adorable. She's petite, like a fairy, but her tiny frame is anything but delicate. She packs a surprising amount of gravitas into that little body and doesn't hesitate to share her formidable opinion on all matters verbal:

> "Don't tell me *approximately* what the author says. Look at the passage—no, *look* at the passage; tell me *exactly* what the author is saying. Exactly, as in word for word."

> "The SAT does precisely what it was designed to do. It reveals persistent weaknesses in comprehension."

> "The SAT is not a literature test. It's a vocabulary-based reasoning test."

> "This isn't about teenagers being teenagers. The French lycée students I've worked with are taught in a system that drills this kind of precision *mercilessly*. They have absolutely no problem telling me the function of a paragraph in the context of an argument, or the relationship between the first and second sentences in a paragraph."

She corrected me if I made a grammatical error in conversation, mostly because she couldn't help herself.

"Are you okay with that?" she asked.

"Absolutely," I said, and it was true, because I knew she was coming from a place of passion, which I appreciated. The only other person who ever corrected me was my mother, and I love her for that. Most people won't tell the unvarnished truth; they think it's impolite. Not *my* mother. She sees it as constructive. Don't ask her something if you don't want to hear the truth, and don't ask rhetorical questions because "Does this make me look fat?" could very well end in tears if you're not prepared.

Erica saw patterns in the SAT's arrangement of grammar questions and could predict the error type by question number like it was a party trick. "Faulty comparisons almost always show up in the last three Identifying Sentence Errors questions," she said, "and tricky subject-verb agreement questions as well."

I was mesmerized.

"*More!*" I'd say, and she seemed perfectly content to humor me with grammar tricks as long as I kept enthusing, which I did. She knew the test so well her expertise verged on suspicious. One day she peppered me with the following reminders: "The final Improving Sentences question is usually complicated parallelism . . . an underlined pronoun often points to a pronoun error . . . and an underlined verb in the *present tense* usually means 'subject-verb agreement error.'"

I couldn't get enough. I wrote down every word as if I were taking dictation. I was a dream catcher, trapping goodies for my children— saving them for a day when they'd finally be able to make use of these precious gifts.

THE THREE MOST FREQUENTLY TESTED ERRORS
ON THE ERROR ID QUESTIONS

Erica knows *precisely* which types of errors appear most frequently, as well as those that are rarely covered or not tested at all. Below, in order of frequency, are the three most frequently tested errors on the Error ID portion of the writing section, along with a tidbit of Erica's advice on the matter.

1. **VERB TENSE:** Don't change the tense unless there's a good reason to do so. A sentence with a date in the past (e.g., 1492) usually requires the simple past ("went," not "has gone").

2. **SUBJECT-VERB AGREEMENT:** "Is/are," "was/were," and "have/has" are the most commonly tested verbs. When you see one underlined, check its subject first. Otherwise, remember that *singular* verbs have an *s* at the end, plural verbs don't (he run*s*/they run).

3. **PRONOUN-ANTECEDENT AGREEMENT:** The antecedent is the noun that a pronoun refers to. Singular nouns must agree with singular pronouns (it/its), and plural nouns must agree with plural pronouns (they/their). Whenever you see "it(s)" or "they/their" underlined, check the antecedent for disagreement. Remember that *collective* nouns such as "group," "city," "agency," and "team" are singular and require singular pronouns (e.g., "The agency wanted *its* payment," not "The agency wanted their payment.")

We talked on about the SAT until late into the night. Erica told us she'd seen passages from Catherine's book *Animals in Translation* in the critical reading section. (Later on, when Erica found out about Catherine's 10 on the essay, she started telling all her students the story. Erica had always said the essay scoring was so erratic that students should shoot for a 10 on the essay and focus their energies on the multiple-choice questions, and now she had proof. Or close to it. Anyway, she said, if a writer whose work is actually on the SAT can't get higher than a 10, it doesn't make sense for seventeen-year-olds to spend their prep time trying to hit 11 or 12.)

Every once in a while my kids came down to check on us and make sure the adults were still holding down the fort. They'd look out at our table, noses pressed up against the screen door, and I'd always ask, "Are you sure you don't want to join us?"

They didn't. They weren't ready to have a conversation with grown-ups about the SAT; they *were* checking out the passion, though. I wanted so badly for each of them to take one little bite—a nibble, that's all—just to see if they liked it.

When it was time to say good-bye, I wasn't ready for the night to end. I wanted more, plus I wanted to see if Erica might be able to transmit any of her zeal for grammar to my children, who seemed to have *no* interest that summer in anything academic. Looking back, that evening shines like the north star of good times during the most trying summer of my life.

The Work of Understanding

Once again, blinded by my own enthusiasm, I scheduled an appointment with Erica—*for the children*—without discussing it with them first. (Will I never learn?) I don't remember why they refused to go that day; the whole summer is a blur of adolescent anger (them) and misery (me): misery because I had lost all authority over my children, and I was scared. I had always been the disciplinarian in the family, but now if I said "no" the kids would walk to their father's house and get a different answer. The four of us had become ensnared in a monster case of postdivorce triangulation. I don't think any of us wanted it that way, including my ex-husband, but that's where we were.

Given the way things were going, it didn't take much convincing for me to throw up my hands and say, "Fine, do what you want."

I showed up for my first meeting with Erica alone, and I arrived without children for every session thereafter. As I drove into the city to meet her, I tried to convince myself it didn't hurt as much as it really did, but there was no way I could conjure enough self-deception to believe my own story. The project was supposed to be about bonding with Ethan, and now, doing it alone, I felt I had failed as a mother.

Where had I gone so wrong?

There was no choice at that point but to pull it together, so I told myself I was going into the city to hunt and gather for my cubs, and they'd be grateful someday—on their time, not mine. That eased the pain just enough for me to walk into the café with my head held high and say to

Erica, without tears or even so much as an explanation, "I'm going to take the session today—for myself."

Grammar Plunge

That first meeting with Erica at a café in the city lasted for hours, as did every *verbal* session thereafter. Each get-together was like happy hour in an alternate universe where people liked the SAT instead of hating and dreading it. I always left our sessions slightly intoxicated, as if I'd eaten too much and needed a nap. Erica chose the cafés, which were usually on the loud side and not the type of venue I would have chosen. I prefer to work in a quiet space, like a library; instead, on that first day, we sat upstairs in a noisy café, right next to the stairwell. The couches were uncomfortably low to the ground and flanked by mismatched coffee tables that wobbled. Everything looked like old Ikea floor models to me—randomly acquired and spritzed with a whiff of *college dorm*.

After we ordered lunch, I asked Erica to tell me her high school SAT story. She said that the first time she took the test she'd stayed up until four in the morning the night before, upset about something she no longer remembered. She scored "only" a 710 on the verbal, which she thought was "completely unacceptable" given that she'd spent ten years with her nose in a book. As far as she was concerned, anything less than an 800 was unreasonable. Of course, this was after the tests had been recentered; her 710 was equivalent to a 650 on the old scale. So she had a point.

Her mother signed her up for a Kaplan course about which she remembers three things: two good pieces of SAT advice and one lecture that she gave her very perplexed Kaplan instructor about the meaning of the word "magnanimous." She thought the word was "Dostoyevskian" and was intent on making sure that he fully understood this.

She also remembered that before she took her second SAT, she went to a bookstore, where she sat on the floor with a Red Book (precursor to the Blue Book) in her lap and looked over the official material, though she never went so far as to purchase the book.

She felt different from the other kids on the retake—as if she had X-ray vision. She saw right through the test: how it was constructed and the faulty reasoning behind the wrong answer choices. She was like an SAT clairvoyant. "It was weird," she told me—weird enough to take home an 800.

Math was another story. She expected to come in somewhere in the 500s because she'd been a B student with a mediocre math education (she scored a 580). And yet at the same time she could *almost* make out what they were doing in that section too, but she couldn't crack it because she didn't have the skills to apply what she could see, the way she did with the verbal.

After we ate, we got down to work, and the golden grammar tips began to sprinkle from her chitchat—tons of them. Erica is sweet and salty, like chocolate-covered pretzels. Her corrections can sometimes hurt a little, but they come from a good heart. I scribbled down every word she uttered, catching the gems as fast as I could in my marble notebook.

> *Wait until you've mastered the material before turning on the clock and taking the sections timed.*

> *Forget it's a multiple-choice test and just answer the questions on your own. The right answer choice will pop out at you after you've already answered it.*

I tested her method right there, in the midst of the noisy café, and she was right—the correct answers *do* pop when you come up with your own answer first.

I told Erica I lived in fear of option E ("no error") on the Identifying Sentence Errors portion of the writing section, and she said *everyone* lives in fear of option E, which made me feel better until she added that she'd seen SATs where option E was the correct answer *three times in a row*.

That's just cruel.

Erica had advice for dealing with "E," too.

Make a checklist and then you'll feel safe choosing E.

She told me the College Board doesn't test all grammar on the SAT, so the trick is to know what they do and don't test and how frequently. Then you prioritize.

SAT GRAMMAR

Not all grammar is tested on the SAT. Erica has dissected the Blue Book as well as every test the College Board has ever released. She knows precisely which rules are tested, how often they are tested, and how the questions are constructed.

- Keys to the Improving Sentences portion of the writing section:

    a) Identify the error and fix it yourself, *then* look for the answer that matches. Don't look at the multiple-choice options before coming up with your own answer.

    b) Shorter is better (start with the shortest answer and work from there).

    c) "-ing" (especially "being") is *usually* wrong on the SAT (*but not always*).

    d) The passive voice is usually wrong (e.g., "I drink the water" is correct versus "The water is drunk by me," which is often incorrect).

- Keys to the Identifying Sentence Errors portion of the writing section:

    a) Faulty comparisons, tricky subject-verb agreement, and diction (vocabulary) questions tend to appear in the last three questions.

    b) An underlined pronoun, especially "it/its" or "they/their," often signals a pronoun error.

    c) An underlined verb in the present tense (most often "is/are," "has/have") frequently signals a subject-verb agreement error.

    d) Comparisons such as "more than" or "less than" at the end of the identifying sentence errors section almost always signal a faulty comparison.

e) Sometimes the answer really is E ("no error"). If you can't find a problem in a sentence, don't pick a letter other than "E" just because you think there must be an error. Remember: the answer "E" can appear more than once in a row.

I didn't know a lick of grammar until I met Ms. Erica Meltzer. It was *embarrassing*. Sure, I could point you to a verb or a noun, an adjective or an adverb—but there would be a very long pause if I had to come up with a dangling modifier or a gerund, not to mention a "relative pronoun" or an "ambiguous antecedent." My ear could take me to a certain point and then I'd hit a wall, at which point Erica would ask, "Is it weird, or is it wrong?"

And I'd say, "I don't know."

After the grammar lesson, we moved on to critical reading. Erica taught me her method, demonstrating the technique using the Blue Book. She has a distinctive style of SAT reading, which starts with putting on her glasses. Then she moves in, *very* close, to the passage—nose to nose, like she's examining a photograph with a magnifying loupe. She always works in pencil and marks up the passage briskly, using some sort of hieroglyphics she's invented. When she's done, the passage is very messy, with circles and symbols all over the page. I'd never seen anyone read like this before.

ERICA'S ABBREVIATED CRITICAL READING METHOD

Erica learned her method from Laura Wilson at WilsonDailyPrep and tells me she would still have no idea how to *teach* critical reading were it not for Laura.

- Circle transition words or phrases such as "and," "however," "but," "therefore," "because," and "on the other hand."

- Circle "interesting" punctuation (colons, semicolons, italicization, quotes).
- Circle strong language. In critical reading passages, transition words, "interesting" punctuation, and strong language mark the locations where ideas are presented, defined, emphasized, or questioned.
- After reading the passage, jot down the tone (positive/negative) and, in four to six words, the main point—or underline the main idea if it's stated directly in the passage.
- The *main point* is usually found in (a) the last sentence of the first paragraph, (b) the first sentence of the second paragraph, or (c) the last sentence of the passage.
- Line number–referenced questions: Read the sentence before *and* after the line that is referenced. If the line is near the beginning of the paragraph, read from the beginning of the paragraph. The topic sentence is always important.
- Tone questions: Note whether the passage is positive or negative and begin by eliminating answers that indicate the opposite. A sentence that includes a "strong" word such as "only" or "never" will have an "emphatic" or "decisive" tone. Extreme answers are unlikely to be correct.
- Look for answers that contain *synonyms* for words in the passage. Choices that use exact wording from the passage are usually wrong.
- Skip and come back to questions that take too long (e.g., "all of the following EXCEPT" questions).
- Identify the main idea, then skim the rest, *except* for the conclusion, which must always be read carefully, especially the last sentence. If a question asks about a skimmed detail, *go back to the passage.* This only works if students can identify the main idea. A kid who has difficulty identifying main ideas is better off looking at the "detail" questions first. No one size fits all!

"*Go back to the passage*" sounds simple, right? And yet it's harder than you might think because few answers to critical reading questions are stated explicitly in the text. For example, a question might ask about the significance of a word in the context of the larger argument, or about the function of the word inside the paragraph. To give you an idea of how difficult such judgments can be for young readers, the word "although" can function to concede a point, to establish a contrast, or to express a contradiction that is only apparent—all depending upon the passage.

Moreover, authors do not give all words equal weight, and the answer often hinges on a key word or phrase in the text. Such questions test a student's ability to detect emphasis, to understand what is central to the author's argument and what is peripheral.

For me, the inference questions were the most challenging. Erica said inference questions tend to be hardest for most students because they're based on information that is suggested but not stated in the text. For inference questions the correct answer is usually a simple rephrasing of the statement from a slightly different point of view: same idea, different words—but a much shorter leap than most people are expecting.

The questions can also be difficult because of the reader's tendency to extrapolate beyond what is on the page. For example, many students will interpret a passage depicting one character behaving unpleasantly toward another character as meaning that the first character is a bad person or is poorly behaved in general, which goes beyond what the author has actually suggested in the passage itself.

Critical reading passages are not out to trick students. They test whether students can follow what a passage is saying, both at the level of individual sentences and at the more abstract level of the larger point or argument the passage is making. The focus is on the author's meaning or intent, which is not necessarily what is taught in most high school English classes, where students are asked to make personal connections to the text or to discuss themes, symbols, and meaning. What students are not being asked to do is to read closely so as to understand how particular linguistic and stylistic choices shape the impression the author wants to convey. That is what the SAT is asking.

Erica would watch me read, which was stressful, and then ask me questions. Invariably my eyes would roll up to the sky, as if I were searching for the answer in my head, which is the wrong place to find answers for this test. You find the answers via close reading of the text. Then I'd open with something like *"Well, I feel like—"* and before I could finish my thought she'd interrupt and say, *"Look at the passage*—no, *look* at the passage—and tell me *exactly* what the author is saying. Exactly, as in word for word."

Erica and I met about a dozen times over the summer, each time for many enjoyable hours—but we didn't have time to work on every aspect of the verbal sections. We didn't really touch on the Sentence Completions because those came easily to me, and I assumed there was nothing more to know about them other than what I could learn by studying vocabulary.

Sentence Completions are sentences in which one or two words have been omitted. To me, Sentence Completion looked like a straightforward vocabulary test. But when I (finally) began SAT work with Ethan, I was surprised by the degree of difficulty he had answering the questions, and I realized there was more to it than that. Ethan is a strong reader with a fairly broad vocabulary for a kid his age, but he often missed more Sentence Completions than he did reading questions, which seemed absolutely ludicrous to me because the reading-passage questions were the hard ones, or so it seemed to me. It made no sense.

Granted, he didn't begin studying vocabulary in earnest until after our college tour in February of his junior year, which in retrospect was way too late. But even after he buckled down, he continued to have a tougher time with the Sentence Completions than made sense to me. (He'd probably say the same about my troubles with SAT math.) I used to say vocabulary was the low-hanging fruit of the critical reading section, but apparently that's not true for everyone.

The Sentence Completion questions are hard because the answer choices include many words high school students don't know, which means they have to figure the meaning out from context. Being older and much better read than a high school junior, I usually knew the vocabulary, but when I didn't I got the right answer by using a process of elimination via educated guessing. Often, it was the deceptively simple-looking words, for which I needed to know a second- or third-level definition, that gave me the most trouble.

Erica and I also devoted only passing attention to the Improving Paragraphs portion of the writing section, which she called "Critical Reading Lite: Half Reading/Half Writing." These six little questions always reside at the end of a long writing section and leave the impression that they've been tacked on as an afterthought. That said, I had to master them. Missing just four questions on the writing section can bring your score down from an 800 to a 700, and on my first four SATs I missed one or two Improving Paragraphs questions per test.

With Erica's help, I quickly started getting all of the Improving Paragraphs questions right. Erica explained that the questions generally fall into two categories: grammar-and-style questions or paragraph organization and rhetoric questions. To do well, you have to know which questions require which approach. Once I categorized questions according to her scheme and learned her method for tackling the section, I had no more problems.

ERICA'S METHOD FOR IMPROVING PARAGRAPHS QUESTIONS

The Improving Paragraphs questions appear at the end of the long writing section and consist of a short reading passage followed by six questions related to grammar, style, or paragraph organization.

- Skim the paragraphs and jot down the main idea. If short on time, don't even skim; just go straight to the questions and work backward. The passages are not complex and rarely require pre-reading to answer the questions. (Mark anything that sounds funny to your ear; there will usually be a related question.)

- Grammar and style questions: eliminate answers using Erica's rules for Improving Sentences questions ("-ing" words are usually wrong; shorter is better; passive voice is bad, etc.).
- Paragraph organization questions on rhetoric: these are essentially reading questions that can be answered by using Erica's method for the critical reading questions (i.e., main point is essential, tone, etc.).

Relationship Issues

I had bigger fish to fry than Improving Paragraphs. The much-loathed "paired passages and paragraphs" in the critical reading section were a killer for me, and Erica said they're everyone's least favorite part of the test. They come in different flavors—long or short—and demand a level of focus (and working memory) that goes beyond anything I'd ever experienced because they require juggling multiple points of view (and not necessarily opposing points of view, either) at the same time. To answer the questions, you have to remember the first passage, remember the second passage, remember the question, *and analyze all three in relationship to each other.* All of those feats are performed by working memory, and, Cogmed or no, working memory is not my strong suit.

The first double passage I tried with Erica was from Ethan's tenth-grade PSAT. In one section, there were two long paired passages about dualism, the genomes, and neuroscience. Passage 1 discussed Descartes, Passage 2 Copernicus. The authors of both passages agreed that they disagreed with dualism, but the differences between the two viewpoints were subtle.

I read the passages with Erica watching, then followed her reading recipe, which included writing everything down to alleviate the issue of working memory overload. After I finished she asked me a question that left me flummoxed. "What's the *relationship* between the passages?" she asked.

Blank stare. What did she mean by *"relationship"*?

"Ask me the main idea," I said, "or the tone. I can tell you the tone."

I didn't know about "the relationship." I didn't even understand what she was asking me—it wasn't as if one passage was pro and the other con. Both authors agreed: dualism is bad. "They have a *good* relationship," I said, well aware this was not what she had in mind. We went round and round until finally I said I had to go because my head hurt.

Erica e-mailed me later and said she didn't know what to make of the trouble I'd had with that question. "You were getting caught up in the details and couldn't see that the two things were the same idea."

Well, sort of, I thought. In fact, I did see that the two passages were talking about the same concept; that was the problem. I couldn't understand how to describe a relationship between two passages that had basically the same take on the same subject. I think Erica was probably asking me to say that the authors agreed on the issue but came at it from different angles . . . which seems obvious today but flummoxed me at the time. Months later, Catherine read the passages and said the relationship was that Passage 2 was blathering about the brain, and Passage 1 was blathering about blather. (Catherine never really warmed up to critical reading.)

I struggled with the double passage questions until the bitter end. They added an extra dimension of "laborious" to the critical reading section, which was plenty grueling without them, as far as I was concerned.

Which is why the SAT has such a bad rap—it takes mental fitness to a whole other level.

THE DOUBLE READING PASSAGES

Erica explained that it helps to think of the double reading passages—two separate reading passages on the same topic—as being constructed using four templates:

1. Most common: opposing views on the same topic, pro and con.
2. The authors agree on the issue at hand but have different focuses.
3. The authors discuss *different* aspects or interpretations of one event. For example, Passage 1 focuses on how an event was perceived by the press, and Passage 2 focuses on how the same event affected women.
4. One passage provides an example of an idea described in the other passage.

On critical reading, understanding the relationship between the two passages is important, first and foremost because the SAT often asks that question explicitly. More challenging are questions asking what one author would think about the ideas of the other author. These questions aren't so hard when the authors disagree across the board, but they can be very tricky when the authors disagree on everything *except* the one issue being asked about in the question. The correct answer might come down to a single key detail, often buried in the middle of a passage.

Many smart, high-achieving kids have trouble nailing the relationship between passages, and it's crucial not to lose *too* much time trying to figure it out, especially before the more straightforward questions have been answered. Erica advises scanning all of the questions for both passages and answering those that ask about just one passage first (sometimes there aren't any) before moving on to relationship questions.

I spent a lot of time trying to articulate to Erica the relationship between passages. She told me I should write down the crucial details and pretend I was doing a math problem—to reason my way to the answer using *just* the information that was written down on the page in front of me.

You have to be systematic with these questions—that's the bottom line. As tedious as that sounds, it does help.

Think Love

I often thought that if I could just inhale Erica, in one big gulp, it would be so much more efficient than trying to consume everything she knew one lesson at a time. The truth, though, was that the more I practiced the reading section, the more I began to enjoy the passages. No one believes me when I say that, but it's true: I started to love the reading passages. I even found myself referring to them in everyday conversations (though I never admitted it at the time, not unless I was with another member of the tribe).

But here's the interesting part: the more I loved them, the more they loved me—confirming the advice of "Noitaraperp," a College Confidential regular who claimed to have moved her (his?) critical reading score from a 500 to an 800. Noitaraperp had posted a piece called "How to Attack the Critical Reading Section," which included the observation that:

> . . . You MUST love the passage you are reading. Force
> yourself to love it—throw yourself into the passage with
> gusto. It works.

As I read this, a light went off. This was the same advice I'd been giving for years.

Running publicity departments for publishing companies, I would tell the publicists that you have to find something to love about a book to get the job done.

At least once a week a publicist would come to me, frustrated, and confess some variant of "I hate the book." I'd sit them down and debrief them.

"What about the author?" I'd ask. "Can you love the author?"

Not infrequently this was a "no" as well.

"How about the author's spouse?"

"The children?"

"The main character's boyfriend?"

"Is there *anything* you can find to love?"

We'd always come up with something because I was absolutely sure you needed it.

Love was where the rubber met the road. I was so sure this was true that I'd extended the theory across the board.

"Just try to love it," I'd tell my kids.

"Keep an open mind, because the love changes everything."

Now I was discovering that "Love your work" was good advice for test prep, too.

Erica disagreed.

"You don't have to love it," she'd say. "You don't even have to like it. You need to look at the test objectively and not take it personally."

We'd argue the issue for hours, neither one of us conceding any ground. Then we'd get back to prepping me for the test.

Just after my work with Erica was done, Ethan decided he was finished rebelling and was ready to get along with me again (thank God), not to mention follow my house rules without seeking a second opinion from his dad.

He didn't come right out and announce his change of heart. His return to the nest was a gesture: "Do you wanna do some SAT work together?" he asked one day.

To which I responded, "Are you kidding?" And without missing a beat, I grabbed both our Blue Books and some freshly sharpened No. 2 pencils and started to tell him everything I could think of that I'd learned from Erica. I'd been waiting so patiently to try out my new tips on Ethan, and he played along, acting like he was genuinely interested in what I was saying.

"Extreme words are usually wrong."

"Read *every word* in the answer choices."

"Before you answer a question *go back to the passage*." (I could hear little Erica's voice in my head as I spoke.)

There weren't enough buckets on the planet to catch my tears of joy when Ethan said those magic words, coming as they did in the wake of the summer's anger and alienation. I knew he wasn't asking to do SAT work because he actually wanted to prepare for the test. He still had no interest in that. This was his olive branch. Our relationship would mend.

I had learned a lesson about not overstaying my welcome, so I kept it brief. After our connection had been reestablished, I told him I had one more tip, and then he could go. It was a tip I'd discovered all on my own, and I wanted to be absolutely sure that he really understood that this was the secret sauce.

He sat at attention, waiting to hear what I'd say—probably humoring me a bit by playing the role of "interested son"—and when I was absolutely sure he was listening, I put it out there: "Love it and it will love you back," I said.

I felt the little smirk he was holding back, because, really, who else but his mother would come up with this kind of advice? But he also knew exactly what I meant, and that I was right. I'd doled out variations on this theme before. "Keep an open mind," I'd say, whenever he'd complain about having to do something that wasn't a choice. "Try to imagine that it might *not* be as horrible as you're expecting," I would say, which would usually elicit an eye roll.

One time when he was particularly grumpy, I gave him a meditation book and told him to read one page every day, which of course got me an earful of reasons explaining *why* that wouldn't make him feel better. But a few days later I found the meditation book with a little yellow sticky note on top, and inscribed on the sticky was a note, in Ethan's trademark chicken scratch: "Thank you. These *did* make me feel better."

"How can I improve on the critical reading?" is the question I'm most frequently asked. I have a list of things I tell people, but I always end by saying, "Love it and it will love you back," and invariably I hear back after the test, "It works!"

I know it does.

17

WHAT *IS* DELIBERATE PRACTICE?
(AND AM I DOING IT?)

Not All Practice Is Created Equal

In 1993, K. Anders Ericsson, a cognitive psychologist studying expertise, published a paper on practice and expert performance. His argument: genius is made, not born. Elite performers in any field are elite because they've spent more time practicing than everyone else.

On the face of it, this may not seem surprising. However, most of us assume talent is innate, not learned. Talented people seem to pick things up easily because they have an inborn proclivity to be good at sports or music or math or whatever it is they excel in. They have a *gift*. Especially during the school years, we tend to divide children who are good at something into two groups: the naturals and the grinds. It's the naturals we expect to reach the top.

But that's not what Ericsson found. Ericsson found that the top performers are always grinds: without exception, top performers have worked harder than performers ranked just below them. Even small differences *within* the top group are directly related to the amount of time individuals have devoted to practice—specifically, to something Ericsson calls *deliberate practice*. More *deliberate practice* means better performance.

Deliberate practice is different from the kind of thing kids do when their parents tell them to go practice the piano. Kids—and grown-ups—like to practice things they already know how to do. Unfortunately, repetition of the familiar does not advance skill. As Ericsson puts it, "research across domains shows that it is only by working at what you can't do that you turn into the expert you want to be."

Systematically working on the things you can't do (or can't do as well as you need or want to) is the essence of deliberate practice. A regimen of deliberate practice is sustained, structured, difficult, and demanding; and it requires an intensity of concentration so taxing that even very high-level performers are unable to complete more than four or five hours at a time. Deliberate practice is *hard*.

Outside academia, Ericsson's research is referred to interchangeably as the 10,000-hour and/or the ten-year rule (though whether or not Ericsson ever promulgated a 10,000-hour rule is apparently in dispute. See below.)* The rule as propounded by popular sources: becoming an elite performer requires a minimum of 10,000 hours of deliberate practice over ten years' time.

The 10,000-hour rule had crossed my radar before I declared my intention to achieve standardized perfection in 2011; I'd just never calculated how many hours there were in a year (8,765, if you don't sleep). Nor had I looked into the probability of achieving my goal (less than .023 percent).

I had no idea what I was taking on. I was going on gut.

Unfortunately, Ericsson's research also shows that your gut is a reliable guide only when you're already an expert, in which case you've developed expert intuition.

The last time my gut had had any experience with the SAT was thirty years ago.

---

* Ericsson in 2007 (*Harvard Business Review*): "Our research shows that even the most gifted performers need a minimum of ten years (or 10,000 hours) of intense training before they win international competitions."
Ericsson in 2012 (in a reply to an *Association for Psychological Science Observer* article on the web): "In fact, the 10,000 hour rule was invented by Malcolm Gladwell."

The other element essential to outstanding performance is a great teacher. The teacher identifies which skills need to be improved, designs the student's practice, observes the results, and gives feedback. For the top performers, different teachers perform these tasks at different stages. The more advanced the student, the more advanced the teacher needs to be.

The Teacher

The teacher has to be an expert, but if you're not an expert yourself and you're looking to hire a teacher (or a trainer or tutor) who is, how do you know how to choose?

You can't necessarily go by experience. Ericsson says expertise can actually decline over time for skills the expert doesn't use often.

A real expert produces consistently superior, measurable results that can be replicated in a laboratory.

But I didn't know any of this then.

Here's what I knew: PWN had scored a perfect SAT score in 2007.

2007 PERFECT **SAT** SCORES (2400)

- Total SAT takers (high school seniors): 1,534,457
- Total perfect scores (high school seniors): 273 (0.018 percent)

PWN was an elite tester, though not one of the 273 listed by the College Board. That figure includes only high school seniors. In official College Board tallies, PWN's score disappears or becomes part of the larger pool of all testers—or maybe part of a smaller pool of wackadoodle grown-ups who've taken the test long after it's required. The College Board doesn't release those numbers.

PWN moved to New York City in 2003 after graduating from Brown, where he studied psychology and philosophy. A series of unlikely events led him into the world of high-stakes SAT prep, and, as part of his initiation into the world of high-end SAT tutoring, he took the SAT and scored a perfect 2400. From what I gather, PWN has always been a 99th-percentile guy. Some kids are good at sports; PWN is good at standardized tests. And video games—he's *very* good at video games, especially Portal.

He's also a really good teacher.

I verified this by calling on him incessantly after our first phone call in May, right before my third SAT. And I didn't even feel like I was imposing because he seemed to genuinely enjoy teaching me as much as I loved being taught by him, which made it easy to keep knocking on his door even as I worked with Erica, did Kumon and Cogmed, and had my IQ tested.

Of course, I never forgot the lucky omen: that Transformer sticker on the rear window of his car. PWN, I was convinced, was going to help me bridge the gap between loathing the test and loving it (or at least warming up to it)—for Ethan. I was counting on PWN to use video games, Transformers, boy stuff, whatever it took, to get Ethan across the divide and onto my side. But every time I'd ask he'd say, "I don't have time." *That's okay.* I was content to wait because I was absolutely sure he was the connector.

In the meantime, I called on PWN to help *me*, and he was always available to answer my questions with ample patience and fresh tricks, which I needed, because things didn't always stick the first go-around. Comprehension wasn't my problem—I had a case of forgetting what I'd learned if I had to think fast, especially under testing conditions.

I started to write his advice on recipe cards so I didn't have to keep calling him to ask the same questions over and over. I'd cut out each problem we discussed and paste it on an extra-large index card, then write down his step-by-step instructions in colored markers, so they looked pretty. Eventually, there were so many cards I had to organize them by category in a recipe box, like I was Betty Crocker, making sure the casserole and the crockpot recipes weren't mixed up together.

I called them my "Don't Eff with Me" cards because the math section started to feel more like a test of your ability not to be messed with by the College Board than your ability to do math. One time I wrote a blog post saying SAT math wasn't school math, and the math people jumped all over me, insisting that it was.

Perhaps they were right, though when I discovered Catherine was making her own list of the same sorts of math problems (tricky, not complicated or advanced), I started to think there must be some truth to the idea. Not to mention, PWN is a math guy, and he says it's best to think of the math section like shrimp ramen. School math is the shrimp.

I still remember my first "Don't Eff with Me" card—it was a "Double Stuffed Function," my pet name for this particular genre of function problem. I could *never* remember how to solve them, which was infuriating, though apparently I'm in good company. Erik the Red says they destroy kids. Still, I couldn't bear to ask PWN to explain them to me one more time, so I made a card, and then I made two cards, and after I had a few more they started to remind me of those *Good Housekeeping* recipe cards I remember moms collecting when I was little.

A SAMPLE "DOUBLE-STUFFED FUNCTION"

Question: Let the function h be defined by $h(x) = 4x - 8$ for all values of x. If $h(8) = t$, what is the value of $h(t)$?

$h(8)$ is read: "h of 8." For readers who weren't taught function notation in school:

$h(x) = 4x - 8$

is identical to

$y = 4x - 8$

A function takes an input number and creates an output number using a "recipe." In this problem, the letter h is the name of the recipe. The notation says x is the input number, and the recipe to find the output number is: multiply the input number by 4 and subtract 8.

The double-stuffed part comes in when the question asks you to cook the recipe twice. First you find $h(8)$, then you take the answer to $h(8)$ and apply the h function to that value.

Solution:

1. $h(8) = 4(8) - 8$
2. $h(8) = 24$
3. $h(8) = t$
   If $h(8) = 24$, and $h(8) = t$, then $t = 24$.
4. $t = 24$
5. $h(24) = 4(24) - 8 = 88$

Answer: $h(t) = 88$

Yes, I do realize this is child's play for some. But not for me, especially not on a timed test. I could easily solve function problems in the privacy of my own home, including the double-stuffed variant, but I'd freeze up when I ran into one on the test.

PWN made up silly names for math problems, too. We both like to have fun with weird word associations. So, while everyone else was stressing out about "the SAT," PWN and I were renaming math problems so they'd be funnier. He calls the triangle inequality theorem a "Sadness Gap" (so much better, right?)—and he has a silly little anecdote that explains the theorem, *his way*, with an accompanying visual image, to make it stick better.

TRIANGLE INEQUALITY THEOREM—À LA PWN

Official Explanation:

The triangle inequality theorem states that the sum of any two sides of a triangle must be greater than the measure of the third side.

PWN's Version (aka "The Sadness Gap"):

Imagine your forearms (apologies to my armless friends) are two sides of a triangle, and the imaginary line that connects your elbows is the third side. If you touch your fingertips together and pull your elbows apart, eventually your fingertips have to disconnect . . . that's when the length between your elbows is longer than the sum of the lengths of your forearms. The Sadness Gap is the space between the two hands. Neat, huh?

Sadness Gap Example:

A triangle has one side with length 8 and another side with length 10. All of the following could be the length of the third side EXCEPT

    A) 1
    B) √5 (approximately 2.24)
    C) 4
    D) 6
    E) 12

The answer is A.

In the literature on expertise, outstanding performers report that deliberate practice is "less inherently enjoyable than leisure." I may have been having too much fun with PWN for my work with him to be considered deliberate practice.

Tuesdays with PWN

Midway through summer I decided it was high time to make PWN's status as my tutor official. PWN was still saying he couldn't work with Ethan, and his website did say that it was "*not* an advertisement for his tutoring services," but he'd never said he wouldn't tutor *me*. Thankfully, he agreed to be my personal trainer for the October test when I asked.

From then on, he arrived at my house every Tuesday morning at ten o'clock on the nose. I don't think he was one minute late, ever. He always carried a black bag, which made me think of a doctor making house calls.

Our sessions would last almost the entire day, the hourly schedule following a circadian groove determined by my stamina, which was amazingly predictable. We'd spend the first three hours in my office going over my work from the week before until I ran out of brain juice at exactly one p.m., after which I would always attempt *one more problem*, which was pointless because there was nothing left in the tank.

I think what we were doing probably does qualify as deliberate practice. The work was hard; it was sustained; and it was structured and supervised by a master teacher. Ericsson writes that "most expert teachers and scientists set aside only a couple of hours a day, typically in the morning, for their most demanding mental activities, such as writing about new ideas." I had three, and then my brain was done.

After we reached brain fritz, PWN and I would switch tasks and move to a different station, the kitchen, where we'd start with the next phase of the session—vocabulary—while I cooked lunch. This part of the day was my own initiative and was inspired by a joy for new words, rather than born out of necessity, like the math. If I couldn't *precisely* define a word in the critical reading section, that word got a flash card. That was the rule.

I had fun trying out rarely used words in everyday conversation. It added an element of surprise, and most people were impressed enough not to question whether I was using the word correctly, though I did have a few friends who'd call me on it if I wandered out of context or pronounced something wrong, which I appreciated.

I liked it when PWN would use my words in his own sentences because then I'd gain another context to help me remember them. I'd throw his word images into my own pot, and by the end of lunch we'd have a twisted game of word associations. It was like a Rorschach test—those inkblots that psychologists use to analyze personalities.

phlegmatic—Alfred Hitchcock ("Whenever I think about Hitchcock's phlegmatic voice, I have the urge to clear my throat.")

temporize—administrator ("The superintendent temporized, hoping we'd all go away.")

supine—yoga ("Supine in the sand . . .")

salvo—boy ("A salvo of spitballs . . .")

portent—falling stars ("The dark cloud was a portent of disaster.")

There wasn't enough PWN in the world, as far as I was concerned. As soon as he realized traditional methods weren't sticking for me, he became a wizard, breaking out new teaching tricks like pulling rabbits from a hat.

Late one night I received an e-mail from PWN:

Subject: A Radical Thought

Your homework this week is to write 5 SAT math questions:
- *1 symbol function question*
- *1 shaded region area question involving triangles*
- *1 Sadness Gap question*
- *1 parabola question about a mystery x-intercept*

> - *1 function question where the function is*
>   *represented in a table (like if f(2) = a, what is f(a))*

> *For each, make sure you include 5 answer choices, and try to*
> *make the INCORRECT choices all seem tempting to a tester*
> *who might now know fully what he's doing.*

"I hate that idea," I wrote back.

Of course, a form of practice that sounds miserable definitely provides an opportunity to get outside your comfort zone, which I had by then discovered Ericsson says is essential to improvement.

No doubt part of me realized this because after the tiniest bit of squawking, I agreed to the challenge—and then immediately discovered that I liked writing SAT questions (which makes me wonder whether writing SAT function questions counts toward the 10,000 hours I would apparently need to put in to get all the function problems right on an actual test).

My goal was always the same: *stump the tutor.*

I came up with a method for writing the questions that I found to be soothing and meditative.

I'd spend hours picking through the Blue Book, looking for questions in whatever category I happened to be working on at that moment; then I'd draft my own version of the question, trying to use as many "best of" elements from the official questions as I could. I'd usually start out easy, but then I'd revise—and revise and revise—each time making my question harder until I was pretty sure I might stump PWN, my perfect-scoring tutor.

I never sent the question to him right away, though. I'd let it bake overnight, and if I couldn't answer my own question the next morning, I knew it was cooked just right and ready to be e-mailed to PWN.

I always received a response back within an hour.

"I *love* the function table," he'd write. "That's an amazing question. Awesome trap answer."

I made a trap answer? PWN was like a friend who always laughs at your jokes and makes you feel good.

Then came the constructive criticism, which was often disguised as a compliment. His comments always made me dig deeper, and think harder, and do another draft, and before I knew it I was questioning my own question.

He'd say something like "That shaded region problem is *so cool*," and I'd feel really smart and reply, "Really? Did I *get* you? How long did it take you to figure out the answer?"

"Oh, it was *very hard*," he'd say, and then he'd slip in something like "but the figure's not drawn to scale, so you need to tell me everything that's perpendicular . . ."

"Okay, I can do that . . ."

Then he'd continue, "And it's awesome that you have a few Pythagorean triples in there, but they're not solving the problem right now—they're distractions. Is there a way to make them necessary to solve the problem—to find the lengths you need to find the area?"

Hmmm . . . let me see if I can do that . . .

Do you see what he did there?

I hardly noticed that I was back at the drawing board. It was a powerful way to engage with the test. I started to feel like I could see through the test, the way Erica said she did on the verbal.

HOW WRITING YOUR OWN SAT QUESTIONS CAN HELP

Writing questions is a powerful way to engage with the material that's tested on the SAT—and is an approach used by *Mathematics 6*, a classic Russian textbook available in English. Writing questions forces you to put yourself in the examiner's head, or try to, helping you see how the test is constructed.

The objectives:

- To gain an understanding of the SAT's precision and lack of ambiguity.

- To reinforce important concepts and techniques.
- To understand *which* concepts are tested on the SAT.
- To anticipate missteps by deconstructing the College Board's answer choices.
- To gain insight into the way multiple concepts are often tested within a single question.

PWN and I worked on more than just math and vocabulary. We revisited a lot of the same territory I'd studied with Erica and Stacey, which is what you're supposed to do when you're learning new material: repeat, repeat, repeat.

I also found it helpful to study the same concepts again with a different teacher because you never know whose magic words will take root. Regardless of the teacher, what didn't work for me were "boy metaphors." I couldn't retain a thing if it was explained via baseball, truck, or car-wash similes. Stacey, the highest score–improving tutor-mom, would use "mommy metaphors," which, not surprisingly, were much more effective. She'd say something like, "An integer is a number that *my eight-year-old would know*—like 0, or 3 or –2," and then she'd ask, "Is 4.5 an integer?"

Now, that would stick: an integer is a whole number without a decimal point at the end. Got it.

Yin and Yang

There was a little bit of overlap in the time I spent with PWN and Erica, which was interesting because they couldn't have been more different. They're like flip sides of the same coin—both right and both fabulous.

For example, compare their reactions to their high school SAT scores:

ERICA: I *only* scored a 710 on the verbal. That was completely unacceptable. Anything less than an 800 was unreasonable.

PWN: I remember that I was devastated when my scores came back that I'd *only* scored a 730 in math. I'd done better than that in reading! FFFFFFFUUUUUUUUU.

Sometimes I felt like a child of divorced parents. Should I use Daddy's laid-back, hang-loose approach? Or try Mommy's super-intense, really precise method?

IDENTIFYING SENTENCE ERRORS CHECKLISTS— PWN VS. ERICA

PWN recommends that test takers be meticulous and check every Identifying Sentence Error question against what he calls the "VPP" list (verbs, pronouns, parallelism). He groups all the other potential errors into a miscellaneous list of "some other things you might see."

PWN's VPP List:

1. **VERB AGREEMENT:** If a verb is underlined in the sentence, check for subject-verb agreement and verb tenses.
2. **PRONOUN AGREEMENT:** After you check the verbs, check *all* underlined pronouns to make sure they have a proper antecedent.
3. **PARALLELISM:** All elements must be parallel (e.g., "<u>setting</u> a zombie on fire and <u>shooting</u> him in the head" rather than "<u>setting</u> a zombie on fire and <u>a shot</u> to the head").

Erica breaks her Identifying Sentence Errors checklist into *sixteen* very precise categories, listed below in approximate order of frequency. She notes that errors involving verbs and pronouns are by far the most common.

Erica's List of Sixteen Categories:

1. Subject-verb agreement
2. Verb tense

3. Pronoun-antecedent

4. Pronoun case

5. Adjective versus adverb

6. Parallel structure: lists

7. Prepositions

8. Faulty comparison

9. Word pairs

10. Noun agreement

11. Comparative versus superlative ("more" versus "most")

12. Relative pronouns ("which," "that," "who," "where," "when")

13. Double positives/double negatives

14. Conjunctions

15. Redundancy

16. Diction

Looking for a 12

PWN and I spent a generous amount of time working on the essay, which I hadn't done before. He suggested I practice writing a timed essay every day, so I committed to an essay a day with my morning coffee. I used College Board prompts and a timer and discovered that writing the essay gets a lot easier *very fast*—an effect that persisted only with daily practice, however. Whenever I fell off the wagon for just a couple of days, I felt like the rusted tin man looking for his can of oil.

I'd send my essay to PWN as soon as I was finished, and he'd reply with a score and a comment. The College Board's robo essay grader *always* gave me 12's, which was not only misleading but lacked the critical ingredient for improvement: feedback. PWN's scoring had meat on the bones.

"This is a solid ten," he'd say.

> "STRENGTHS: Solid example in the Tiger Mom book,
> and explained in such a way that I, as a reader, don't feel
> like I'm reading a book-report plot summary. . . .

WEAKNESSES: You basically wrote two intro paragraphs, and that cost you valuable time and space where
you could have been making other points. . . ."

"You don't address the question enough. . . ."

"New rule: no brand-new ideas after 1.5 pages. . . ."

PWN'S ESSAY ADVICE

- Answer the question *directly*. Yes or no—pick a side.
- Pretend you're on the debate team and *convince* the reader.
- Don't waffle. Stick to your side of the argument.
- Passion is good.
- Short intros are good.
- Don't give away too much in the intro—just hint and expand later.
- *No* grammar errors (*especially* in the opening paragraph).
- Don't go outside the lines.
- Be specific . . . use concrete examples and details. Don't be vague or make hypothetical statements.
- *Show* it, don't *say* it.

Observation

According to Ericsson, "The development of expertise requires coaches
who are capable of giving constructive, even painful feedback." I was
getting bountiful feedback, but until one Tuesday in early fall, I'm not
sure I felt any pain.

It was a Tuesday just like all others—9:59:59 a.m.

Ding-dong.

"Hi," I said, excited as always to see PWN at my door, trusty black
bag in hand. "How are you?"

"Good," he said, but he looked *different* that day—slightly mischievous . . . or something.

Oh no . . .

"I have a new idea," he said as he walked inside. "I'd like to watch you take a math section today—to see if we can get to the bottom of what's giving you so much trouble."

Everything he said garbled up as my brain did a remix of his words, and "*Why are you so slowwww . . . ?*" was all I could hear.

I had no problem embarrassing myself in front of him with misused vocabulary, but the thought of PWN watching me do math took things to a whole new level, somehow. I would have preferred to jump out of an airplane than to have PWN *watch me take a math section.*

"Um, okay," I said, mustering every bit of calm I could summon to avert a full-blown panic attack. We headed downstairs to my office, though instead of chatting joyfully as I usually did, I was looking for an escape hatch in the stairwell.

We sat down at my desk, just like we did every week.

"I need some ChapStick," I said, which was actually true. I never work without ChapStick. I ran upstairs and rifled through my drawers till I found some, then went back to my office and took my seat.

I was in the midst of organizing my testing paraphernalia—the pencils, my sharpener, the calculator—when I noticed that PWN had taken out a stopwatch. *He* was ready to begin.

"I need a bite of chocolate," I said. I could hear my heart thumping in my ears. I climbed out of my chair again and ran back up the stairs, this time to the fridge, where I kept a stash of dark chocolate for times like these. I was in dire need of energy and comfort.

I stuffed a few squares in my mouth and ran back down to my office, where PWN was waiting to observe me.

"Okay," I said, "I'm ready," and he started his stopwatch. To say that those twenty-five minutes felt like twenty-five hours would not do justice to the misery I experienced. I could see PWN from the corner of my eye taking notes as I worked, jotting down how long I spent on each problem, what method I used, and so on. After a few minutes, he faded into the background and I was left alone in my own, private cocoon of panic.

I walked away from this experience with valuable advice: in the future, PWN told me, I was to "MacGyver it."

After PWN left, I Googled "MacGyver" to find out what I would be doing if and when I MacGyvered the math section on a future SAT. MacGyver, I learned, was a TV character who solved complicated problems with nothing more than a little duct tape and a Swiss Army knife. MacGyver was nimble.

I was not nimble at all. PWN said I took *six* excruciating minutes trying to solve one problem—and never even got to the answer. That kind of move will kill your score on test day. I needed to be more flexible with my approaches to problem solving, he said, and I should switch methods more quickly when something didn't work.

He also told me that most of the time, on the SAT, the fastest way to solve a counting problem is simply to list the possibilities and count them. Because the test is calculator-optional, problems typically use small numbers, which makes the counting problems amenable to listing and counting 1-2-3.

A COUNTING PROBLEM, COURTESY OF PWN

A science teacher is trying to create a lab group consisting of two seniors and one junior. If there are three seniors in his class, and five juniors, what is the total number of different groups he can create?

(A) 15   (B) 18   (C) 24   (D) 30   (E) 36

Most students pick answer D (i.e., $3 \times 2 \times 5 = 30$), which is the wrong answer.

The best way to answer this question is to methodically make lists of each and every possibility. The SAT often uses small numbers, making this a more foolproof method than using the formula.

Start with Everything You Know

During the final month before the October SAT, I'd started to worry I was going to embarrass PWN if I got a bad score. I was still having trouble thinking fast and I wanted to let everyone know: *It's not his fault.* PWN said not to worry, but I feared I was a new kind of challenge, and that he was in uncharted waters trying to teach an old dog new tricks.

On the Tuesday before my fifth SAT, PWN arrived at ten in the morning, just like always. "We're going to do something different today," he said (again). "Start with everything you know," he said.

"Excuse me?"

"I want you to tell me *everything* you know about the SAT, and write it down in your notebook," he said. "And don't use your recipe cards. Just tell me what you remember." And so I did—for *three straight hours* with PWN sitting by my side, patiently listening as I listed everything I could think of, section by section. His patience was nothing short of astounding.

The next time I saw PWN was four days later at an old Italian restaurant in the Bronx. I walked in, having just finished my fifth SAT, and saw him sitting at a table (patiently).

It was October 1, 2011. "I nailed it," I said as soon as I saw him. I was energized.

He looked up at me—the one and only time I ever saw PWN worried.

18

FIRST-SERVE DEBBIE

Lesson Learned

I took my fifth SAT on October 1, 2011, at DeWitt Clinton High School in the Bronx.

Like throwing on an accessory as an afterthought, I'd added a last-minute twist to the "twelve methods/one year" concept. I decided to try out as many different test centers as possible, to see if location plays any role in the "standardized" experience.

It does.

I took the first four tests in the affluent suburban towns of Westchester County, the first in a fancy private school, the following three in public schools. These were apples-to-apples experiences with slight variations in the proctor's delivery or the type of desk or room (gymnasium versus classroom), but generally: same test experience, slightly different seasonings.

I tried to change up my fourth SAT experience by taking the test in Ossining, New York (home to Sing Sing, the legendary maximum-security state prison). Median family income in Ossining, though high compared to the rest of the country, was about two-thirds that of Irvington, and Wikipedia listed 35 percent of the town as black or Hispanic, as opposed to around 5 percent for the "river towns," where I lived and had taken my first three tests. I wondered whether the experience would be different.

It wasn't. Ossining High School was just like all the others in Westchester: suburban and middle class. The test takers were slightly more diverse. One girl showed up late, and the proctor passed out calculators—the only time I saw that happen—but that was the only detail that distinguished my Ossining SAT from the other three.

For my fifth SAT, I wanted to broaden my horizons.

On the way to my son's school in the Bronx there was a school I'd passed about which I knew just two things: it was urban, and it was called DeWitt Clinton High School. I also knew how to drive there, which was important because I'm prone to getting lost (poor visual recall). One thing I didn't need to add to my test experience was the stress of taking the wrong route and ending up miles from where I was supposed to be.

So I signed up to take SAT No. 5 at DeWitt Clinton. It was only after the test that I learned more about the school's rich history as well as its current dysfunction. In decades past, DeWitt's graduates included photographer Richard Avedon, writer James Baldwin, actor Burt Lancaster, fashion designer Ralph Lauren, U.S. congressman Charles Rangel, movie director Gary Marshall, and Pulitzer Prize–winning playwright Neil Simon. But by 2011 the school's story line had changed. Searching the *Times* for recent news of DeWitt, I found a 2005 story on student reaction to the installation of metal detectors inside the front doors. Fifteen hundred students had cut classes to demonstrate in protest. More recently, the school had earned a series of F's from the New York City Department of Education, putting it in the bottom 4 percent of the city's high schools.

I didn't know any of this on the morning of October 1, 2011, when I arrived to take the test. I had made a plan to meet Akil Bello, founder of a test-prep company called Bell Curves, in front of the school. Akil had been planning to take the test that day, too, so we decided to make an outing of it. Before test day I'd met him only once, but we'd been friends on Twitter ever since I had witnessed an exchange he'd had with Kaplan just before the May SAT and decided he was my kind of test-prep guy.

Kaplan had been doling out misleading advice over Twitter, and Akil was not about to let that slide. The advice read:

> *"Relatively prime" numbers are integers with no common*
> *factor other than 1. Ex. 35 & 54 are relatively prime.*

A few of the other test-prep folks retweeted the tip. The problem was that while the tweet was true, it wasn't a tip. Relatively prime numbers aren't tested on the SAT or the ACT.

Akil let it slide the first time around, or maybe he didn't catch it. But when Kaplan sent out the same tweet again, this time as an "ACT tip," Akil called them on it:

> *@kaplansatact Has the ACT ever tested the definition of*
> *relatively prime?*

I assumed some hapless intern was behind the tweet and unaware of the minor ruckus he was creating. Surprisingly, though, Kaplan responded:

> *@akilbello No, that's not tested on the ACT!*

To which Akil responded:

> *@Kaplansatact So why do you keep tweeting it?*

Awkward silence over Twitter.

Akil is funny and smart, and he's even funnier in person when he's not limited to 140 characters. He's been doing test prep for a very long time, so you do not want to mess with Akil when it comes to tweeting tips.

Akil graduated from a high school in the Virgin Islands in 1989 with a 510 in verbal and a 470 in math (590 and 500 in today's scores) and began his test-prep career in 1990 with a proctoring job for The Princeton Review. By 1992 they'd trained him to teach the SAT. (He graduated from the Pratt Institute with a degree in architecture in 1995.)

Ten years later, Akil had taught hundreds of students and answered thousands of SAT questions, and was by that point regularly scoring in the 99th percentile on the SAT himself. His November 2002 SAT scores were 800 verbal and 740 math. In 2003, he founded a test-prep company he called Bell Curves with his brother and father—the latter an educator with over four decades of experience, including positions as a junior high school teacher, a vice principal, a deputy commissioner of a district, and a college professor. Their mission: to help students from disadvantaged and underserved communities overcome barriers to education.

"We teach them what they need to know," Akil told me, and I believed him. He is a man who knows his purpose in life.

We're Not in Kansas Anymore

The morning of the test, I left my house at seven o'clock and drove twenty minutes in the rain to DeWitt Clinton High School in the Bronx. I'd planned to park my car in the school's parking lot, which I'd scoped out during the week in an effort to avoid all potential glitches on test morning. But when I pulled up to the school that Saturday, I found the lot closed off behind a chain-link fence topped with a coiled strand of barbed wire.

I've never seen barbed wire in Dobbs Ferry.

I parked around the corner and went in search of Akil.

He was easy to spot, and not because he was nearly a quarter century older than everyone else standing outside the school waiting to be admitted. Akil is the youngest-looking forty-year-old I've ever seen, lean and lanky, and was wearing a hoodie that morning and carrying a backpack just like the kids, as though he'd been laminated at the age of sixteen.

There was just one telltale sign that he wasn't a student: he was waving at me and smiling broadly. No one waiting to take the SAT smiles like that—no student who feels like his or her life chances are about to be determined by the next four hours, that is.

"Good morning," Akil greeted me, speaking with gusto. He was enjoying himself. "I bought you some coffee and a doughnut."

A doughnut? I hadn't had a doughnut for breakfast in years, having swapped pastries for the kind of fare people my age are supposed to eat, like fruit, nuts, and almond milk. I pulled the sugary lump of dough from the bag and took a bite. It was so sinfully sweet it made my teeth hurt.

I was starting to smile broadly myself.

We were waiting together in line, chatting over our sticky doughnuts, when a few of Akil's students spotted him. They gave us friendly hellos in plain sight of their friends, not the *"We don't say hi to grown-ups"* snub I'd encountered in Westchester.

Maybe they didn't realize Akil was a grown-up.

Say No 2 Knives

The doors opened at 8:00 a.m. sharp, and the crowd began to file in, moving at a crawl. As I got closer to the doors I could see the holdup: the metal detectors whose installation students had protested six years before. Everyone had to be inspected as if we were boarding an airplane, except our final destination was a four-hour-long high-stakes standardized test. As I waited my turn, I read the posters on the walls: "Use Your No. 2 Pencil Wisely on Test Day," said one. "SAY NO 2 KNIVES," read another. After we passed through the metal detector, our bags were checked by a police officer, and my trusty bottle of seltzer was confiscated.

Once inside, Akil and I followed the crowd to the auditorium, where everyone was instructed to wait while the rest of the testers made it through inspection. We checked our room numbers on our way in and passed by the list for the "Accommodations Room"—which was visibly shorter than the list in Dobbs Ferry, where there were at least five times more kids taking the test with accommodations than I now saw at De-Witt Clinton.

In Dobbs Ferry, I'd accidentally discovered the huge number of students taking the test with accommodations when I stood in the accommodations line, the only line I had seen as I walked inside the door. It was very long.

I had been waiting a good ten minutes when a proctor came by and announced, "Make sure you're in the *right* line. This is the line for accommodations."

"Excuse me?" I asked. "There's *another* line? Besides this one?" It was hard to imagine there were *more* kids waiting someplace else.

The Accommodations (Not the Kind You'll Find at a B & B)

To be eligible for testing accommodations, students must show a physical or mental condition that "substantially influences their ability to participate in College Board tests." For students who document such a condition, a wide array of testing accommodations are available for the SAT, starting with but by no means limited to large print, use of a highlighter, braille, frequent breaks, extended breaks, dictation to a scribe, specified time of day, special furniture, special lighting, screens to block distractions, and visual magnification or auditory amplification.

The simplest way to apply for accommodations is to ask your high school's guidance department to do it for you, which is the norm. If your application is approved, an official letter and SSD (Services for Students with Disabilities) registration code are sent out. If your request is denied, you can appeal.

College admissions officers have no way of knowing whether a student took the test under "non-standard conditions." Prior to 2003, the scores of students who had been given testing accommodations were marked by an asterisk, but the College Board dropped the asterisk in 2003. Since then, the number of students asking for and being granted accommodations has increased substantially.

The enormously long line of students with accommodations in Dobbs Ferry compared to the very short line of students with accommodations in the Bronx made me wonder about the demographics of students taking the test with accommodations.

SAT ACCOMMODATIONS

The process through which students receive SAT testing accommodations can be somewhat complicated if you're handling it yourself. Fortunately, school guidance offices usually make the request and provide the necessary documentation.

- **START EARLY:** The entire process takes approximately five weeks from submission of request to the decision, seven weeks if the College Board requests a documentation review. If you apply for accommodations yourself, without using your guidance department, the College Board requires a documentation review as a matter of course, and the full seven weeks will elapse before you have your answer.

- **EXAMPLES OF TESTING ACCOMMODATIONS:** Extended time, private room, special lighting, large print, a "reader." The College Board's website posts a long (though not exhaustive) list of possible accommodations.

- **STUDENTS WITH EXTENDED TIME** (usually time and a half) complete nine sections of the SAT; the experimental section is not included in their exams. A student who receives extended time cannot leave the test room early.

- **APPROVED ACCOMMODATIONS:** Once the approval has gone through, the accommodation applies to *all* College Board exams, including the PSAT and AP exams, the SAT subject tests, and the SAT.

- **IF YOU PLAN TO MAKE THE REQUEST YOURSELF:** Start by finding and downloading the two-page Student Eligibility

Form. On the College Board website, find "Services for Students with Disabilities," then click through the various pages until you see a reference to "students who want to request accommodations without the assistance of their school." That page will include a link to the form. (In my experience, College Board URLs seemed to change rather often, but the pages on accommodations are easy to find.) **REMEMBER:** Documentation review is required of all students (and parents) making their own requests, and the DIY process takes seven weeks from submission of application to College Board decision.

Extended time—usually time and a half—is the most common testing accommodation students receive. More rarely, double time is given, in which case the SAT is administered over two days.

The extended-time accommodation sounded like a great idea (I'm speaking as a person who scored significantly higher in the privacy of my home without the pressure of time), until I realized it meant having to sit through a longer test. I'm not sure I could have focused any longer, given how wrung out I typically felt after the regular-length test.

HOW DOES EXTENDED TIME AFFECT SCORES?

Studies showed that extended time increased scores for *both* learning disabled *and* nondisabled students.

- Medium- and high-ability students (both with and without learning disabilities) were helped most by extended time.
- Math gains due to extended time were greater than verbal gains.
- Female scores improved more than male scores did.

Don't Mess with Me

Akil and I followed the crowd of students up and down the halls until we found our testing rooms. My room was run-down, with tattered shades on the windows and walls that needed paint. I felt at home as soon as I walked through the door and spotted an overhead projector—the same kind we had when I was in school, back in the day. All the classrooms in my town's public schools have SmartBoards now.

Catherine wrote a blog post on *Kitchen Table Math* explaining the "SmartBoard equity" in our district. Apparently those were the actual words the administrators and then–school board members used. *Smart-Board equity.* There were kids in classrooms with SmartBoards, and there were *other* kids in *other* classrooms *without* SmartBoards. Not fair!

Hence: SmartBoard equity.

What really stood out about my testing experience in the Bronx: the kids at DeWitt Clinton High School were quiet as little church mice, and deferential too. I didn't hear a single wisecrack anytime during the test (a first), and after the proctor took us through the directions, which went quickly without all the adolescent quips interrupting the spiel, we went straight to work. I didn't talk to any of the students that day or any other day, so I don't know how they were feeling about the test. But they seemed serious and focused in a way that the test takers in my neighborhood didn't, at least on the outside.

I wasn't my normal Debbie self that day, either. A different Debbie showed up to take SAT No. 5: *Confident Debbie.*

Normal Debbie lingers over questions and second-guesses herself, changing right answers to wrong ones.

Confident Debbie took the October test all in first serves. I answered every question and never looked back. I was *aggressive*, which is not me at all; and I ran like the wind. *It felt so good.*

After the test, I met Akil in front of the school, in the same spot where we'd met hours earlier. Time felt compressed, as if those four hours had occurred in time-lapse photography. I walked out of SAT No. 5 with a bounce in my step, buoyant, like those boys who'd skipped by me after my first test, bantering about how easy the test was, while I hobbled, bleary-eyed and delirious, trying to find my car keys.

"How'd it go?" Akil asked when he saw me.

I inhaled a nice deep breath and said: "Akil, I took that test like a man. I was all gut. SAT No. 5 will be a test of how good my gut is."

Akil was noncommittal. Up to this point, we'd been mostly Twitter friends, so he didn't have much to go on.

PWN, on the other hand, does know *Normal Debbie*, and when Akil and I met him for a bowl of spaghetti at a nearby restaurant after the test, he looked concerned.

"Well," he said, tentatively, "we'll just have to wait and see how that approach worked out for you."

That was it—that was *all* I could get out of him. Not a single tea-leaf prediction, no Magic 8-Ball message, not so much as a whiff of the clairvoyance I was looking for. PWN refused to play the "How do you think I did?" game. He was like a doctor who doesn't speculate before all the tests come back. So frustrating.

I think *First-Serve Debbie* made him nervous.

Late that afternoon, we said our good-byes and I drove home still feeling great. I was on such a high from that test, it was all I could do to pry myself from the forums on College Confidential, which were hopping for weeks with speculation over this and that answer. Catherine and Chris had also taken the test that day and were only too happy to waste hours with me discussing the minutiae of a test gone by.

"Was the answer to the Bob Fleece question 'eccentric'?" (Catherine said "eccentric," though she thought it was possible she and the College Board might not see eye to eye on that one. As it turned out, the College Board also thought Bob Fleece was eccentric.)

"What about the tone in those dual passages about nuclear power . . . was it disparaging?"

"Was the Walden passage human or scientific?"

"I got a Disney passage. Did you? Was that the experimental section?"

"The overlapping circles problem—what was the central angle of the smaller arc?"

And on and on. I *should* have been studying. If I had taken even a moment to glance at my calendar, I would have realized there was no time to relax. The next SAT was scheduled for November 5, and I should have been mapping out and executing a strategy to improve, not obsessing over answers from the last test.

Now We're Talkin'

October 20, 2011, was my favorite day of my lucky year.

It was the day my scores came back for SAT No. 5, and while I did not get the 2400 I had set out to achieve, I did get a perfect score on the writing section. That was enough to overshadow everything else for the entire week.

			OCTOBER SCORES		
	Jan. 22	Mar. 12	May 7	June 4	Oct. 1
CRITICAL READING	680	690	690	720	740
MATH	510	530	530	570	560
WRITING	610	690	700	680	**800**
ESSAY	9	9	10	9	10

My 800 on the writing section came with a 10 on my essay, so, yes, it really *is* possible to achieve a perfect score on writing with a 10 on the essay as long as you make no mistakes on the multiple-choice questions. In fact, I've heard of some SATs on which it was possible to score an 800 with a 9 on the essay, though it depends on the curve of the test that month.

I still wanted a 12 on the essay, but for that week a 10 was just fine.

A 740 on the critical reading section put me in the 98th percentile, which felt good. The test had included dual passages on nuclear power that killed my chances for a perfect reading score that day. Other than the questions about those passages, I only made one critical reading error on the whole test. Catherine got a perfect reading score that day.

And the math—my beloved nemesis! I scored 560, 10 points lower than my previous score four months before, in June. I could hardly believe it. A statistician would say 560 and 570 are essentially the same score, that I was in my range. But I was incredulous. After all that Kumon and Cogmed, the question writing and the hours and hours of practice—not to mention my love and devotion to improving my performance in math—I felt betrayed.

A 560 made no sense whatsoever. It even occurred to me that perhaps there'd been a scoring error in my math section.

Stranger things have happened.

Scoring Snafus

After the October 2005 SAT, four thousand tests (1 percent of the total) were scored incorrectly, a mistake discovered when two students asked that their scores be reexamined. News of the blunder unfolded for months, each announcement from the College Board revealing more scoring errors—some as high as 400 points—until finally a $3 million class-action lawsuit was filed.

Imagine being one of the students whose tests were underscored by 400 points. Or one of the group who learned they'd been robbed of 200 SAT points *after* they'd received their college rejection letters.

Imagine coming out of the SAT thinking you've scored in the 2000 range just like you did on all those practice tests, only to have the report come back with a 1700. Then you learn, months later, that there has been a "scanning machine error" and that your test was affected—by 200 points. Oh boy, I'd be mad.

The colleges all claimed they'd done their best to reconsider applicants who had been affected by the scoring glitch, but I would have found that cold comfort if it had happened to one of my children.

So what do you do if you believe there's been a scoring error on your test?

You do what my friend Akil did after the test we took together. Akil has been teaching the SAT for decades, coaching hundreds of students, analyzing thousands of questions, reviewing, training, proctoring—this is a man with serious standardized test experience. He takes the test numerous times each and every year, so *he knows*. When he saw his October scores—800 on math, 720 on writing, and 730 on critical reading—he wasn't doing the same happy dance I was. He was scratching his head over his critical reading score, especially after he received his score report and saw that he'd gotten two "easy" questions wrong. Akil never gets easy questions wrong.

There was just no way.

Now *my* math score, which, personally, I found hard to believe . . . there was a way. My skepticism was more along the lines of "Hmmm, maybe they scored my test wrong." Wishful disbelief.

Akil's disbelief had nothing to do with hoping against hope. When he saw he'd gotten two easy questions wrong, he was sure he'd been robbed—or perhaps he'd misbubbled—but whatever it was, he wanted to know. So he did what you're supposed to do if you believe there's been a mistake. He asked the College Board to hand-score his test.

The College Board will hand-score an SAT for an extra fifty-five dollars (plus another fifty-five dollars to hand-score the essay, which means only that someone rereads the two essay *scores*, not the essay itself). If an error is found on their end, the fee is refunded. The service can be requested for up to five months after the testing date and takes five weeks to complete. The new score, if there is one, replaces the old score, so it's possible for a score to decrease as well as increase.

Akil was certain there'd been a mistake, so he forked over the money to have his score verified by hand. It turned out he was right, though he'll never know exactly how right because the College Board's response was cryptic. Five weeks after his request, he received a letter:

> *Re: Score Change*
>
> *Dear Akil,*   .
>
> *After making adjustments with the scoring key, our hand-scoring specialists confirmed that you misplaced responses in the critical reading section of the test. As a result of hand scoring your critical reading score increased.*

And then they added 10 points to his critical reading score—boosting it from a 730 to a 740.

Excuse me?

That's not a fifty-five-dollar explanation. The letter refers to "misplaced responses," which implies that more than one response was misplaced. But 10 extra points is only one question on most tests. What happened to the other points? And which questions were misbubbled?

There was no closure as far as I was concerned, but Akil was ready to move on.

SAT Allies

By early fall, Ethan was finally ready to begin focusing on the test (the PSAT was coming up in October), and I had passed the halfway mark of the project. I was still far from the expert I had hoped I'd be by that point, but I had my bearings.

We started out doing sections together during the month of September, and I must tell you—we had *a lot* of fun, not that Ethan would ever admit that. But we did. Ethan would teach me the math problems, and I loved torturing him with vocabulary. He'd use our everyday life scenarios to write mock SAT questions, and I even received a few apology notes after bad behavior, written in "SAT words," which of course warmed my SAT heart.

Dear Mom,

I am extremely <u>remorseful</u> for the past few days. I will try harder to achieve the <u>amiable</u> qualities that you want me to have. I don't want to <u>antagonize</u> you and make you <u>hostile</u>. I have been <u>cantankerous</u> lately and only want you to think of me with <u>laudable</u> qualities.

Love,
Ethan

Those notes are now safely stored in Ethan's treasure chest, along with his first tooth and his baby footprint from the hospital on the day he was born.

He took the PSAT eleven days after my October test. I spent much of the night before trying to make sure his bag was well stocked, which annoyed Ethan and probably didn't do much to soothe my nerves, either, truth be told.

"I don't need a fresh pencil for every section," he said.

I didn't care—*what did he know?* I'd sharpened the whole box of Dixon No. 2's—my favorites—and he was taking them whether he liked it or not.

"It helps to have lots of sharp pencils," I said. "I know what I'm talking about."

I picked him up from the train station after the test, which he'd taken at his school, just a few blocks down the street from DeWitt Clinton High. "How'd it go?!" I asked, unable to contain myself. I wanted to hear every detail and he hadn't even closed the car door yet. "Did you like it?" . . . "How many kids were in the room with you?" . . . "Did you eat the chocolate I packed?" . . . "What kind of desk did you have?" . . . "What was the proctor like?"

I peppered him with questions about the test the entire ride home.

"I'm pretty sure I got everything on the first math section right," he said earnestly. "The second math section I may have gotten two or three wrong."

"Good . . . good . . . keep going," I said. "I want *all* the details."

"There were one or two vocab words I didn't know," he continued, "but most were the ones we studied." He sounded confident, which, at the time, I thought was an excellent sign. Ethan and I were going to have to learn the hard way that feeling like you know something is not the same thing as actually knowing it. (It was only after I'd taken all seven SATs that I discovered the literature on metacognition and "judgment of learning.")

And you know, he humored me that whole ride home, recounting the minutiae in vivid detail, just the way I like it. I'm pretty sure I picked up a trace of joy in his voice, too, though he'd never admit that to a soul. To this day, the best I can get out of him is, "It was less bad than it would have been if you hadn't done it with me."

It would be a few months before we received his scores—which, when they arrived, turned out to provide exactly the motivation Ethan needed to set his own goal. His goal for himself wasn't *my* goal for him (at first), but that turned out to be for the best. I learned later, talking to the founder of Advantage Testing, that it's important for the student to choose the goal. When students aren't motivated, it's usually because the objective has been set by parents rather than themselves.

It's true he didn't love the test the way I did. But he didn't hate it the way his friends did, either. Good enough.

The real magic of the project, though I didn't know it at the time, was that what *I* thought about the SAT became more important to Ethan than what his friends thought. I embedded myself in my teenage son's life at the very moment when those forces of nature—*the peers*—are most powerful, and most dangerous.

When your children are little, they listen to you. Then, when they become teenagers, they stop. A lot of them stop, at any rate, my kids included. I knew parents whose teenage kids still listened to them, but I didn't know what those families were doing differently. Today, I sometimes think my SAT project, as over the top as it looked from the outside, was a kind of remedial parenting—*intensive* remedial parenting. My kids and I had a lot of ground to make up and not much time to do it.

Of course, this wasn't what I was supposed to be doing, according to the books (and according to most of the people I knew). It's normal for teens to "separate" and "individuate" during high school, everyone knows that! Friends are supposed to assume an ever-larger role in the adolescent's life, and parents are supposed to fade. That's *normal*.

But what if normal is wrong?

What if normal isn't normal at all?

Before World War II, teenagers didn't exist. There were teenage people, obviously, but no teenagers in the sense of adolescent children with their own "youth culture," separate from the culture of their parents. Teenage children lived in a world dominated by adults, not by other teens.

That older world, I now see, never really went away for the people I knew whose teenage children still listened to them. In those families, the adults were more important than the friends.

Knowing what I know now, I think it's a *terrible* idea to let your child's friends become more important than you. Adolescents are out of their minds! They're impulsive, they make terrible decisions, and they think they're going to live forever, which leads to lots more terrible decisions. Plus they're addicted to their cell phones. Teenagers should not be running anything, least of all each other's lives.

This is why God invented parents.

So while many of Ethan's peers were busy separating, he was sitting next to me at the kitchen table—explaining functions to his math-challenged mama, arguing over the virtues of studying vocabulary, and learning how to spot a dangling modifier. We spent hours upon hours discussing all the trimmings that are part and parcel of the SAT experience, and in the process I reclaimed my authority over my son's values, at least where school was concerned.

For the last two years of high school, Ethan grew steadily more serious about his studies, and about college. He was no longer the boy who would obligingly tell a school psychologist he was happy getting B's he hadn't worked for.

And by the end, I was no longer the besieged parent I had been just two years before. My children had come back.

19

A STANDARDIZED EXPERIENCE

Derailment Is a Symptom?

Thursday, October 20: learned of perfect writing score. *Best. Day. Ever.*

The very *next* day, everything fell apart.

I discovered my bank accounts had had a security breach and I would have to close down the accounts and change all of my passwords. The ripple effect seemed to touch every aspect of my existence. The next three weeks—the weeks leading up to my sixth, and next to last, SAT—were a frenzy of thwarting bounced checks, fallout from missed appointments (somehow, my calendar disappeared in the password switch), sick children who needed picking up from school and tending to, migraine headaches, and school buses that failed to show without so much as a call to warn me. The havoc that followed my perfect writing score was epic.

Over the course of those weeks I developed a whole new phobia: fear of interruptions. Every time I sat down to study, the phone would ring or the doorbell would buzz, and it was always some catastrophe that needed my prompt attention.

It felt biblical, like the plagues.

I'm an optimist by nature (more than I should be, at times), but those few weeks put my positive nature to the test. I tried everything I could think of to keep seeing the glass as half full—but it was starting to look pretty empty. I wrote positive messages on index cards and tacked them all around the house to remind myself how to get back to my beautiful life:

"Practice Staying Strong (*Never* Fall Apart)" was posted above my desk.

"I Can Choose My Thoughts" was taped to the fridge.

"When You Think About Others, Think Love" was posted on the bathroom mirror.

The signs helped, a little.

But there came a day—a morning my daughter's school bus didn't show because of a torrential downpour and I had to drive her to school myself—when I arrived home, feeling shaky, and made an executive decision: it was time for my problems to hit the back burner. I had just over one week left until my next SAT, and I'd done nary a thing to prepare.

I unplugged the phones, locked the doors, pulled down the shades, and went down to my office, where I hoped to finally isolate myself in peace and quiet. Before shutting off the Internet, I decided to scan my e-mails, just to be 100 percent sure there wasn't an obstacle that couldn't wait a few hours.

As I scrolled through my unread messages, I noticed a subject line that offered help with math. The e-mail was from a tutor whom I'd never met. People—and by people, I mean complete strangers—had been so generous with their offers to help me improve my score that I got excited and clicked it open to see what she had to say.

But this message was not nice, as the other e-mails had been. This was a drive-by attack, via e-mail, by a total stranger.

> *You need to choose whether you want to admit that you are*
> *ignorant about math and did not receive a proper education*
> *or whether you are simply stupid. You seem to be choosing*
> *willfully stupid, which is too bad.*

The tutor went on for a good long page, maybe two, berating me with her "advice," and finished by saying she was available to help as long as I didn't share her name.

I didn't even know who this person was; for all I knew, this alleged tutor wasn't even a tutor. She sounded like an Internet troll. It didn't matter, though, because the e-mail had arrived at the wrong time. I cried and cried and cried, all day long—weeks' worth of pent-up tears of exasperation and frustration from all the derailments—all unleashed by the unkind words of a person I'd never met.

Months later, after everything was said and done, I received a book in the mail from another complete stranger. It was titled *Test Success!: How to Be Calm, Confident and Focused on Any Test,* and in it the author, Dr. Ben Bernstein, lists the signs of test anxiety and offers remedies for improving test performance. I flipped through the book and was struck by what I read: Dr. Bernstein lists problems that were the same as mine under the heading "Excuses, Laments, Protests—and an Antidote."

The idea that my problems might be *symptoms* had never occurred to me. Was it possible that all the alarms and derailments I was experiencing were actually a form of test anxiety?

I'd always thought of test anxiety as mental: as negative thoughts, or feelings of panic, or lack of confidence . . . none of which afflicted me, I thought. In fact, my frame of mind was the opposite of test anxiety, or so it seemed to me. I was confident and self-assured, and I was certain that if I could just find a little peace and quiet, I'd ace the test once and for all and I could call it a day, knowing I'd accomplished my goal, which was to teach my son a lesson about what a little hard work and some determination can achieve. I had a case of "the problems," not test anxiety.

But to do well on high-stakes tests, Dr. Bernstein writes, one must *cultivate* the ability to focus—despite problems.

STRESS AND PERFORMANCE

When stress is either too high or too low, performance suffers. Think *Goldilocks*: you need a little bit of stress to be energized and alert, but not too much. Athletes know that the perfect amount of stress will take you into "the zone," where you need to be to achieve maximum performance.

Among the signs of performance anxiety that Dr. Bernstein lists:

- You're calm *during* the test, but distracted while *preparing* for the test.
- You're preoccupied with nonessential tasks (e-mail, phone calls, lunch, bills, exercise).
- You engage in a flurry of multitasking.
- You second-guess yourself after the test.
- You display poor self-assessment skills.
- You experience disorganized thinking.

I displayed all of those signs, and more. What I did *not* have was any awareness they were signs of anything deeper than a spate of bad luck.

On the morning of November 5, I arrived for my sixth SAT feeling relaxed—not a good sign. Dr. Bernstein would say I was experiencing "disconnection," which he describes as a form of performance anxiety. Some of us react to fear by disconnecting from the experience, like a phone line that's been cut off.

If I'd known to be on the lookout for these camouflaged symptoms, I would have been only too willing to employ the remedies Dr. Bernstein recommends. "Cultivating awareness" and "taking deep, steady breaths" are right up my alley. I'm a good little yogi. I meditate. I seek enlightenment. If you tell me you'll surround me with "white light" for protection—I might believe you.

Dr. Bernstein advises "grounding yourself" by placing both feet on the floor and consciously feeling the ground beneath your feet. He suggests uncrossing your arms and legs and making sure you aren't slumping or flinching (I'm a flincher), writing the word "breathe" on top of your test—simple, noninvasive exercises to try.

Location, Location, Location

For the love of God, who *were* those kids taking the SAT in November? I wasn't the only one who strolled in that day with a laissez-faire attitude. *Everyone* at the test seemed nonchalant to the point of oblivion, even the proctors, who were downright blasé.

For that sixth test, I had returned to the private school where I'd taken my first SAT ten months before. I'd had to abandon the "different location for each test" plan because when I tried to sign up four weeks before the November test, every other test location in my vicinity was booked. Unbeknownst to me, November is a very popular month for the SAT. October is the most popular, followed in order by June, November, May, December, March, and finally January.

When I realized it might be possible to get shut out altogether, I went ahead and signed up for a seat for the December SAT too, at the public school in Dobbs Ferry (same venue as SAT No. 2). I figured I could always switch locations if it turned out I had time to search for other test sites.

In hindsight, that was a bad move.

Test location is worth taking the time to consider, and had I spent time contemplating this variable, it might have occurred to me that the Masters School was not a location I wanted to revisit. At Masters, the test is administered in a gymnasium lined with rows of pork-chop desks (those classic wood chairs with a pork chop–shaped arm attached).

The Masters School is located on beautiful grounds, and testing in a location just a mile away from my house was a plus, but beautiful grounds and proximity don't even come close to compensating for taking the test inside a loud, echoey room on a desk that's way too small.

That morning, the crowd seemed different, and not only because of their nonchalance. They looked young to me, for starters. I got my first inkling of what was different when I heard foreign-language students discussing CD players with one of the proctors. There was confusion as to whether the test center was supposed to provide CD players for the listening portion of the SAT II language subject tests or whether that responsibility fell to the student. (CD players are the student's responsibility.)

"Don't worry," the proctor told a young-looking boy who'd shown up without his CD player. "Take it next year, or the year after." I was right—these students were young. The boy must have been a student at the school because the proctor knew what grade he was in. "You have plenty of time," he assured the kid. "Take a different subject test today." (On the SAT II subjects, students can choose on test day which subjects they want to be tested on. A student can take from one to three different subject tests per sitting.)

The boy looked unfazed.

My next clue came when I walked into the gym and saw that the room had been divided in half instead of into three sections, as it had been the last time. At this November test, half of the gym was cordoned off for SAT II subject testers. I don't remember even noticing the SAT subject testers before that day. Later I learned that the popularity of the November SAT is due in part to the subject testers. November is the only month all year when the listening portion of the language test is offered.

The other half of the gym was allocated for the rest of us.

As soon as I saw the little armchair desks lined up in tidy rows, my heart sank because I remembered: although they meet SAT guidelines for desk size (twelve by fifteen inches) pork-chop desks are way too small. Having to shuffle pencils, eraser, calculator, test booklet, and answer sheet from desk to lap to floor and back is not only discombobulating, it wastes essential time you need to answer the questions. Especially on the math sections, you don't have one second to spare. So take your test at a regular desk inside a proper classroom if you possibly can.

CLUNK . . . *clunk* . . . *clunk* . . . *clunk* . . . As soon as I heard that first clunk of a calculator hitting the gym floor, it all came right back— the echoes in the gym when stuff falls off the desks.

TEST CENTER VARIABLES

Although the SAT is a standardized test, test locations are not uniform. Some schools give the test in a quiet classroom with a single proctor while others use the school gym (which echoes) or a cafeteria (also noisy). Test location details such as desk size and room type can make a big difference in the experience and in your score.

Official Test Center Rules:

- Desks must have a minimum writing surface of twelve by fifteen inches.
- Desks are to be a minimum of four feet apart in every direction.
- A working clock must be visible.
- Staff must possess unquestionable integrity and sound judgment.
- Test rooms should be away from noisy and distracting activities.

Test Center Suggestions (Based on Experience):

- Desks should be *larger* than twelve by fifteen inches for optimal performance.
- Tests should be taken in classrooms, which have fewer distractions than gyms and cafeterias.
- Choose a front-row seat to minimize visual distractions.
- A wristwatch is essential. Don't assume the proctor will keep time properly. Practice giving yourself your own five-minute warnings.
- *Expect* distractions.

That day, I purposely chose a seat in the front of the gym, as opposed to the last time I tested there, when I ended up in the middle, not wanting to call attention to myself. After the test, I learned that students taking the SAT aren't supposed to choose their own seats. Allowing students to sit where they please is a violation of protocol serious enough to warrant invalidation of test scores.

Six months after SAT No. 6, ETS actually did cancel the scores of 199 students who'd taken the May 2012 SAT at Packer Collegiate Institute in Brooklyn, New York. Among the violations cited were "students who were able to sit where they wanted." Other violations included "proctors who left the exam booklets unattended, desks that were seated too closely together, and proctors who were inattentive."

To make matters worse, while other seniors were focused on graduation ceremonies and parties, the teenagers affected by the rule-breaking proctors at Packer Collegiate had their makeup test abruptly canceled the night before it was scheduled due to "logistical problems."

The Proctor Effect

The best proctors are probably the ones you don't remember. I remember the proctor from my sixth SAT *vividly*.

The problems started with the essay, Section 1. The proctor read the instructions from the script, just like all the other proctors, though his rendition was lackluster. Then, just as we were about to begin writing, he went off script.

Proctors never go off script during the SAT. The SAT is a *standardized* test; test-taking conditions are supposed to be the same across testing centers.

The proctor told us he couldn't find chalk to write the end time on the board in the front of the gym, so we should use the clock on the wall. Then he pointed out the clock: high up behind the basketball net. I crouched down and cocked my head, staring up in the direction the proctor was pointing, and sure enough there *was* a clock up there, though I could barely see it because it was covered by a protective metal grating.

I had a watch with me, of course, but I'd never had to use it during a test, and it wasn't just a watch, it was a *Mission: Impossible*–style gizmo, an atomic watch my father had given Ethan when he was ten. It had doodads and dials, stuff ten-year-old boys like: a compass, a calendar, an alarm clock, a stopwatch. I should have read the instruction pamphlet before taking it to the test—or, better yet, bought a simpler watch. Regrettably, I did neither. I'd grown complacent because my first five proctors had kept the time perfectly, as they are supposed to do.

After pointing out the barely visible clock, the proctor returned to the script and told us to begin writing. The prompt that day asked whether individuals should take responsibility for issues that didn't affect them directly, and I thought *Yes they should!* and then—nothing. I stared at the blank lines in my answer booklet, trying to think of examples of people taking responsibility for something that didn't directly affect them that could be raised to the level of universal principle. And thought, and thought.

Nothing came to mind. My thoughts were a wide-open meadow of nothingness; if I had been meditating, this would have been the perfect zone. Alas, I was not meditating. I was taking my sixth SAT, and time was flying, and not because I was having fun. I tried to focus. *Still* nothing. As I sat there, straining to come up with something—anything—to say, I heard someone reading out loud: *"For those of you who are planning to take an SAT subject test in mathematics . . ."*

It was the proctor again, reading instructions to the SAT II subject testers sitting on the other side of the partition dividing the gym. I could hear him clear as a bell, as though he were standing directly beside my desk reading to me personally and leaning in close to make sure I heard. *I was on the wrong channel.*

I glanced around the gym to see if anyone else was bothered, but my fellow testers seemed oblivious to the racket coming from the other side of the gym. They were writing their essays, not trying to think of their first example—they were focused. I began to feel faint, as though I might have a panic attack—*at age forty-seven, in the middle of an SAT writing section*—so I stopped trying to think and wrote down a sentence in my answer book: "It is essential that individuals take responsibility for issues and problems that do not affect them directly."

It was a start.

I got through the rest of the paragraph in one piece but then, hitting the second paragraph, I drove the bus off the cliff. *I needed more words to fill the lines*—and I didn't have them, and at some point I more or less panicked. I started writing stream of consciousness—something about the inadequacies of American education. Even worse, I was writing the essay as myself, myself being in this case a disgruntled parent who was paying for Catholic high school and had clearly forgotten that her essay graders might be the very same educators about whom she was ranting in response to an SAT prompt about people taking or not taking responsibility.

A few paragraphs later I came to and wondered how much time we had left. There was no telling. I'd forgotten to write down the start time, rendering my atomic chronometer useless, and I had no idea how long I'd been laboring over my essay. I glanced up to the front of the gym, thinking I might catch the proctor's eye and wave him over, and it was then that I noticed a handwritten sign on the chalkboard I hadn't noticed before. The sign read: "6:06 a.m."

Now, why would it say 6:06 a.m.? I thought. *We started the test around 8:30.*

I spent what seemed like a few minutes contemplating this mystery before realizing I'd lost focus (again). All around me the other test takers were still writing, no more fazed by the "6:06 a.m." sign than they'd been by the proctor reading math directions a few minutes before. I seemed to be the only person in the room suffering an attention deficit. I should have been in the distraction-free room, for students taking the test with accommodations.

I managed to pick up where I'd left off, but then abruptly changed topics to pollution. I'd just watched a documentary about a garbage dump, and it was the only thing I could think of to write about besides education.

Finally the words started to flow and I found my groove—for about three minutes, at which point the proctor announced, out of the blue, "Stop work and put your pencil down." No five-minute warning, as I was accustomed to, just "Section's over," and that was that. I was mid-sentence and hadn't even begun to write a conclusion.

Where was my warning?

It turned out that, at SAT No. 6, five-minute warnings were delivered at random, per the proctor's prerogative. One time he gave a seven-minute warning, another time he gave us the two-minute mark. A few times, nothing. I wondered whether the five-minute warnings I'd had at the other tests were a favor doled out by the nice proctors, as opposed to the erratic proctors who couldn't find chalk and gave warnings at random intervals or not at all. (Answer: Five-minute warnings are a requirement, as is having a "visible clock" in the testing room. At least, both were requirements according to the ETS Proctor Manual I found on the Internet. The manual has since been removed.)

I hustled back from the ladies' room during the first break because I wanted to ask the proctor why the sign said "6:06 a.m."

"Hi," I said, a little out of breath from the rush.

"Hello," he said in a friendly but very deep voice. "How are you?" He appeared to remember me from the last time I'd taken the test. He'd been the first proctor to ask why I was there.

"Why does that sign say 6:06?" I asked, pointing to the board and noticing that it now read "6:42 a.m."

"That's Pacific Time," he said, and gestured toward the clock behind the basketball hoop. "It's in *Pacific* Time—I didn't want to confuse anyone."

Confuse anyone?

Why on earth would a proctor supervising a test in New York State think it would be helpful to post California times?

"Take your seats," said the proctor. Our first five-minute break was over.

KEEP YOUR OWN TIME

- Stacey Howe-Lott, the Seattle tutor, instructs students never to rely on proctors to keep time or give five-minute warnings.
- She advises bringing an analog watch to the test.
- Stacey tells her students to reset the minute hand of their watches to twelve at the beginning of each section, which makes time calculations unnecessary during the test. All seven 25-minute sections end at 25 minutes past the hour, and the two 20-minute sections end at 20 past the hour. Because elapsed time is obvious *at a glance*, test takers can devote all of their time and mental energy to answering questions, not figuring out how much time they have left if the proctor has written "8:48" on the board and their watch says "8:33."

The time-zone switch turned out to be just one of many timing flubs the proctor made that day, the most egregious of which I now refer to as "the big time lop." Midway through Section 5—for me, a double passage in the critical reading section—the proctor stood up at the front of the gym and cleared his throat. I'd been carefully monitoring my pace and knew *exactly* where I needed to be and at what point I should begin reading the last passage in the section and answering these questions. I was precisely on schedule, having calculated my progress based on the California end time the proctor had written on the board in the front of the room. (He had located a marker and paper during one of the breaks and posted the time on a sign.) What on earth could he possibly have to say *right that minute* that couldn't wait until the end of the section?

"Uh, excuse me," he said confidently. "That time on the board is wrong. You have five minutes less than that." And with that, he sat back down in his chair and resumed reading his newspaper, leaving us with seven minutes to finish the section rather than the twelve minutes I thought I had.

I was hysterical.

There was no way I had time to read the passage *and* do the questions. *It could not be done.* I panicked for about two seconds, then went directly into fight-or-flight, though I'm not sure which option my brain actually chose—probably *fight*, seeing as how I didn't get up and run out of the room. I found myself skipping the passages completely and racing to the questions, which I read in a gulp, then racing back to the passages, scanning for anything that looked even conceivably like an answer. This was probably the best strategy available to me under the circumstances, but answering critical reading questions without actually *reading* felt dreadful.

At the next break, still furious (and shaken), I approached the proctor again. "Excuse me," I said. "*What happened to our five minutes?*"

The proctor was chatting with one of the kids taking the test. There must have been an edge to my voice, because the boy he was talking to instantly stepped aside. He had that look on his face kids get when Mom is on the warpath and they're pretty sure *they're* not the one who messed up, but on the other hand they'd just as soon not attract undue attention to themselves at the moment.

"What can I do for you?" the proctor said, less chummy than he'd been before. The kid stood nearby, within earshot, listening in as we spoke.

My voice was trembling. "*What happened in that section?*"

"You should have used your watch," the proctor said with an astounding tone of conviction, not to mention a complete and total lack of personal accountability for actually performing his job.

"I did use my watch," I said. "I used *my* watch with *your* end time."

"It was the lesser of two evils," he added, as if this explained everything.

The proctor turned back to the student, who, after shooting me a quick glance, picked up where he'd left off.

CRITICAL READING—*WITHOUT*
READING THE PASSAGE

Warning: Strategy *not* foolproof.

This is a panic-button tactic. Not advisable for everyday use on the SAT.

- Answer line-reference questions first. ("In lines 16–18, the author suggests . . .") Answers will *usually* be in the sentence above or below the line referenced and definitely *somewhere* within the paragraph.
- Extreme language choices are *usually* wrong. Avoid answers that use words such as "all," "only," and "never" and superlatives such as "best" or "most."
- Emotional extremes are often wrong, as are answers that contain negative emotions and use words such as "bitter" or "harsh."
- Bland answer choices are often correct—that is, answers with words that leave wiggle room and are complaint-proof and unobjectionable. Key words include "some," "may," "might," "possibly," "can," "illustrate," and "exemplify."
- Politically correct answers—ones that are sympathetic toward educators, researchers, racial minorities, artists, and writers— are often correct.

Years ago, I'd read an old Malcolm Gladwell article in *The New Yorker* that said SAT critics had "long made a parlor game" of answering SAT reading questions without reading the passage. Until SAT No. 6, I had never attempted this feat and had no interest in doing so. I *wanted* to read the passages, especially after I began to find them interesting, and if I got the answer wrong, I wanted to know why the correct answer was right. So I hadn't given the parlor game much thought.

At one point, the parents at *Kitchen Table Math* debated the issue.

Several felt that if it *was* possible to answer reading questions without reading the passages, that was a bad thing. Catherine thought it was a natural thing—a good reader should be able to spot right answers blind at a rate higher than chance, she said—and a lot of back-and-forth ensued about whether the critical reading section did or did not have an "implied author." Catherine insisted that it did.

After being forced to play a variant of the parlor game for real (I didn't read the passages, but I did look at them while I was answering the questions), I think good readers—readers who pick up on style and voice—can probably choose correct answers at a rate better than chance by looking for tone and style cues in the answer choices. My own percent correct was far above chance: I answered at least half the questions correctly, where I should have gotten only 20 percent right,* guessing randomly. Apparently, eleven months spent answering critical reading questions had etched the fuddy-duddy voice of the SAT into my psyche. (Now that the Blue Book comes bundled with a DVD, students can hear a real person—the narrator, a middle-aged man who looks like he's dressed to attend his Princeton reunion—speaking in *the voice*.)

I took my seat, pondering the proctor's lesser-of-two-evils pronouncement. We still had Sections 7, 8, 9, and 10 to get through, all in a row, without any more breaks. And then my sixth SAT could rest in peace, where it belonged, in the past tense.

But first, things had to get worse before they could get better. As we began Section 7, I was clinging to a ledge; my "attentional apparatus" (as I kept seeing it called in brain books) could not handle *one more thing*. Then, halfway into the section, the SAT II subject testers on the other side of the partition finished their test and began hootin' and hollerin' as if they were watching a basketball game and their team had just won by two points in overtime.

I became completely unglued.

I flapped my arms, trying to get the proctor's attention so he could

---

* I don't know the exact percentage because my score report doesn't show which question the double-passage section began with.

quiet things down, but he was reading his newspaper, oblivious to the hoopla going on just yards away.

Apparently, he had not read the official manual for proctors, which clearly states:

Proctors are to remain vigilant at all times during testing. Do not engage in activities that are not related to testing (such as talking on a cell phone or grading papers).

It was hopeless. The proctor could not be roused, and the room could not be quieted. I looked around to see how my fellow testers were coping with the situation, but no one gave any visible sign of distress or concern.

My previous proctors must have been outliers, because "inattentive proctors" are listed in the official manual as one of the most common student complaints.

Chief Complaints

Apparently, I'd been lucky for my first five SATs. The proctors kept time, the rooms were reasonably quiet, I was given regular five-minute warnings, and the test experiences were unmemorable (which is good).

But by all accounts, my sixth SAT was not unique.

I wrote a blog post about the experience and received dozens of e-mails from students, tutors, and moms wanting to share their botched-SAT stories.

From a tutor:

> *My kids had a proctor preparing her wedding flower ar-*
> *rangements by pouring glass beads into glass bowls and then*
> *arranging flowers—and she didn't keep her eye on the clock.*

From a mom:

> *My son had a terrible proctor, who didn't keep track of the*
> *minutes. This messed up my son on the writing. I'd read*

*your post and told him to bring a watch with him, but you
know teenagers.*

I heard a story about a marching band that practiced right outside the testing room, another about a proctor who, while students were testing, played Angry Birds—*with the sound turned on.* There were multiple stories of proctors giving inaccurate information, including one who told the kids, "Points aren't taken off for wrong answers." In that case, a student in the room corrected the proctor. The worst anecdote as far as I was concerned was about a student vomiting during the test and no one bothering to clean it up until the test was over.

One student noted that it's hypocritical of the College Board to say they encourage the reporting of problems because the College Board also tells students that their scores might be delayed by an investigation. "Who wants to take that risk," he wrote, "especially if the test date is at the end of the year and the student needs the score for applications."

He has a point.

The Office of Testing Integrity

The Educational Testing Service (ETS) is a nonprofit organization that develops and administers various standardized tests, including the SAT. Among the many departments within ETS is an entity called the "Office of Testing Integrity." It was an auditor from this office who reported the seating violation at Packer Collegiate Institute, leading to the cancellation of 199 SAT scores six months after my own proctor fiasco.

The scrutiny of Packer was probably the result of a larger SAT cheating scandal in Great Neck, Long Island, that was unfolding on front pages across the country during the fall of my perfect score project. The Long Island cheating scandal began in late 2010 with the report of a single rule having been broken during test administration. The investigation that followed found several suspicious sets of high SAT/low GPA correlations among the testers. Investigators confirmed the cheating through handwriting analysis, which established that one student had taken multiple

SATs. That student was a nineteen-year-old college freshman named Sam Eshaghoff, who was charged with accepting fees of up to $3,600 from fifteen different students (including one girl) to take the SAT for them. This amount could buy you a score of somewhere between 2170 and 2220, depending on the day. The charges ultimately grew to encompass more schools, more impersonators, more cheaters; the various actors were charged with misdemeanors and felonies; and in the end the College Board announced a new set of "Enhanced Security Measures" for the SAT.

The New *Rules*

On March 27, 2012, the College Board issued a press release announcing a new set of security measures designed to "help keep the tests fair."

The press release began: "The College Board is steadfastly committed to ensuring the validity and security of the SAT ... these enhancements—developed with the input of the Freeh Group International Solutions, LLC—are designed to effectively address the issue of test-taker impersonation without creating unnecessary barriers that might prevent students—particularly those traditionally underrepresented in higher education—from pursuing their college dreams."

It droned on, delivering more high-minded statements about integrity, fair test environments, registration and test-day enhancements, and the like. I labored my way through two pages of assurances and commitments and saw not one word about the proctor problem. All of the new measures were focused on catching the cheaters, none of them on shaping up the proctors.

The *only* item I managed to find on the matter of negligent proctors was a comment on the *New York Times* website. At the end of a story titled "Questions for the SAT's Top Cop," I found a comment from an SAT test center coordinator:

> *As a testing coordinator/supervisor for a college entrance*
> *exam testing center, I am required to train testing "proctors"*
> *on how to check a student's acceptable photo ID against the*

*actual student, admissions ticket and roster. This must be
checked every time the student leaves and reenters the room
(i.e., after breaks). What we are not trained on, however, is
how to determine if an ID is fake.*

Bob Schaeffer, the founder of FairTest, had posted a comment, too:
"SAT test-day security relies on overworked and underpaid proctors and
supervisors who are often swamped by huge numbers of students." In 2011,
the *New York Times* reported that proctors were paid $75 for the day.

2012–2013 SECURITY ENHANCEMENTS

Effective with the 2012–2013 academic year, ETS and the College
Board implemented new security measures that were designed to
maintain a fair testing environment for the three million students
who take the SAT each year. Changes were made to the registration, test-day, and post-test-day process, including the following:

Enhancements:

- Acceptable photo required for admission ticket.
- Walk-in standby testers no longer admitted.
- Test-day changes no longer permitted.
- Test takers subject to additional ID checks throughout test.
- More comprehensive certification statement on the SAT an-
  swer sheet.

It's a Wonderful Life

Creeeeeek . . . thunk.

The Masters School gym door closed behind me. I'd been chewed
up and spit out into the parking lot, finally. The afternoon was crisp and
bright. It was 1:15 p.m.—*Eastern* Standard Time.

"What do you want for lunch?" I asked Ethan when I got home.

He was playing *World of Warcraft* and barely looked up. The novelty of having a mother who was taking seven SATs in one year had worn off.

"Can I have eggs?" he asked.

"Sure," I said. "How many?"

"Six," he said. Ethan had recently become obsessed with CrossFit and the paleo diet, activities I had been striving mightily to enliven with SAT vocabulary words.

"Can I have broccoli too?"

"Sure," I said. "How about an omelet?"

"Great," he said, eyes still not leaving the screen. "Do we have green tea?"

"Yup," I said. "We sure do."

"Thanks, Mom. I love you."

"I love you too, sweetie."

The best part of the project was the fun I was having with Ethan. Mother-son bonding aside, I put to good use every scrap of lowdown I gathered that year when it came time for *my* little cub to take the SAT.

> *Dear Ms. Heffler,*
>
> *My son will be taking the SAT on May 5. His name is Ethan. Will there be full-size desks in there (as opposed to those little deskettes)? And if not, can I please request that he have a full-size desk? Also, the two of us are extremely noise sensitive (I guess, who isn't, right?!)—so if you could make sure the doors stay shut, that would be great. I know that helped me enormously. It's very distracting when you can hear kids in the hall—especially when you've got one of those double reading passages or something! Hope you are well, and many thanks for everything.*
>
> *Best,*
> *Debbie*

Anyone can contact a test center supervisor and ask what kinds of desks and rooms the school uses for the SAT. It's not cheating, and trust me—it's worth knowing before test day.

November Scores

Had this been the real deal for me—had that November SAT been part of my college application—I would have seriously considered canceling my scores, which students can do any day until the first Wednesday after the test. I also thought about reporting the many irregularities, but in the end I decided not to because I didn't want to mess up any seniors who might have taken the test with me that day.

I often wonder if that proctor ever learned the real rule about "overtiming" (giving students too much time to complete a section) after the November 2011 SAT. According to an ETS manual I discovered online, which addresses the matter of overtiming: *Make no adjustment. Note the section affected.*

My scores arrived a few weeks later.

SAT No. 6 was the one and only test that year for which my scores came back better than I expected.

NOVEMBER SCORES						
	Jan. 22	Mar. 12	May 7	June 4	Oct. 1	Nov. 5
CRITICAL READING	680	690	690	720	740	630
MATH	510	530	530	570	560	540
WRITING	610	690	700	680	800	780
ESSAY	9	9	10	9	10	9

As Dr. Ben Bernstein says, faulty self-assessment is often a sign of test anxiety.

20

SAT No. 7: MY BUDDHA

One day you finally knew
what you had to do, and began,
though the voices around you
kept shouting
their bad advice . . .

—MARY OLIVER, "THE JOURNEY"

Patience

I knew *exactly* where I was going.

I'd first heard about them before I started the project, but I resisted for an entire year. It felt over the top, not to mention there was *no way* I could afford it.

SCENE:

Thanksgiving dinner, 2010, two months before my project began. I'm at the home of longtime family friends—coincidentally, the exact same location where way too many hours were squandered thirty years before, when I was a junior in high school. My host (a real-estate mogul) discusses the SAT while topping his guests' champagne flutes.

> HOST (*keeping his voice down*): Call Advantage . . . really . . .
> they're the *best*. (*A pause.*) Why waste time?

ME (*thinking hard*): Right . . .

HOST (*still sotto voce, so as not to be trumpeting his daughter's expensive tutoring and high-end scores*): Patience studied with Advantage and she got a perfect score. *Everyone* uses them. (*He gestures toward his wife, who is chatting with guests across the living room.*)

ME (*looking quizzical*): *Everyone?*

HOST (*to wife, who's now at his side*): Jenny, do you remember that guy's name? The one who tutored Patience for the SAT? You remember—the guy from Advantage. What was his name? Ted something, right?

HOST (*turning back to me*): He tutors *all the kids* at Miss Fine's. Jenny, you still have his number, right?

JENNY (*smiling*): *Yeeessss . . .* I'm sure I've got it *somewhere.* Let me look for it, Debbie. I'll call you, okay? He really was *faaaabulous . . .*

ME (*pause, sip, sip*): That would be *great.*

In my next life I want to come back as Patience and live with *her* parents, in *that* house, and be tutored by Advantage Testing—*the best.* We clinked glasses and wandered into the dining room to seat ourselves at the table, which had been set for twenty the week before. As we carried on discussing the SAT the feast was served, a meal that could have been drawn from the pages of an Edith Wharton novel: *The Age of Innocence . . . and the SAT.*

The next day I bought a Blue Book and charged twenty dollars to my credit card.

TOP-DRAWER TEST PREP

Advantage Testing was founded in 1986 by Arun Alagappan, a Princeton grad with a degree from Harvard Law and a passion for tutoring. The company's approach is systematic, long-term, and rigorous.

- Length of study varies, though Advantage recommends studying for an entire academic year before taking the SAT.
- On average, Advantage students complete forty-five to fifty-five sessions that run fifty to one hundred minutes in length.
- Homework averages twenty minutes per night.
- Advantage does not guarantee score gains, although the *New York Times* calls their results "stunning."

"Have you tried Advantage?"

Invariably, someone would ask that question when I mentioned the project.

"*No*," I'd always say, rolling my eyes. "I have *not* tried Advantage."

Why would people think I had a spare fortune to indulge myself in a service like that? I didn't have that kind of money to spend on Ethan, who was going to need high scores if he had any hope of winning merit aid, let alone on me.

Of course, I had never actually *called* Advantage to find out what they charged. I was too intimidated by the word on the street, which was always delivered in a hushed voice—"A thousand dollars an hour."

If I'd taken the time to substantiate their rates, I would have discovered that the $1,000-an-hour figure is something of an urban legend. Sessions actually range from $95 to almost $800 an hour. Better, but still out of my league.

I'm more the DIY type—scrappy. That jewel on my ring is a fake. I drive an old Subaru, and my jeans come from the sale rack at the Gap. So I spent the twelve months after that Thanksgiving dinner thinking there was *no way* I could ever afford Advantage, especially not with the kind of year I'd had.

Cut to almost exactly one year later, six SATs down the hatch, and two and a half weeks left before my final SAT of the project.

By that point, I would have considered refinancing my home to make *it* happen. After all the fuss I'd made, how could I ever face my little chickadees without a perfect score?

I can hear what you're thinking: "Who left *her* in charge of the money? Look at those math scores."

What can I say—there's nothing like a little humble pie to activate your impulsive side . . .

You're Kidding, Right?

Advantage Testing has not turned anyone away for financial reasons in over twenty-five years.

That's what Arun Alagappan, president of Advantage, told me when I brought up the issue of elitism at our first meeting. Arun founded the company in 1986, after a year spent moonlighting as a tutor while working at a prestigious law firm. He finally left law to follow his true calling: tutoring.

He had tutored his first student, a Greek woman who wanted to learn math, at age seventeen. He'd loved the experience so much that he's been doing it ever since. He tutored all through his undergraduate years at Princeton and his law school years at Harvard "for relaxation."

Arun thinks tutoring is fun. After that first session with the Greek woman he did a happy dance in her garage before leaving because he loved it so much. Decades later, he still sounds giddy when he talks about tutoring.

By the time I called Advantage Testing in November 2011, Arun's company had grown to twenty-two locations, including twenty-one in the United States and one in Paris, France. (Correction: In my next life I'd like to be tutored by Arun—*in Paris*—as Patience.)

It took nearly a year for me to achieve an Advantage-friendly frame of mind, which is when I finally picked up the phone. The very notion of elite tutors preparing elite kids for the SAT is . . . well, it was disheartening.

"What about the middle class?" I asked Arun at our first meeting. "What are *we* supposed to do?"

That's when he told me he'd never turned a student down for financial reasons. In fact, the availability of financial assistance is plainly stated on their website, which explains that it is the company's "explicit goal to enroll motivated students [for example, *me*] regardless of their ability to pay."

Advantage is surprisingly egalitarian. They offer a wide range of financial assistance—including pro bono tutoring for families who qualify. And they have a public charity, the Advantage Testing Foundation, whose mission is to "advance the academic and professional ambitions of students of modest means."

Advantage does, however, decline to work with financially strapped perfect-SAT-score-seeking *mothers* who have less than three weeks to prepare. They're all about long-term prep. When I called to ask, "How much and when can I start?" Janna, the young woman who answered the phone, told me politely, "That's just *not* what we do." I spilled the whole crazy story—my goal, my son, the "math issue," yadda, yadda, yadda. "I don't think we can help," she said, apologetically. "We don't normally take on last-minute cases. There's not enough time to get results."

"But I'll *pay*," I said. "*Please*—I *need* your biggest score raiser." ("Why waste time?" as Patience's father had said.)

Silence.

"Let me see what I can do," she said.

Two days passed before I heard back from her in an e-mail. The news was bad. Janna said they were delighted that I shared their belief that "with hard work and rigorous study, everyone can improve," but the answer was still no.

Damn.

I read on.

Even though Advantage would not be able to tutor me, Janna wrote, the president wanted to meet with me in person to explain his hesitation about taking me on as a client.

Ooh la la! . . . My pinky toe was sticking through the crack of that door.

"I would *love* to speak with Mr. Alagappan," I wrote back exactly one second after reading the offer. "When and where?"

Let It Shine

Arun is a man on a mission. He believes standardized tests can be a powerful tool for learning, but that students must prepare "rigorously and cheerfully." I'm certainly with him on that.

When I arrived at his office a few days later, he was on the phone with a student and asked me to have a seat and wait, which I was delighted to do. I loved listening in as he exuberantly explained a math problem to some student on the other end of the phone line. I used the few extra minutes to strategize how to turn Arun's "no" into a "yes."

It took just over an hour.

Who Are These People?

Arun refused payment because he didn't think my goal of achieving a perfect score with two weeks of tutoring was realistic, and I would likely be unsatisfied with the results. So we agreed that if I wanted to pay something for the service, I could make a donation to any organization whose mission is to improve access to high-quality education. Then he phoned Janna and asked her to schedule time for me with two of the company's tutors.

I saw Arun as a kindred spirit. He had the same positive perspective on the SAT that I did (and do), and while he advised against expecting a higher score in two weeks—even with exposure to the Advantage material and tutors (*I* still believed it was possible)—he did agree with my underlying premise: an SAT score can be improved through sustained hard work.

But here's the catch: you have to be methodical. My original game plan—a method a month—was probably as close to the opposite of methodical as you can get.

Janna put me in touch with my new tutors, and I quickly nestled my way into every unoccupied nook and cranny on their calendars. My first appointment, with John Roberts, was a few days later, thirteen days before the test and four days before Thanksgiving, which was scheduled to take place at the same house, with the same cast of characters, as the year before.

John is regal. He holds a PhD in English literature from New York University and a master's in theological studies from the Harvard Divinity School. He graduated from Oberlin and taught at NYU and, of course, was a National Merit Finalist. John is a leader within Advantage, responsible for mentoring other tutors as well as representing the organization to families. Beyond tutoring, he is the president of the Board of Trustees for LEDA (Leadership Enterprise for a Diverse America), a seven-week summer pro bono program supported generously by the Advantage Testing Foundation. He's a kind of poster child for Advantage: elite, yet egalitarian.

Advantage tutors are all well pedigreed. A quick scan of their bios on the website could make even the most confident and well educated break out in a cold sweat. The write-ups are chock-full of formidable distinctions: summa and magna cum laude degrees from the most prestigious colleges and universities; Phi Beta Kappa honors; prizes; fellowships.

These are the top one-percenters, each tutor carefully chosen from hundreds of applicants. *Crain's New York Business* reported that in 2003, nine hundred people applied for tutoring positions at Advantage Testing and only five were hired. Every Advantage tutor has scored in the top 1 percent on the tests he or she tutors, and to work for Advantage, tutors must be effective motivators—dedicated and energetic. Advantage Testing charges "professional rates" comparable to those of top lawyers and doctors because its tutors are highly credentialed and qualified. Arun told me that the company tries to create as many quality educational opportunities as possible for a broad range of students while simultaneously creating respected professional careers for its tutors.

THE ADVANTAGE TESTING TUTORS

An impressive 98 percent of Advantage Testing students report being "overwhelmingly happy" with their experience. A family quoted in *The Wall Street Journal* characterizes its Advantage experience as somewhere between "spectacular and indescribable."

- Tutoring is a full-time job for Advantage tutors (although some, like one of my tutors, who was an actor, have outside interests).
- Individual rates for tutors depend on student evaluations, score increases, and level of experience.
- Tutors must score in the top 1 percent of any test they will be teaching.
- Tutors primarily consist of high honors graduates from leading colleges and universities. Many hold graduate or professional degrees.
- Tutors are selected out of hundreds of applicants.
- Tutors are trained by directors and senior tutors prior to working with students.

Incidentally, Arun was raised in a middle-class family and was not tutored. He was, however, a very hard worker. If a teacher assigned five math problems, or five vocabulary words, he did ten.

The Journey

My first meeting with John lasted four hours. We met at his office, which is in one of the Advantage Testing locations on the Upper East Side. Advantage has a handful of locations in New York, all within a few blocks of each other, and I was surprised to find that their offices were sort of dumpy. For that kind of money, I was expecting lavish. But no. The furniture was mismatched, and there were stacks of papers and books everywhere; the rooms looked like they'd been decorated by boys who didn't care.

I'm probably as oversensitive to visuals as I am to sounds, and I feel best when my surroundings are homey, or tasteful, or elegant—or basically anything but messy and/or strictly utilitarian. But I had more fun in those unadorned offices than I would have had on a dozen Caribbean vacations with all my favorite friends and family. I came to see dumpy as a good thing in a tutor's office. Like the dumpy you see in some professors' offices.

I wrote Arun as soon as I got home to let him know how much I'd enjoyed that first session:

> *Dear Arun,*
>
> *I'm so exhausted I can hardly string a sentence together, but I wanted to say "WOW!" before the day was over. You're the Martha Stewart of test prep. That was truly an extraordinary experience that I will savor for a very long time.*
>
> *Do you have any idea how much I covet one of those notebooks?*
>
> *I'll be dreaming of prime factorization tonight.*
>
> *All the best and many thanks,*
> *Debbie*

The Method to the Madness

I'd brought along my October SAT test booklet, which had just arrived in the mail, and since John hadn't seen the test yet, he was excited. All the tutors light up when the actual test booklets come out three times a year—it's like Christmas morning for the test-prep industry. He flipped to the last math problem in Section 8: question number sixteen. Always the hardest one in the section. He'd heard about number sixteen from his students and wanted to see it for himself. Apparently it was a twist on a classic SAT problem he'd seen before, though a *devilish* twist, which seemed to impress him. He nodded and smiled, as if to say, "Good one."

Then he said, "I'll be right back" and left the room. When he returned, he handed me a stack of lined loose-leaf paper—heavy-gauge loose leaf, the kind I love, with reinforced holes so it won't tear—and scissors.

Have I mentioned before that I'm really into office supplies? And that "organizing"—scrapbooking, decoupage, Magic Markers, ribbons, rainbow-colored tissue paper, stickers, and generally any sort of arts and crafts activity—is relaxing for me, probably the same way tutoring is for Arun? John was a little formal at the beginning of our first session, but he loosened up about ten minutes in when he broke out his scissors and Scotch tape and saw how excited I got.

John cut the math problem out of my test booklet and pasted it onto a sheet of loose leaf, which he handed to me, saying, "Write this down." And he proceeded to explain the solution while I took dictation.

John told me to start a fresh notebook at home just for my work with Advantage. Apparently that's what all the kids at Advantage Testing do: they make personal SAT notebooks in their own handwriting, with the problems they need to learn taped to the page and the solutions written in their own hand in words that have been dictated by their tutors and explained to them very precisely. In the notebook, problems are organized by category: distance formula, equally spaced lists, exponents, percentages, ratios, Venn diagrams, patterns, combinations and permutations.

Did someone say "notebook"?

How could I not have thought of this myself? I'd gone so far as to make SAT math recipe cards—why had I stopped there? I was Queen of the Notebook—I could have *invented* the notebook if someone else hadn't thought of it first—it made so much sense to organize material this way. My recipe cards required constant shuffling and reordering; a notebook was so fabulously methodical.

I couldn't wait to get home and start mine.

"The kids *love* making these," I asked. "Right?"

"Well," he said, "some of them get into it, but not all."

John was into it, though—that much I knew. You don't keep a stash of heavy-gauge reinforced loose leaf at your fingertips unless you appreciate nice notebooks. "Every student makes one," he told me. "And that becomes the book they study from before the test."

I couldn't wait to show Ethan, though Daisy was really the one who would appreciate it. But it was far too early to be bringing up SAT notebooks with Daisy. She would have snarled and said I was "pressuring" her, or something along those lines.

For the rest of the session John and I went over basic math terms, things I'd learned in grade school and probably hadn't thought about since. "Write this down," John would say for each term, and I did exactly as he told me. "Make three columns, and at the top of the columns write, respectively, 'Term,' 'Definition,' and 'Examples.'"

Then he defined the terms and I wrote down what he said.

Term	Definition	Examples
THROUGH	Including the first and last numbers (same as "inclusive")	The integers from 7 through 9 are 7, 8, and 9. The integers from 7 to 9 inclusive are also 7, 8, and 9.
BETWEEN	Not including the first and last numbers	The integers between 7 and 10 are 8 and 9.
FACTOR	A number that divides into the original number without a remainder. On the SAT, factors are less than or equal to the original number. Algebraic expressions can also be factors.	Examples: 1, 2, 3, and 6 are factors of 6, and $(x + 2)$ and $(x - 4)$ are factors of $x^2 - 2x - 8$. Note: 1 is a factor of every whole number.

Here's the thing about the SAT that I don't think I fully realized until the very end of my project: there is reading in the math section, and math in the reading section. That's what makes the SAT so hard, and so interesting. You *must* learn math vocabulary to do well, and there are reading questions that require math. Imagine you're in the midst of a four-hour exam, and you get hit with something like this:

What is the sum of the least prime number and the greatest
negative even integer?

There's no time on test day to scratch your head and wonder, *What's
the greatest negative even integer?* Or: *Is 1 a prime number?* You have to
fly like the wind, and you can't miss a single word. And this is the *math*
section we're talking about.

THE ADVANTAGE METHOD

Advantage Testing emphasizes the fundamentals, and tutors are
trained to teach the core subjects covered on the SAT in a systematic fashion.

- Students are taught core subjects and test-taking strategies,
  not tricks.
- Course material is based on twenty-five years' worth of officially released tests.
- Emphasis is placed on critical reasoning, content review, and
  efficient methods for problem solving.
- The intent is to deepen understanding of concepts taught in
  school and to teach methods for applying them on the SAT.
- Practice tests are administered on weekends at rented schools,
  using official College Board material. The mock tests are
  timed and proctored to simulate test-day conditions. Advantage students typically complete *fifteen* practice tests before
  ever taking a real one.

As I left John's office, he handed me a packet of juicy-looking math
that was titled "Math Summary Review #1." At first glance it looked
easy. *Piece of cake*, I thought.

Ha!

The problems took tricky to a whole other level. Interestingly, these questions didn't try to mimic the test but, rather, were clearly intended to serve some other purpose, which I soon realized was to expose one's weaknesses—*fast*. I arrived at my second session with John with my tail between my legs and my worksheets covered in question marks.

My other Advantage tutor, also working with me on math, was a man named Michael Kayne. Michael was from a different tribe. Where John was earnest, intense, and passionate, Michael was an entertainer. He had graduated from New York University and attended Oxford University, then performed with the Harlem Globetrotters and onstage at Carnegie Hall, Lincoln Center, Madison Square Garden, and the Rainbow Room. Working with Michael, I had a lot of belly laughs, one of which nearly killed me when I choked on a piece of apple because he had me laughing so hard.

"Write this down," he would say (just like John):

"Samson leaves Namibia traveling at 80 mph. Four hours later, Octavius gives chase along the same route at 100 mph . . ."

"And when Consuela finally returns from her trip to France, what is her average speed, round trip?"

"Debbie has to assemble a basketball team . . ."

"Now Debbie's making a bouquet . . ."

He'd go on and on, spinning stories and regaling me with animated tales of ratios and percents while scribbling numbers on the board.

"Tell me another one!" I'd say. "And use probability this time!"

And he'd launch into some story about koalas and gorillas and leprechauns, always eliciting giggles and pleas for more. It was SAT improv. I bet he's the *best* dad.

Michael didn't seem to have the same zeal for the SAT notebooks that John and I shared. I realized this at our very first session when Michael said, "Write this down" and I looked up, waiting to be handed sheets of heavy-gauge loose leaf. After that first session with John, I'd assumed loose leaf was part of the package.

"Do you have paper?" I asked.

He seemed perplexed that I would have shown up without something to take notes on, but he didn't make a big deal about it—he just left his office in search of something for me to write on.

When he came back and handed me thin yellow sheets of lined paper torn from a legal pad, I didn't have the heart to tell him what was so *wrong* with that. (John would have known.)

As soon as I got home, I copied my notes onto *good* paper and packed a stash of the good stuff for future sessions.

No *Freaking Out*

I spent the better part of the two weeks before my last SAT camped out in the Advantage Testing offices. When John and Michael were busy tutoring students, I'd wait for them in the waiting room, if that's the correct term to describe the space between their offices where I sat.

Between sessions, I made myself at home with the real SAT students. After a few days I felt comfortable enough to buzz people into the building if I heard the bell ring. I can only imagine what those kids were thinking when they'd pass by and see me sprawled out with supplies and my *own* SAT scrapbook.

Who's that lady with the notebook?

On my next to last day, I asked John if we could discuss the essay. I still wanted a 12. He pulled out essays his students had written on the SAT and we played Guess the Score: he read each essay out loud, I graded. I dished out a lot of 9's and 10's, though I rated one essay as "a 7—*tops*." The writer hadn't answered the question *or* written a conclusion.

It turned out every single essay had earned an 11 or a 12 except one, which had received a 10. (I should add that Advantage shows real clients the full range of essays and scores, not just 11's and 12's.)

I was outraged. I'd been writing with integrity and passion, straight from the heart and intelligently (I believed). I thought the 11's and 12's John was reading were terrible. Fake fancy, strewn with arcane examples and ten-dollar words, without soul. And they were winning.

I couldn't write like that even if I'd wanted to. I didn't have it in me.

I didn't even know where to shop for a gown to wear to that ball. In fact, I didn't want to attend that party now that I knew who was there. I wanted a 12 on my own terms: I wanted a 12 for writing with integrity, seriously and well, as myself.

No wonder I went to Bennington. Two nights before my last SAT and I was having an identity crisis. Which did I want more—a perfect score, or to be "myself"?

I arrived the next day for my last session with Advantage tired and worn out. Both my kids had been giving me a hard time in the way only teenagers can when they see an opening. I'd taken my eye off the parenting ball for those last few weeks, devoting my full attention to the SAT, and they'd taken advantage. Now we were embroiled in arguments and recriminations.

When I walked into Michael's office, the first thing he said was "Leave Debbie home tomorrow, okay?" Apparently he'd been briefed by John.

I often had the feeling the Advantage staff shared notes after I left, because they all knew everything I'd said to each of them. Even Kathy, the program consultant assigned to coordinate my program—Kathy knew all the details, too. It was a little 007. Maybe it was part of "the method"; maybe everyone got that amenity at Advantage. In any event, it was a luxury not having to explain everything to everyone all the time.

By early evening I was packing my stuff, getting ready to head home for a good night's sleep before my final test. As I said good-bye to Michael, he suddenly produced one more lesson. "Write this down," he said, slightly more authoritative than usual.

I grabbed a sheet of loose leaf.

"No freaking out," he said. I wrote that down.

"*Nothing* distracts us." I scribbled that down too.

Then he moved on to a line of questioning, as if preparing me for a military operation.

"What happens if the building's on fire?"

I paused.

"You don't *move*," he answered. "You keep working."

He went on: "What if someone throws up?" My eyes must have opened very wide at that one because I *hate* throw-up, and I was inwardly praying this was nothing more than a hypothetical example. *"You keep working,"* he said.

For the next fifteen minutes he dictated the final instructions and I wrote down every word. Then I drove home and did *exactly* as he'd said.

MICHAEL'S FINAL TIPS

Michael Kayne has been a tutor at Advantage Testing since 2003. He tailors last-minute tips for each student. Below are his final tips for *me*.

The Night Before:

- Do not answer the phone.
- Do not look at Facebook or Twitter.
- Do not make videos or blog posts.
- Do not look at a computer.

During the Test:

- Think: Did I answer the question they asked?
- Think: Did I use my calculator?
- Think: There are *no new questions*.

Good Morning, Sun in My Face

I did *exactly* as Michael advised and slept like a baby that night, sound and unworried. I awoke at six o'clock and cooked myself breakfast, even though breakfast is not really my thing. There would be no stone left unturned this time, and I was *leaving Debbie home*. Over a plate of scrambled eggs I paged through my homemade notebook, then—resolute—I left the house for my last test, just a short drive down the street.

I was in the zone.

When I got to the school I didn't speak to a soul. I made no attempt to establish eye contact, nor did I notice whether there were any kids there I knew who were ignoring me. I seated myself in the front row and tried not to move a single muscle that wasn't absolutely necessary to the test. Now that I'd finally found my focus, I was terrified to lose it.

For five straight hours I didn't go to the ladies' room; I didn't eat a snack; I barely breathed. I remember clenching a few times—literally, physically flinching so my mind wouldn't drift. And when I walked out at the end, I can say, from the bottom of my heart, that I'd given it my all. There was nothing left—*that was it.*

The first thing I did was eat a big bowl of spaghetti (by now, a post-test tradition). The next thing I did was write a note to Arun to say thank you.

> *Dear Arun,*
>
> *My last SAT is now behind me. It was a great experience and I feel as though I gave it my all. That feels good. I'm hopeful that the amazing tutelage of Michael and John is reflected in my score. If not, it is no reflection on them. I am surprisingly resistant to doing well on this test, which makes no sense to me, but that's another story for a day when I'm less exhausted.*
>
> *I came out of there feeling stronger than I ever have before, which I hope is a good sign.*
>
> *I'm sure I aced the essay this time (hopefully, the graders will agree with me). I did everything John and Michael said to do and if I don't improve on the math, something's wrong with that test!*
>
> *It will be nothing less than sheer absurdity if my score doesn't finally improve (a great deal, I might add).*
>
> *I'll be in touch when the scores come back. In the meantime, thank you!*
>
> *All the best,*
> *Debbie*

When I woke up the next day, I couldn't move a muscle. Literally, I could not get out of bed. I felt like I had the flu, except I never got the flu. And my present condition was much more painful than any virus I had come down with in the past. My entire body hurt.

The phone rang and I picked up. It was my daughter.

"Hi, sweetie," I said from flat on my back, calves propped on the coffee table in an effort to find a comfortable position.

"I *hate* your SAT project," she said, out of the blue.

I spent the next four months nursing my aching body back to health. I was sure I had Lyme disease or something terrible, but everyone kept saying, "It's stress."

My back hurt constantly. I had never had back problems in my life; now I was never without them. I couldn't sit at my desk and I could read only lying down with my knees up and the book on my stomach. My dad kept telling me to see a chiropractor, and I kept resisting, until I couldn't hold out any longer. Then I saw my chiropractor four times a week for four months.

No one ever knew what struck me, but I think it was all the flinching I did during the last test. I clenched my entire body for more than five hours, then ached for four months after.

Thank goodness the pain is gone now.

There'll Be Days Like This

The final scores arrived on the morning of December 22, 2011.

	Jan. 22	Mar. 12	May 7	June 4	Oct. 1	Nov. 5	Dec. 3
CRITICAL READING	680	690	690	720	740	630	760
MATH	510	530	530	570	560	540	530
WRITING	610	690	700	680	800	780	730
ESSAY	9	9	10	9	10	9	10

I felt like the wind had been knocked out of me.

I was up to my eyeballs in disappointment and shock. How could I have gotten a *10* on the essay? My seventh and final effort had been a home-run essay if I ever saw one. Show me an essay grader who can write better than that in less than twenty-five minutes.

I was bitter.

And my math score—oooofff. I was crestfallen.

The worst part was telling Ethan. He looked at me with I-can't-believe-my-mom-didn't-do-it eyes and said, "*Really?*" I must have had him convinced that I would prevail. Now I had to break it to him that Wonder Woman was just pretend.

But after that moment's look of disbelief, Ethan waved my math scores aside and headed straight for my reading and writing scores, telling me how great they were and conveying firmly the view that his mother's failed attempt to better herself in SAT math said nothing about the success or failure of his mother's perfect-score quest. To Ethan, sweet boy and loyal son, I had done it. Just about.

That *did* make me feel better. Not Ethan's sensible focus on my new and improved superscore, although a 330-point gain on the SAT is very large, especially when you consider that the College Board reports that studies show test prep has minimal impact: on average 5 to 20 points.

What made me feel better was Ethan himself. In all the commotion (the family had other things going on, some of them wrenching), I had missed the fact that Ethan really wasn't a boy anymore. He had become a sensitive young man. Ethan, the boy who had moved out of my house after one too many botched errands in the hot sun and a math test his mom made him take at Kumon, was now a nearly grown son who felt stricken at seeing his mother sad. We had come a long way.

And of course, I was tickled pink to see what a natural-born optimist he was—like his mama. Ethan wasn't *just* trying to buck me up. A part of him seemed actually to believe I had come close. He'd become more me than me.

The consoling e-mails from family and friends helped a lot, too, though I couldn't help feeling like a high school senior who'd just found out she hadn't gotten into her first-choice school. "You can always transfer" . . . "It wasn't meant to be" . . . "There's a *better* school out there for you." All true enough, but the facts of the matter remain the same.

At the end of the day, I received an e-mail from a total stranger that lifted my spirits. It was from a high school senior, who wrote:

> *SAT scores came out today! How did you do? I hope you did well. I know you'll get a good score, and congrats on completing the project! What you did was very inspiring, especially for high school seniors. I just thought that I would let you know that you motivated me to study, and I went from a 1630 (520R 600M 510W) (junior year) to a 2300 (700R 800M 800W) (senior year).*

I turned the corner after reading that note.

The SAT Hand

My visions of PWN came true.

He agreed to work with Ethan (and Chris, too) and he really was an SAT Transformer, just the way I knew he'd be.

Ethan and PWN started working together at my house shortly before Ethan's junior year. Then, in the fall, Ethan would stop off at PWN's apartment in the Bronx once a week on his way home from school. They'd do a little SAT work and then play video games until Ethan left to catch his train.

I could feel the momentum building, little by little. First came the bonding. Ethan loved PWN. All the kids do. Pretty soon I saw the attitude change: from *I'm humoring my mother* to *It's not so bad*, Ethan's new outlook on life.

By October, when Ethan took his junior-year PSAT, I could swear I caught a note of glee in his voice as he recounted the details to me on the car ride home from the train. And by the time his scores came back in mid-December, he'd picked up a full head of steam and now, for the first time, set his own score goal for the SAT—nearly 200 points beyond what his PSAT performance predicted he was likely to achieve.

PWN agreed with Ethan's goal, and the two of them mapped out a strategy, which I embellished with decorative charts and graphs, and implemented with equal parts enthusiasm and colorful office supplies.

Ethan took his first SAT in January, exactly one year after I took my first for the project. He wasn't ready, but he wanted to take it at his school with all his friends, so he did. He scored only 30 points below his goal.

Then, in late February, while taking his first college tour, he really saw the light: *SAT = college*. Suddenly, Ethan wanted to kick it into high gear for himself, not just to mollify his mother, who was pushing and prodding and trying to set an example.

We blocked off every Saturday for full, timed practice tests, which Ethan took at the dining-room table while I worked in my basement office just below. At the five-minute breaks he'd bring down the sections he'd finished, and I would correct them while he worked on the next set.

Occasionally, I'd see patterns to his mistakes and I'd peek my head into the dining room.

"Ethan, stop the clock for a second."

He'd look up attentively. He was serious; he wanted to reach his goal so he could put the test behind him and move on. "You're rushing at the end of the sections," I'd tell him. "Pay attention to the questions at the end." Or: "Read every word in the answer choices."

"Okay, Mom," he'd say, and go back to work, making a small adjustment here and there.

By April he wanted me to break out the charts I'd made of his scores, the ones he'd cracked jokes about just a few months before. Now he asked me to update the charts to see if he'd made any progress—and he had! We'd collected enough data to be able to see the line moving in the right direction, slowly but unmistakably. That line on the graph was definitely a motivator.

So was the girl who lived down the street. She and Ethan had known each other since they were little, and she was *into* it, taking those practice tests on the weekends too. She was a better student than Ethan—in the way girls often tend to be (better organized and more focused)—and the two of them were neck and neck in their practice scores. She also happened to be a competitive tennis player, and some of that fierce athletic energy came into the picture, which kept Ethan on his toes because he wanted to beat her.

In the end she beat him, but not by much, and he exceeded his goal by 30 points.

Good enough for Ethan to call it a day and feel good about moving on.

I, on the other hand, wanted him to take another crack at the test because there had been three eleventh-hour snafus, only two of which I can write about, that had to have depressed his scores, I thought.

The first, just a few days before the test, was Ethan's hand. His left hand, the SAT hand. (Ethan's a lefty.) He broke his hand horsing around on a soccer field and came home from school needing a cast. I've never had a broken bone in my life, and this was probably Ethan's fifth fracture, and he was only sixteen years old. Only sixteen and taking his second SAT. With a broken hand.

Needless to say, we'd never factored "broken SAT hand" into our test prep, and although Ethan could move his fingers I was nervous he wouldn't be able to bubble properly. Meanwhile Ethan was insisting that he take the test as planned, cast and all.

"Let me see you bubble," I'd say, and he would practice, but I could hear little whimpers of pain as he colored in the circles. He didn't care. He'd had his standardized test strategy all mapped out for months in advance—the SAT, the AP exam, the SAT II subject tests—and as far as he was concerned, there was no room in his spring-of-junior-year schedule to make any last-minute test-date adjustments. He could have postponed the test till the fall, which is what the College Board told me when I called and tried to persuade them to give my son a personal bubbler as a "special circumstance accommodation." They said no. The College Board won't get involved with the medical issues of juniors because the kids can still take the SAT the fall of their senior year.

The night before the test, I spotted Ethan playing Halo, which I took to be a good sign. I figured if he could work a video game controller, he could bubble.

The other mini-crisis—the full dimensions of which I only learned after the test—was that Ethan had an abscessed tooth. When I picked him up after the test, I found him holding his jaw and complaining that his head ached. We headed straight to the dentist, who said Ethan needed an emergency root canal.

So Ethan ended up taking his second and final SAT with a broken SAT hand and an abscessed tooth—and I couldn't convince him for the life of me to take the test again, without the cast and the abscess.

It's probably just as well. Ethan's attitude wasn't just a question of *I hit my goal, I'm done.* He also believed that if he bumped his scores up any higher his application would look less attractive to colleges, not more, because the mismatch between his grades and his scores would be so wide that it would raise a flag. He needed to spend his time raising his grades, he said, not his scores.

At the time, having looked into the connection between SAT scores and merit aid, I didn't think that was right. But I do know at least one student with an extremely wide discrepancy between his scores and his GPA who was rejected by schools he was more than prepared for. Which gives me pause.

In the end, Ethan got into eight of the ten colleges he applied to, including two of his three top choices. Three of the colleges, including the University of Vermont, made generous offers of merit aid (merit, not need based)—up to $60,000 over four years, in one case—though his two favorites did not, I'm sorry to say. And his grades kept going up. He applied to colleges with a 3.24 GPA and learned at the end of his senior year that his final GPA for the year, the only year *sans catastrophe*, would be a 3.54, his highest GPA in all of high school.

Best of all, he finished with a B+ in honors calculus, which he insists has nothing whatsoever to do with the fifteen minutes a day he spent doing Kumon worksheets over breakfast this year. Jennifer, the den mother at our local Kumon, started him off on Level H last summer; now he's finished Level K, the step just *before* calculus, which is why Ethan thinks it didn't help. Maybe one of his professors will explain the cumulative nature of math. Heaven knows I've tried.

Here's the kicker.

Ethan got an 11 on his essay.

My little boy, the one with the chicken scratch for handwriting, who couldn't fill two pages to save his life, scored higher than yours truly, the supposed writer in the family, who happened to care much more deeply about the essay than he did.

There has to be a lesson in there somewhere.

The Moment of Dawn

In the end, I superscored my way into the 97th percentile, which feels much better than saying my highest math score was a 570. And Ethan brought home a percentile almost that high, which is excellent.

I learned so many lessons that year. It's hard to know where to begin.

First of all, I understand now that it takes much longer to master a subject than I could possibly have understood without going through the experience of working very hard to learn math and failing to move the needle on the SAT math section by even one point.

I had no problem learning math, nor did I have trouble understanding the math Stacey, PWN, John, Michael, and Catherine taught me.

What I could not accomplish in one year's time was *mastery*: I could not develop the instant recall and ease in applying new learning to unfamiliar problems that comes with time and practice. Over that year I learned a great deal of the high school math I missed as a teen, but I didn't become proficient, and proficiency is what the SAT tests.

Proficiency takes time. Anders Ericsson didn't pull his 10,000 hours out of thin air. After studying SAT math for a year, I was still a novice.

Second: I can also safely say that none of the tricks in this book or any other can compensate for a weak foundation. This was a painful lesson for me when it came to math. The math section was my favorite by far; it was the section I spent the most time on and, of the three, the one I was most emotionally invested in. And my scores went nowhere.

I hope parents and educators will see my experience as a ringing endorsement of all those mathematicians who keep telling us that American students need a *coherent curriculum in mathematics*: a curriculum that starts at the beginning and moves forward sequentially, each new concept building on and incorporating the previous concept, the connections among them made clear.

SAT test prep is not a coherent curriculum in *math* (though a good SAT course can offer a coherent curriculum in the SAT). Test prep is test prep, not math prep; test prep assumes students have *already* spent many years learning math. Unfortunately, an awful lot of students have spent many years taking math but not learning math, and I'm one of them. I gave up in math at some point during tenth-grade geometry. After acing algebra the year before, I couldn't seem to make it through that low point in the struggle. So as I prepared for the SAT I was learning new math concepts in the order they come up on the test, and devoting time to them proportionate to the frequency with which they appear on the test, and that is pretty much the exact opposite of a coherent curriculum in math.

Catherine's experience prepping both herself and Chris bears this out. Her rural school didn't teach her much math—the three years of math she took were the equivalent of about one year in a good private school—but what she did learn, she learned well. It's in her bones. Chris's math education wasn't good, but Catherine retaught math at home from the time Chris was ten (she retaught herself, too), so while his foundation wasn't exactly strong, it was better than mine. Catherine raised both their math scores by about 100 points. She said she absolutely could not go further without taking a real Algebra II course. She could do all the quadratic function problems, but she couldn't do them fast—and she wasn't going to be able to do them fast until she took Algebra II. Test prep works only when you have something to build on.

Last but not least, if your child has a solid foundation in reading, writing, and math, test prep works. My critical reading score went up by 80 points, writing by 110. According to the research, that isn't supposed to happen—especially not on critical reading, which is universally acknowledged as the most difficult of the three sections to tutor.

My 80-point gain in reading and 110-point gain in writing were the result of expert test prep. As a veteran of the publishing industry, I started the project with rock-solid foundations in both, which I had built over the course of twenty-plus years of exacting practice in all things verbal. Without that base, no amount of test prep could have saved me.

If I were to do it all over again, I'd start the year with Kumon and stick with it. I would also enroll in my local community college and take the high school math courses I slept through the first go-around. For those of you who've never checked out the campus bookstore of a non-selective college, institutions of higher learning today offer math courses going all the way back to grade-school arithmetic. *With multiple sections.*

A former boyfriend used to say that I could bend a spoon with my will, but apparently Ethan's will is stronger than mine because there really was nothing I could do to make him take the test one more time. Ethan kept his goal ambitious, but realistic, and that is to his credit.

There is one other thing I would do differently. If I had it to do over again, I would take him on those college tours earlier than the spring of junior year. There is *nothing* more motivating than seeing the "perfect school," and realizing you only have a so-so chance of getting in. I thought junior year is when you're *supposed* to take the tours, but that's too late for a student to make any big changes in GPA. By junior year, the cake is almost baked.

How It Pertained to Everything

I didn't anticipate how sweet the best part of the project would be.

In the beginning, I threw myself into it expecting great things: days and nights of happy bonding with my children over their studies and the approaching SAT. We three would undertake this quest together, our relationship would deepen, and we would grow memories to cherish. Plus we would have great scores.

Seven months later, both my kids had moved out of my house in protest, and I had lost my confidence as a parent. The family was in crisis.

In the end, what the project brought to my life was . . . *happy bonding with my children*. (And great scores!) Happy bonding with Ethan, at any rate; Daisy's turn is coming.

To the amazement of my friends and family (ask them!), and to my own astonishment, after the chaotic summer when my children left, the Family SAT Project worked. I learned so much about my son reading his practice essays, which told me who he was and what he thought; he had grown into a young man of character with opinions about politics, history, and literature I might never have known had the College Board not prompted him to tell me. And I will always remember sitting side by side, practice test after practice test, as Ethan explained the math problems to me; and watching movies together and feeling a nudge when an actor uttered an SAT word. We still do that today.

When I'm ninety years old and sitting on my front porch in a rocking chair, watching my great-grandchildren frolic around the yard, I'm not going to care about our scores. I may still be able to reel them off by heart, since that's the nature of the beast, but I won't care.

I *will* remember the joy we had pursuing those scores, and the tussles we had, and the sadness we had, too.

All that we went through together: I will remember.

ACKNOWLEDGMENTS

When I was an editor and people would come to me with a book idea, I'd say, "Great idea! Now go write the book." *Writing* the book is the hardest part of . . . *writing a book.* Of course, I knew that on some level, from all the times I'd doled out those words and never heard back again. What I did not know was how much rocket fuel it takes to propel the engines through to the finish. "It takes a village" does not begin to encompass the many generous individuals who helped bring this book to the light of day. There were so many allies without whom I never would have made it to these acknowledgments, that it's hard to know where to begin thanking.

I will start with my son, Ethan, who not only inspired the project, but unflinchingly tolerated his often obsessed, and sometimes possessed, mother. I am forever grateful for his participation in my experiment and for his willingness to allow me to share our story. Studying for the SAT was easy; writing the book about the journey was the real test of how strong our relationship had become. Let's just say this: I kicked those stress tires hard, and Ethan never flinched. I've never seen anything like the reservoirs of strength and good-natured outlook on life that he displayed the year I was writing.

It was the year Ethan learned how to cook, clean, get himself to and from school, fill out college applications, and keep track of his own schoolwork. It was the year I took away the safety net that his seventh grade special ed teacher had told me to shed years before. It was the year I had to block out the world, and Ethan sat by my side every step of the way. He listened to me read draft after draft and corrected little details, such as which video game he played or what drink I served with the scrambled eggs. And he played the piano every day, I'm sure in large part because he knows that piano playing always makes me feel better. Without Ethan, there would have been no project, no book, and certainly there would have been a lot less joy in my life.

Daisy gets an extra large helping of gratitude, too. Like any mother, I always thought she was special, but little did I know that she'd be a catalyst for change in an entire family, and that the ripples of her experience would touch people I hardly knew. Daisy's trials and tribulations during the year I wrote this book forced me to re-think everything I thought I believed in about love and family, and ultimately pushed me to grow as a person and a mother. I have my darling Daisy to thank for making me a better person. I rewrote the book after the skies cleared and flavored it with everything I learned along the way.

I would be remiss if I did not express deep gratitude for my wise cousin, Cindy Leavitt, who crossed my path fortuitously at a fork in the road and introduced me to the work of Gordon Neufeld; and to Colleen Drobot, who stepped into my life as a sagacious messenger and set me free to finish the book.

I'm grateful to my parents, Judy and Ed, for their unwavering support, especially when life seemed so crazy that this silly SAT project started to seem like a really bad idea. They never stopped believing in me or cheering me on. They read the manuscript more times than love would demand, pointing out typos that not even the finest copyeditors had managed to catch. I think everyone needs someone who believes in his or her dreams. I'm fortunate enough to have an army.

Duncan Mackenzie was the first person I told about the project after it came to me in a flash, fully formed and three-dimensional. He was the first person to encourage me to reconsider my career in corporate

America, an idea that seemed more than a little far-fetched at the time. Duncan's conviction was critical from the get-go, and his encouraging phone calls along the way never failed to come at just the right time. There's a lot of Duncan's wisdom baked into these pages.

Special thanks to Leslie Wells for her contribution to my book proposal. She gave it structure when I lost my way.

Some of those with super-duper powers to motivate should be mentioned by name here. Emily McKhann, you need to bottle your magic and sell it for a million dollars. The world would be a lot better off if everyone could have a little bit of Emily in their life. Bob Miller deserves credit for realizing "that's a book" when I was blogging at the time about studying for the SAT with my son. And Mark Hurst, thank you for being the first to tell me that good test prep is not that complicated: use the Blue Book! (If only I'd listened to your wise words from the start!) Heartfelt thanks to Rick Newman for pointing out the importance of having the book's structure down before starting to write.

Jennifer Lewis's illustrations always inspire me and brighten my day. Susan Danziger and Albert Wenger are my fairy godparents, who believe, support, and encourage. They never forgot me, even when I fell off the face of the Internet.

Gretchen Rubin not only inspired me with her project (*The Happiness Project*), but she encouraged me every step of the way, generously offering ideas and inspiration. Gretchen believed in my project from the get-go, which was affirming and reassuring.

Marcella Moran and Dr. Kutcher, thank God we found you and thank you for your support with Ethan as well as your support for me as an author.

When the book idea came to me, it was fully formed with an agent attached in my mind. I called Lisa Gallagher, who being British knew nothing about the SAT, and informed her she was going be my agent. Undaunted by my audacity, she agreed to take me on. Lisa propped me up when I lost faith, and I don't know if I could have survived without her.

Jon Berry read the first draft of every chapter and unfailingly helped me out of the weeds. Thanks for always reminding me when it was time to add the scrambled eggs.

Thank you to all the wise teachers who guided me: Stacey Howe-Lott, Mike McClenathan (aka PWN the SAT), and Erica Meltzer (thank god we stumbled across each other on the Internet); at Advantage Testing, Arun Alagappan, John Roberts, and Michael Kayne; and Erik the Red, my SAT "Library of Congress," who never failed to answer my incessant cries for help. And finally, thank you Philip Keller, the first person who helped me understand functions—even if it was only for a minute.

At Crown Publishers: thank you to Tina Constable for being a warrior and for believing in me. There is no one I trust more, and I was so grateful when you saw the potential in my proposal. Thank you also to Rick Horgan for allowing me to be "me"—a grammatically imperfect over-italicizer—while making me a better writer. Carisa Hays, it's a miracle that we were brought together to work on this. I couldn't ask for anyone better to be in charge of publicity. Seriously. Thank you also to Tammy Blake and Ellen Folan for your diligence and enthusiasm. I've walked a mile in your shoes. And to Meredith McGinness and Christina Foxley for their hard work and expertise; and to everyone else who played a role in the birth of this book: Candice Chaplin, Christine Edwards, Andy Augusto, Jennifer Ridgeway, Nathan Robertson, Ada Yonenaka, Songhee Kim, Elizabeth Rendfleisch, Rosalie Wieder, and Maria Spano. Matthew Martin, thank you for your heartfelt affirmation.

An extra dollop of appreciation goes to Michael Nagin, the genius behind my jacket design. I must tell you that in all my years in publishing, I never witnessed a first-try jacket hit a home run. You achieved the impossible and captured the essence of everything I wanted to say.

Many thanks to Michelle Young for stepping in with her photographic prowess when the professionals let me down. And also to Skye Levy, for making the smiles real.

The last person I need to thank is my "north star," Catherine Johnson, without whom there would be no project and no book. Catherine Johnson's contributions to this book were so immense that they deserve their own page of acknowledgment.

There are no doubt many others who I should properly acknowledge. In fact, I could go so far as to admit that there is probably no end to the list of people I should thank. And the contributions of those not listed here should not be diminished by my oversight.

Catherine Johnson's blog, *Kitchen Table Math*, was one of my first sources of inspiration for this project. It's where I discovered an entire community of parents who didn't find the idea of studying for the SAT with one's child to be anything out of the ordinary.

Originally, I'd wanted Catherine to coauthor the book, but when logistics made that impossible, she instead stepped in as a guide, a friend, and a mentor. In the final months, as I struggled to finish the last draft, unable to figure out what it was that was missing, Catherine called one night with an insight that added such depth and clarity that I asked her to read the entire book, which thankfully she agreed to do. Ultimately, Catherine polished every word of the final draft with discernment and tender loving care.

Catherine, thank you!

INDEX

About the Author

DEBBIE STIER is a single mother of two teenagers. Her book publishing career has spanned two decades, most of it spent in PR where she was responsible for publicizing dozens of iconic books ranging from *The Notebook* to *Marley and Me*. Frequently covered by the media, including *MediaBistro, New York Observer,* and *New York* magazine, Debbie regularly speaks on topic pertaining to social media and technology as well as, most recently, standardized testing. She has been a contributor to *Time* and *Psychology Today*. She lives with her son and daughter in New York City where she is home schooling her daughter, but you can find her at perfectscoreproject.com.